MOSCOW STORIES

MOSCOW STORIES

LOREN R. GRAHAM

Indiana University Press
BLOOMINGTON AND INDIANAPOLIS

This book is a publication of

Indiana University Press
601 North Morton Street
Bloomington, IN 47404-3797 USA

http://iupress.indiana.edu

Telephone orders   800-842-6796
Fax orders   812-855-7931
Orders by e-mail   iuporder@indiana.edu

Library of Congress Cataloging-in-Publication Data

Graham, Loren R.
Moscow stories / Loren R. Graham.
p. cm.
Includes bibliographical references and index.
ISBN 0-253-34716-5 (cloth : alk. paper) 1. Science—Social
aspects—Soviet Union. 2. Science—Social aspects—Russia (Federation)
3. Soviet Union—Intellectual life. 4. Soviet Union—Social
conditions—1945-1991. 5. Russia (Federation)—Intellectual life—1991-
6. Russia (Federation)—Social conditions—1991- 7. Graham, Loren R.
—Travel—Soviet Union. 8. Graham, Loren R.—Travel—Russia
(Federation) I. Title.
Q175.52.S65G73 2006
303.48'3'0947—dc22
2005022442

1 2 3 4 5 11 10 09 08 07 06

To my friends in Russia,
who have taught me so much

CONTENTS

——

PART IV.
Intelligence, the Cold War, and Security Concerns

PART V.
From the USSR to Post-Communist Russia

PREFACE

TODAY IT IS HARD TO REMEMBER how remote, mysterious and threatening the Soviet Union was for people in the West fifty years ago. It had been described as a riddle wrapped in an enigma, and few Americans, mostly diplomats and a few businessmen with the right connections (Armand Hammer comes to mind), were given visas and permitted to see a very small part of a vast empire, mainly Moscow and its environs. Visitors from the West met only a narrow selection of Russians, ones officially regarded as immunized against capitalist seduction.

But a small number of foreign students was also allowed in, at first largely those from countries friendly to the Soviet Union and considered susceptible to Communist ideology. By 1959, when I applied to go there as a student, the foreign student population was growing slowly but only one small group of Americans had been permitted the previous year to enroll in Moscow and Leningrad universities. Among them was almost none with my declared interest, Soviet science, a highly sensitive subject area for a secretive regime that considered America the "Main Enemy." So I knew that I would be regarded with suspicion, at best, which made me, initially, extremely guarded. Yet I quickly became entranced by a country in which life was almost as difficult for a grudgingly tolerated outsider as it was for ordinary Soviet citizens. I returned to Russia again and again, making at least one, but often three or four, trips there every year. The Soviet Union has vanished, replaced by Russia (and a nominal commonwealth of contiguous independent countries), but its past is as alive for me as its uncertain present.

I believe that this book is one of the few personal and informal accounts of experiences in Russia written by an American academic specialist in Russian affairs, certainly the only one covering such a long span of years. And the adventure goes on, since I have more trips to Russia planned for 2006.

None of the episodes in this book has been published previously, and the book includes information about significant moments in the history of Russia and the United States during my years of research in the former Soviet Union. They range from the election of John F. Kennedy as president in November 1960, the years of rule of Nikita Khrushchev and Leonid Brezhnev, the accession to power of Mikhail Gorbachev in 1985, the collapse of the Soviet Union in December 1991, and the social and terrorist turmoil in Russia in the early years of the twenty-first century. During these years I talked with hundreds of Russians, including a personal exchange with the most infamous scientist of the twentieth century, Trofim Lysenko, who suppressed research in genetics in the Soviet Union and was responsible for the imprisonment or deaths of hundreds of scientists. The book also reveals information from numerous discussions with Mikhail Gorbachev's main advisor, the architect of perestroika, a man I have known for forty-seven years. All names given in this book are the actual names of the people involved, with one exception: one minor figure still alive to whom I have given a pseudonym in order to protect personal privacy.

But this book is not only about Russia; it also about personalities and events in America over the last fifty years. The book opens and closes with the stories of two American communists who were friends of mine, and their views about the Soviet Union, and it also includes a discussion of an expatriate American community in Moscow at the height of the Cold War, many of them sympathetic to the USSR, including the American founder of the Soviet microelectronics industry. Another section scrutinizes the philanthropic activities of the Hungarian-American financier George Soros, with whom I traveled in Russia several times. Yet another analyzes the field of Russian Studies in the United States, showing how it was affected by the Cold War. The impact on my profession had direct personal consequences for me; as a frequent "guest" of the Soviet Union I had to avoid becoming a pawn of intelligence agencies, both those of the USSR and the United States. I once had to jump out of a window in Moscow to escape the KGB, and also rebuffed the FBI in my office in Princeton when they attempted to involve me in intelligence operations.

Anthropologists speak of the potential conflict between being participant and observer. I was both. During my years in Russia I was forced to confront a range of pressing ethical questions, such as the possibility (and desirability) for scientists to maintain political neutrality; the difficulties involved in comparing our own society to the "other"; the tension between independence of thought and the demands of loyalty; the detachment of the anthropologists' "gaze"—to name but a few. I have wrestled with these questions for many years, and I have tried to record here the ways in which I dealt with them. I am very aware that other people would, and did, handle some of these issues differently.

Loren Graham
St. Petersburg, Russia
November 2005

MOSCOW STORIES

PART I

LEARNING TO LEARN ABOUT
RUSSIA AND COMMUNISM

CHAPTER ONE

THE COMMUNISM
PROBLEM IN
FARMERSBURG

THE HELSINKI–MOSCOW TRAIN DISAPPEARED in the distance, leaving me stranded alone in the forests astraddle the Finnish-Soviet border. I had been ejected from the train, along with the enormous amount of luggage that was supposed to sustain me for a year in the Soviet Union. In the fall of 1960 I hoped to be one of the first American students at Moscow University, a beneficiary of the newly established U.S.–USSR exchange agreement. When the Soviet border guard—the first Soviet official I had ever seen in my life—examined my entry documents and passport, which I had been assured by the American exchange officials were all in order, he simply, without a word, gestured with his thumb in an unmistakable way indicating that I had to get off the train. I barely managed to unload my luggage before the train started up and headed toward Moscow, without me. I stood beside the track and looked in both directions. No building or person was in sight, only green pines interspersed with some other trees displaying splotches of colored autumn leaves.

I did not know whether I was in Finland or the Soviet Union. I feared I was already on Soviet territory, since the man who expelled me from the train was a Soviet border guard. I decided to walk back the way the train had come, hoping that I was headed in the direction of Finland—if I wasn't already there. But walking was a challenge; each of my three large suitcases was so heavy that I could carry only one at a time. Furthermore, the sleeves of my heavily insulated Abercrombie & Fitch "duck hunter's coat," recently purchased in New York City, were crammed with additional items that would not fit in the suitcases—

vitamin pills, dried food, coffee, a pair of heavy shoes, and a few novels. I could not wear it, so it amounted to a fourth piece of luggage. I
took each piece separately down the track until I reached the furthest
point at which I could see both piles of my belongings at the same
time, and then returned to the original pile for another trip.

Working in relays for more than half an hour, I finally came to a
small hut beside the tracks. Going up to the door, I knocked, and when
a face appeared in the crack, I spoke in my newly acquired Russian.
The door was immediately slammed in my face, and I got no response
to my hammering on the door. Finally, I cried out in English, "I am an
American student who got kicked off the Russian train. I need help."
The door immediately opened, and the man said, "Why didn't you say
you were an American? I thought you were someone trying to escape
from the Soviet Union, and that only brings me trouble." He turned
out to be a Finnish border official, and he invited me in, gave me some
tea, and asked what the problem was. I explained what had happened,
and he asked to see my documents. He immediately informed me that
my entry visa was valid only for the Moscow airport. "Don't you know
that each Soviet entry visa is good for only one point of entry? You must
wait here for the next train going back to Helsinki, and arrange there
for a flight into Moscow. With these documents they will admit you."

This was my introduction to the Soviet Union. I was twenty-seven
years old, a former Navy officer, but now a graduate student at Columbia University in New York City. I was a native of Indiana, and married
to a fellow Hoosier, my professor's daughter at Purdue University, and
already the father of a three-year-old daughter.

I knew a lot about Russia and communism—but only from books
and classes and research in musty library shelves. The first real, live
communist I knew personally came from Indiana, not Moscow or Leningrad. And he had played a part in an intellectual adventure that took
me to this place, then as distant to most Americans as the moon.

I was nine years old the first time I heard the word "communist."
When I completed the third grade in Farmersburg, a small town in
southern Indiana, my teacher, Mrs. McGarvey, told me not to leave
after the last class; she said that she "wanted to talk to me a bit." Mrs.
McGarvey was a fine teacher, and I was drawn to her. She had disci-
plined me on more than one occasion, however, and I was a bit anxious about what was in store for me.

I waited until all the other members of the class had left, shouting
with joy at being released for the summer, and then timidly ap-

proached her desk. Mrs. McGarvey smiled at me and said, "Loren, you are the brightest student I have ever taught with one exception—Wendell Furry. I sure hope that you do not turn out like he did. I am ashamed of him."

I knew who Wendell Furry was, although he was quite a bit older than I. Wendell's father was the town minister and lived only three houses away from my grandparents' house.

I had been inside the Furry home. If Farmersburg possessed any members of the intelligentsia, the Furrys came as close as anybody to qualifying. My grandfather Graham, despite his interest in learning, ran far behind. Both my Grandfather and Reverend Furry kept books in their houses, but Reverend Furry had a whole room full of books that rivaled the collection of the town library, which reposed in an alcove above a store front on Main Street. The Furry family library had become important to me because I had been expelled from the town library for "indecent behavior." I was afraid that Mrs. McGarvey knew about this incident, and that I was on the same disastrous path as Wendell Furry, whatever that path was. The reason I had been expelled from the town's meager assortment of books was that the librarian had caught me, at age eight, staring at a drawing of a female breast in *Gray's Anatomy.* Several days later I told Reverend Furry that I could not use the town library because I had misbehaved. He did not inquire into the nature of my misdemeanor but offered me books from his library, which I gratefully accepted. All these thoughts ran through my head as I stood before Mrs. McGarvey after being warned that I reminded her of Wendell Furry, and that Wendell had become a shame on the community.

With some trepidation I asked, "How *did* Wendell Furry end up?" I was completely mystified about his sins, since I had heard many times that Wendell Furry was a genius, a boy who could do anything, the pride of the community. Mrs. McGarvey replied, "He is a *communist.*" Again, my mind raced. "What is a communist?" I wondered. Surely, it must be something awful. Maybe it was connected to sex, that mysterious phenomenon which seemed to concern adults so much and had already gotten me into trouble.

I later learned that it had been twenty-six years since Mrs. McGarvey had Wendell Furry in her third-grade class, but her memories were still vivid. Wendell and his fate impelled her to warn me against following the path to perdition blazed by her earlier star pupil. Yet on the few occasions I saw Wendell in Farmersburg when he returned home from Harvard University, where he was a young professor of physics, he seemed like one of the nicest, most intelligent men I had ever known. Mrs. McGarvey assured me that I would eventually find out what a communist is, and would then know how to ask about one, but that I needed to be on my guard not to become one, because smart students like Wendell and me were somehow particularly susceptible to this terrible disease.

Mrs. McGarvey was prescient when she assured me that I would eventually find out what communism was and would know how to ask questions about it. And I never forgot her reference to Wendell Furry; I kept track of him in later life, although I did not know him well. I, like him, eventually became a teacher at Harvard University. During my academic career I was a specialist in the history of Russian science at two of the leading centers of the study of communism in the United States, the Russian Institute at Columbia University and the Russian Research Center at Harvard. But my curiosity back then, when I was nine years old, was much more about Wendell Furry than it was about communism. What were the terrible things that he had done and what he still, apparently, was doing? And how could Farmersburg produce someone who aroused such emotions in my teacher?

Farmersburg, Shelburn, Hymera, and the other small towns near me in the 1930s were far from being idyllic communities; they were racked by economic tensions and suffered from intense social deprivation. Most people, farmers and coal miners, were very poor. Tuberculosis, pneumonia, and diseases like goiters and rickets, which are caused by inadequate nutrition, were common. During my childhood I suffered from the first two. Only a tiny group of people, mostly the mine owners and supervisors, lived well. Even those farmers who had quite a bit of land, like my Grandfather Graham, lived extremely modestly, since the soil was largely clay and yielded poor crops. During the Depression, when I was a child, the conditions were at their worst. Hoboes from the railway came by our house and begged for food. My mother would give them something to eat, but insisted that they sit in the backyard; she would not permit them in the house. At this time my father was unemployed, having been fired from his high school teaching job, and there was very little food in our house.

The politics of the southern Wabash Valley at this time were not greatly different from those in working-class regions of Europe, divided sharply between the left and the right. Many miners looked upon the mine owners and town bankers as class enemies. I felt the tension personally because my grandfather Champion "Champ" McClanahan had been a miner and then a railway worker and my uncle, Charles

Huntworth, was the Farmersburg banker. When the bank in nearby Shelburn failed in the early 1930s an angry mob converged on the home of the town banker, seized him, and rode him out of town on a rail. He was fortunate not to have been killed. Grandmother McClanahan described this incident to me in such detail that I was convinced that either she or a close friend was a part of the crowd accompanying the banker.

Seeking relief from economic marginality, people looked both to the political left and the political right. On the left, the Wabash Valley Socialist Party was active among the miners and railway workers. Radicalism had deep roots in the region; Eugene Debs, a leader of American socialism, and Theodore Dreiser, the radical writer, were both from Terre Haute, an economically depressed town just a few miles to the north. On the right, the Ku Klux Klan was powerful among the Scotch-Irish Protestants of southern Indiana.

As a boy I had often heard rumors that in earlier years my grandparents might have been associated with both of these movements. At first I thought one set of grandparents was radical and the other right wing, but gradually I began to suspect that the same grandfather—Champ McClanahan—had ricocheted from the left to the right. Champ had worked in the coal mines and for the railroads—targets of opportunity for Debs, who frequently visited the local mines, founded the American Railway Union in 1893, the Socialist Party in 1898, and the Industrial Workers of the World (IWW, or "Wobblies") in 1905. Champ McClanahan was born in 1854 and experienced these events in his prime as a working man. He was unhappy about his economic and social situation, and he looked for transforming doctrines that might give him access to a better world.

Champion McClanahan died before I was born, but when I was in high school and was beginning to become interested in political history his widow, Grandmother McClanahan, was still alive. One day in 1948 or 1949, when I was fifteen or sixteen, I gathered up my courage and asked, "Grandmother, were you and Grandfather McClanahan ever members of the Ku Klux Klan?" Her affirmative answer shocked me. This sweet and kind lady, who often baked cookies for me and so obviously adored me, had been a member of an organization that was vehemently opposed to everything I thought was fair and just. Incredulous, I asked her, "But how could that be? Don't you know what the Klan stood for?" My grandmother stared at me with surprised eyes. So far as I know, she had no more than a grammar school education. Her parents, Reece Nesbit and Mary Elizabeth Siner, were, according to family records, unable to read or write. "Loren, I do not know what they are teaching you in school," she replied, "but the Klan arranged the most wonderful potluck church picnics you can imagine, and we all went there with our baskets of chicken and our pies, and we visited with our neighbors, and everyone had a wonderful time." I then asked her if Grandfather McClanahan, who had married her in 1891, had once been a follower of the Wabash Valley Socialist Party, founded by Debs a few years later. Yes, he had, she said, not seeing any contradiction in the two activities. The socialists, she explained, stood for the rights of the workers and protected them against the bankers and mine owners. Furthermore, they too arranged wonderful picnics. Later, when I studied the history of modern Germany and wondered how that country, which in the early years of the twentieth century had the most robust left-wing movement in Europe, could have been the stronghold of right-wing politics after 1933, I would recall this conversation.

Wendell Furry was born in 1907 and, as a young man, experienced the atmosphere of social and economic tension in and around Farmersburg that gave rise to the contradictory political impulses of my grandfather. He was an undergraduate at DePauw University in the 1920s and a graduate student at Harvard in the early thirties. He was a brilliant physicist who had a particular interest in relativistic quantum theory. He gradually became attracted to Marxism and joined the Communist Party in 1938, four years before my conversation with Mrs. McGarvey. During World War II he worked at MIT and occupied an office in Building 20, an ugly structure that housed a famous center of technological innovation. (Many years later I would have an office in that unappealing building.) He received numerous high honors, and in 1950 went to do research in Copenhagen at the invitation of Niels Bohr, one of the century's greatest physicists.

When McCarthyism hit the United States in the early 1950s, Wendell was called before the House Un-American Activities Committee and accused of being a communist, one of the leaders of a cell of subversives active at Harvard and MIT. Suddenly his name was plastered across the front pages of the nation's leading newspapers. Senator McCarthy singled him out as a symbol of "Red Harvard." At first he refused to testify, invoking his Fifth Amendment rights. Later he decided that taking this position only increased suspicions about activities that he considered totally innocent, so he agreed to present his political biography, as it were, both to McCarthy's committee and to the press. In an interview in February 1954 with an undergraduate

Harvard Crimson

Registration Magazine

CAMBRIDGE, MASSACHUSETTS M-1

Was Furry Relates History of Red Unit
uals; At University From 1938 to 1947
'inds

e the once-

ed out an-
al experi-
ry. Stanley
received
aling with
>-acids in
the pass-
through. a
nonia, hy-
awesome
the first
luction of
rom inor-
lly signi-
ams, pro-
it is the
ow much
uired for
nto being

nost pub-
stic year
that the
s a land-
logy and
; link in
no older
en or the
sts found
the con-
modern
ern man
ever to
rld. In-
L. Mo*
Anthro-
he field

y
outlook
ith the

CRIMSON—JOHN B. LOENGARD

WENDELL H. FURRY

Tells of Own Reasons
For Joining, Leaving
Party Group Here

by J. ANTHONY LUKAS
Copyright by the Harvard Crimson
February 3, 1954

A weary, somewhat discouraged man cocked his feet up on his desk yesterday and poured out the long, virtually un-told story of his years in the Communist Party at Harvard.

Apparently relieved to be free at last from the confining gag of the Fifth Amendment, Wendell H. Furry, associate professor of Physics, talked volubly and openly about his reasons for joining the party in 1938 and the nature of the cell here from then up until 1947 when he quit.

Furry said he was glad to be able finally to offer a "bit of explanation of the past" and to "answer the questions many people at the University must be asking on these subjects." Some of what he said had already been told the Corporation last spring, but this is the first time he has told his full story in public.

"It is fashionable these days," he said, "to say that such questions can be answered only by a psychiatrist, but I think the answers I can give are pretty adequate. I do not think that I am by nature at all a political sort of person. Scientific studies are what interest me most and the only things for which I seem to have any appreciable aptitude.

Strong Emotional Drive

"It is unlikely that I would ever have had much to do with political activity in the short of

Wendell H. Furry, Associate Professor of Physics at Harvard University, discusses his membership in a Communist Party cell at Harvard from 1938 to 1947. *The Harvard Crimson*, February 3, 1954.

reporter for *The Harvard Crimson* who would later become famous as a social commentator and author of a book on Boston's desegregation—J. Anthony Lukas—Furry said that in 1938, discouraged by political events in Germany and Spain, he joined the Communist Party and remained a member until 1947.

In the late thirties and during World War II the unit of the Communist Party in which Furry participated met regularly in Cambridge to discuss the political situation and to review books written by radical authors. (Another member of this group was Dirk Struik, mathematician and fellow historian of science at MIT, who lived on to the age of 106, dying in 2000. I would later attend a memorial service for him and ponder the connections between places like patriotic Indiana and atheistic communism.) In the war years Furry said that at his laboratory at MIT, in which radar was being developed, he worked with several colleagues who were also members of the Communist Party. It was Furry's refusal to name these people that so infuriated Senator McCarthy. Furry gave this explanation to Lukas and *The Crimson:*

> At times during the war there were two or three people in the
> group engaged in secret war work, as I was at the M.I.T. Radia-
> tion lab, but we never mentioned the nature of our work and
> there was never the slightest suggestion that we depart from secu-
> rity rules in any way. . . . I believe that membership in the Party at
> that time was quite consistent with being a loyal American.

In March, 1947, Furry left the Party when it, in his words, "violently attacked the United States and began a type of propaganda drastically different from that of the previous seven or eight years." For his refusal to name the other members of the Party who worked with him during the war years Furry was cited for "contempt of Congress," put on trial, and widely criticized by students, faculty, and the administration at Harvard. A few courageous members of the university community defended him, but their voices were lost in the whirlwind.

Furry's wife and young daughters were also victims of this inquisition. The weekly newspaper in Belmont, Massachusetts, became aware that the children of an American communist were studying in the local schools, supported by the town's taxpayers, and began persecuting the children with articles and editorials. Wendell's lawyer, Gerald Berlin, called the Belmont editor and threatened him with legal action if he did not stop harassing the family. The editor realized that there was no legal defense for what he was doing and stopped his cruel campaign.

The trial of Wendell Furry ended in an acquittal on the legal grounds of the pertinacy (relevancy) of the hearing to the matter under investigation. Furry was retained on the faculty of Harvard, his reputation heavily damaged. Nonetheless, his colleagues in the physics department thought highly enough of him to make him head of the department. The ordeal that he went through still frequently comes up in conversations around Harvard.

My first years of association with Harvard University coincided with Wendell Furry's last years there. When my wife and I moved to Cambridge in 1974 I decided to go visit him. I sought him out at his office in the Jefferson Physical Laboratory on the Harvard campus, only a few blocks from where we were setting up house. When I told his secretary that I would like to see Professor Furry, and that I was from the same small town in Indiana where he grew up, she smiled and replied that she detected the similarity in our accents. She made an appointment for me with Wendell, and soon the two of us were together.

Although the difference in our ages, twenty-six years, meant that we had few common close friends, we knew a great many of the same people. He remembered my family well, and our farm. I told him how grateful I was to his father for letting me use his books when the town librarian would not. Wendell remembered both libraries and said he imagined we had read some of the same books. He was a good friend of Percy Self, his old classmate in Farmersburg, who was a relative of mine (Percy's grandfather Frank was my great-grandfather). Percy had become a truck driver, and a member of the Teamsters Union; occasionally Percy, when he and his truck turned out to be near Boston, would drive his giant eighteen-wheel rig into Cambridge and Belmont to visit with Wendell. Percy would park his truck on the street near Wendell's house on Frost Road in Belmont, and the Harvard professor and the teamster would sit together and reminisce about Farmersburg, where Percy still lived. Percy knew that Wendell had been accused of being a communist, but he did not care, belying Mrs. McGarvey's contention that everyone in the town was ashamed of Furry. What was important to Percy was that Wendell was his high school friend and a man who still valued their friendship.

Eventually I mentioned that we had the same third-grade teacher, Mrs. McGarvey. Wendell reacted with pleasure and interest. I then made the kind of tactless remark that was prompted by what might be charitably described as naïveté. I thought that a sophisticated Harvard professor would not be offended if I described my conversation with Mrs. McGarvey over thirty years earlier. I told him, with a laugh, what Mrs. McGarvey had said about him, and how she had warned me not to follow the same path. I instantly regretted my insensitivity when I saw how much my remark had hurt him. All these years later Wendell Furry was still gravely wounded by what had happened to him, and the opinion of his long-deceased third grade teacher added to his pain. I was deeply distressed and did everything I could to soften the blow, making jokes about the anti-communism of small town America, but what had been said could not be unsaid.

I wish I had subsequently had a redemptive opportunity to say what I should have said: I understood why the political and economic conflicts that bedeviled Farmersburg in the late 1920s and 1930s would have inclined a young man to develop a radical point of view. After all, my grandfather, driven by visceral, populist sentiments, had been radicalized (at least by Indiana standards). I would have explained to him somehow that the reason I had not followed the path Mrs. McGarvey warned me against was that I had been fortunate enough to avoid being deceived by the promises of communism, simply because I was born late enough to see Stalinism's most frightful features. Furry had, like so many others, committed himself to a dream of social justice — and been betrayed. But unfortunately I did not have the opportunity to say what I should have said: Wendell Furry died shortly after our first, and only, adult conversation. In the last months of his life, after the death of his wife Betty from cancer, the old physicist was confined to a nursing home near Fresh Pond, in Cambridge, where he had nightmares about the persecution he and his family endured years earlier. In the night, to the stupefaction of the attendants, he would cry out, "The FBI, the FBI, they are after me! Call the American Civil Liberties Union and Gerald Berlin!"

All this obviously happened many, many years ago. But today I often think about those conversations in Indiana and Cambridge and wonder if they do not contain meaning that I have failed to extract. How should I judge today Wendell Furry and my grandparents McClanahan and their political involvements? For that matter, how should I judge myself in trying to judge them? As a faculty member at MIT and Harvard, my sympathies now naturally accrue to Wendell Furry. Like many intellectuals of his generation, he was attracted to Marxism. Even today it is not unusual for intellectuals to be interested in Marxism, while it is quite rare for them, at least in America, to be drawn to fascism. Now, in the year 2005, a few students and faculty at MIT and Harvard study Marx's works in the hope that they will find important and undiscovered truths. However mistaken this hope almost surely is, my grandparents' association with the Ku Klux Klan seems different, and quite indefensible, both intellectually and morally, a truly horrid thing.

But what is my responsibility, given my good fortune—education and hindsight—to make of the lives and beliefs of my grandparents? They did not have the (possibly overrated) benefits of education; they belonged to both socialist and semi-fascist organizations (sequentially). My grandmother made no subtle distinction between them, seeing only two movements that provided social outlets for lonely farmers living on isolated farms. In contrast, both Wendell Furry and I had the benefits of many years of education. By the time Wendell Furry was commanded to appear before the House Un-American Activities Committee many of the horrors of Stalinism should have been already apparent; the Great Purges had peaked in 1937 (the year before Wendell joined the Communist Party), and savage political oppression in the Soviet Union had occurred in the twenties, thirties, and forties. There were plenty of objective observers (like John Dewey and George Orwell) who had seen the Soviet version of socialism and recognized that an implacable ideology was nourished by the blood of millions. While many Western intellectuals like Furry may not have paid attention or given credence to the ghastly reports of events in the Soviet Union almost from its inception, the information was widely available.

Grandfather and Grandmother McClanahan had almost no education and access to very little information. They made mistakes out of ignorance. Wendell Furry made them when he could have found plentiful reasons not to remain faithful to the dream. But he was unfairly and cruelly persecuted because of his mistakes, something that did not happen to my grandparents. Therefore, my sympathy still runs a bit stronger toward him.

But is that right, since we now know that communism claimed even more victims in the past century than fascism? Many millions of lives were sacrificed to the vision that Furry shared with so many others. Yet is there not something morally different between communism and fascism in terms of their basic principles? If the theorists of communism had been right in their principles of economics (they were not) the world might have become a better place, but if the theorists of fascism had been right in their principles of racial inequality (they were not), the world would have become a place of abominations. Should one judge a political ideology by its principles, or by its results? If one judges by results, both systems were disasters of almost unimaginable proportions that made the past century the bloodiest in history.

Sometimes late at night as I think about how these good people— some highly educated, some uneducated—made such serious errors in judgment I despair of the possibility of making good ones. I feel overwhelmed by the suspicion that I am making other mistakes now, along with Wendell, despite "enlightenment," mistakes that are no doubt quite different from those made by my grandparents and Wendell Furry, but ones the generation that follows me will see as clearly and dispassionately as the ones I see in the lives of these people who came before me—sincere dreamers who, despite their mistakes, remain attractive to me.

CHAPTER TWO

TECHNOLOGICAL
COMPETITION AND
THE COLD WAR

WHEN I REACHED COLLEGE AGE in the 1950s the Cold War was at its height. The United States and the Soviet Union were locked in a technological and ideological struggle, and the members of my generation were called upon by our government to be active participants in that contest. Most of us were more than willing to be enrolled, and many accepted government scholarships, as did I, that paid for all or part of our educations in return for our promises to give several years of our lives to the military upon graduation.

Encouraged by my father, who received a college education at a nearby state teachers' college, my three older brothers established the tradition of studying engineering at Purdue University, and I unquestioningly followed their precedent. I later found that although I loved science, I was not enthralled by engineering itself. Furthermore, I discovered after taking an elective course in history that this subject excited me just as much as physics and mathematics. So I would decide in graduate school to combine my affections by becoming a historian of science. But first I finished engineering studies and then fulfilled my three years of obligations as an officer in the United States Navy.

Quite a few of my classmates at Purdue were also engineering students who entered military service, and a special group among them became test pilots engaged in competition with the Soviet Union in an aviation rivalry that would soon turn into a space race. Old Purdue friends who ended up as astronauts in the competition with the Soviet Union to reach the moon included Neil Armstrong, Gene Cernan, Gus Grissom, and Roger Chafee. Several of my close friends died in military plane accidents within a few years of graduation, and Grissom and Chafee would burn up on a rocket launch pad. I was not cut out to be a jet pilot or an astronaut, but I soon learned that the nation also needed people who understood the Soviet Union, and, because of my training in science and engineering, I was a logical person to become a specialist on Russian science. In both my undergraduate and graduate years there was no shortage of financial aid for a person with my interests.

During my navy service an event occurred which symbolized the significance of the Soviet Union and its scientific prowess. One evening in late September 1957, as my ship in the Mediterranean lurched sickeningly in great waves, we received an encoded message from Washington. As communications officer I was responsible for taking it to the "cryptographic shack," installing the right combination of code wheels in the decoding machine, and typing out the message. It read, "Intelligence sources inform us that within the next ten days the Russians are expected to launch an artificial satellite into space. It is expected that this event will attract considerable worldwide attention." A few days later, on October 4, I picked up a BBC broadcast that told us that the Russians had thrown "Sputnik" into orbit. I tuned to the right frequency on the multi-band receiver in the radio shack and listened to its "beep-beep." We also soon heard that the entire world was thrilled by the technological breakthroughs of the Soviet Union, and that Americans were in a frenzy about the need to catch up with the Russians in science and technology. But no one seemed to know much about the history or organization of Russian science and technology, so my future course of studies and research seemed almost inevitable to me.

Three years later I was a graduate student at Moscow University in the USSR, "in the belly of the beast," preparing for a lifetime career as a historian of Russian science and technology. In the intervening years I had engaged in intense study of Russian language and history at Columbia University. At the suggestion of my professors I then applied to the newly established graduate student exchange program between the United States and the Soviet Union.

In Russia I found the same juxtaposition of rural backwardness and technological aspiration I had known as a child in the rural Midwest in an area where horses were occasionally still used. When I saw how entranced Russian citizens were with technology, especially aviation, I understood that, too, from my own experience. In a cemetery near Moscow I found the tombstones of Soviet aviators, men who died

The author standing near Moscow
State University in the fall of 1960.

A horse and wagon in the village of Kolomenskoe, at the
edge of Moscow, winter 1960–1961. Photo by the author.

Graves of Soviet aviators in a Moscow cemetery,
winter 1960–1961. Photo by the author.

young like my close friends and Purdue classmates John Bauerle and
Brook Bray. I immediately felt sympathy for these young Russian men.

While I was in Moscow on that first of many visits, on April 12, 1961,
all the newspapers trumpeted the latest triumph of Soviet technology:
the cosmonaut Iurii Gagarin had circumnavigated the globe in a satellite. A mammoth demonstration was held to celebrate the event, and
my wife Pat and I made our way through the crowded streets to Red
Square. (Pat had joined in the latter part of my first visit to Russia.) In
later years when the Soviet Union became a decrepit and failing society I would often recall that day as the apogee in Soviet citizens' belief
that they held the key to the future of civilization. The celebrations on
the street were genuine and heartfelt. Soviet science was, they were
sure, the best in the world, and Soviet rockets succeeded where American ones failed. The Soviet papers ran pictures of American missiles
exploding on the launching pad in the 1950s and early 1960s and
when, a number of years later, my fellow Purdue graduates Gus Grissom and Roger Chafee died in the Apollo Command Service Module,
I learned about the tragedy from Russian newspapers, which covered
the story in detail.

As Pat and I returned to Moscow University after witnessing the demonstrations in celebration of Gagarin's feat on that April day I was approached by a reporter from Radio Moscow, who had discerned that I was an American, a very rare visitor in those days. He stuck the microphone of his tape recorder in front of my face and said, "So you are an American student at Moscow University. What do you think of Iurii Gagarin and his marvelous flight?" I replied, "I congratulate him and the Soviet Union for this remarkable feat. As an historical event, I think it can be compared to the first circumnavigation of the globe by ship by Magellan." The Moscow Radio reporter turned off his tape recorder and queried, "Who is this Magellan? Progressive or Non-progressive?"

Soon after the demonstration for Iurii Gagarin, another Red Square festival was planned, the May Day Parade. Everyone said that with the triumph of Gagarin still so fresh, this parade would be particularly exuberant. Pat and I wanted to see it, but we soon learned that parades in the Soviet Union were not something you watched, they were something you participated in. The only observers were the members of the ruling Politburo atop Lenin and Stalin's tomb in Red Square and a few invited members of the diplomatic corps in the bleachers alongside.

Pat and I decided to march in the parade in order to see the events. Students from Moscow University were assigned a certain place in the long lines of marchers, and we joined in, sandwiched between students from North Vietnam and East Germany.

As we marched along, red flags flying, trumpets blaring, the thought occurred to me that if anyone took a photograph of Pat and me marching in the May Day Parade in Red Square that came to the attention of the FBI we might have a bit of a problem. And although we were participating in a student exchange sanctioned by the U.S. government, the parallel between my marching in Red Square to Communist tunes while my closest friends were dying in the service of their country in the Cold War made me a bit uncomfortable. To the best of our knowledge the FBI never noticed; later Pat was given FBI clearance for a presidential appointment by President Jimmy Carter. However, the accompanying photographs provide belated evidence that, had the FBI been more efficient, might have caused some difficulty.

When we arrived in front of Lenin and Stalin's tomb in Red Square we saw standing on the top in the center the leader of the government, Nikita Khrushchev, wearing a light-colored coat, and, on his left, Gagarin, waving his white-gloved hand. For Khrushchev, Gagarin was a living symbol of the superiority of the Soviet system, of the strength of Russian technology, and of the glory of Khrushchev's rule.

Line-up for May Day Parade, Moscow, 1961. Signs say
"Hands off Cuba!" "All hail to the socialist unity and solidarity
of nations on the path to socialism and communism!" "To the
complete collapse of colonialism!" Photo by the author.

Patricia Graham, the author's wife, at the Moscow State University
float in the May Day Parade, Moscow, 1961. Photo by the author.

Soviet leaders atop the mausoleum in Red Square, May Day,
1961, taken by the author as he and his wife marched by in the
parade. Cosmonaut Iurii Gagarin, the first man to circumnavi-
gate the globe in a satellite, waves his white-gloved hand. To his
right is the Soviet leader Nikita Khrushchev. The names Lenin
and Stalin are engraved on the stone. Six months later, Stalin's
body and his name were removed from the mausoleum.

I later met Gagarin at a reception and talked briefly to him. His
quiet politeness and coolness immediately reminded me of Neil Armstrong, my classmate who eventually beat the Russians to the moon.
Gagarin was definitely "the right stuff," a man who felt at one with
machines in a way I never would or could. I later heard that his calm-
ness in emergency situations amazed even his Soviet trainers, the
people who chose him because of these qualities. But like many of my
friends, his competence and equanimity did not make him omnipo-
tent—he would be killed in 1968, at age 34, while testing a jet plane.

PART II

STUDENT DAYS AT
MOSCOW UNIVERSITY

CHAPTER THREE

NO SINGING ALLOWED
AT MOSCOW UNIVERSITY

When I departed for my first trip to Russia, I went alone; I had been unable to get permission for my wife and daughter to accompany me. But I soon found that while I might be unaccompanied I was never alone. Life in the Soviet Union was nothing if not communal.

Upon my arrival at Moscow State University (MGU) as a graduate student in the fall of 1960 I found posted on the back of the door of my dormitory room a long list of rules governing student behavior. The list was so long that I pulled up a chair and spent some time reading it. I found that practically everything was forbidden—eating, drinking, rowdy behavior, making noise, keeping pets, singing. Although all this sounded to me like "social behavior" the official announcement lumped them under the heading of "anti-social behavior."

During the year that followed I never met another person who had ever read those rules. Certainly no one paid any attention to them. In fact, eating, drinking, rowdy behavior, making noise, keeping pets, and singing all seemed to be required. Every evening there were raucous parties in the rooms, with particularly heavy drinking. Volodya, the tall and genial floor leader of the Komsomol (Young Communist League), was supposed to enforce the rules, but in the evenings he usually locked himself inside his room and let the parties rage. This divergence between official policy and real life was my first lesson that existence under Soviet "totalitarianism" was not quite as regimented as we in the West were led to believe.

A few years earlier most of Moscow University had been moved from its former location near the Kremlin to "Lenin Hills" (in tsarist times, "Sparrow Hills") near the edge of the city on a high river bank overlooking the entire city. The architecture of the buildings was "late Stalinist," a conglomeration of classical and Soviet features adorning a central skyscraper with a great spire on top, surmounted by the hammer and sickle. Around the central building were arranged wings with dormitories, and I was assigned to "Zone G, Room 805, right half."

My assigned room measured two meters by three meters, about six by nine feet. It seemed to be about the size of three telephone booths. I lived there for an academic year, and for the last three months of that year I was with my wife Pat, who joined me from Denmark, where she had been living near her Danish relatives. The dormitory room was too tiny to hold a double bed, or even a normal single bed. We slept on a slender couch which was so narrow that we simply could not both fit on it, even when we were particularly friendly, which we usually were. We solved that problem by pulling the cushions forward into the room, rolling up blankets and cramming them in the vacated back corner, and carefully placing me in that crucial position, where my greater weight supported Pat, who, cantilever style, slept on the cushions suspended over empty space. If I jumped up in the middle of the night to go to the nearby bathroom, Pat was unceremoniously dumped on the floor. We learned to warn each other of impending bed calamities.

At the head of the bed, attached to the wall about a foot from our heads, was a "wire radio." Wire radios were very common in the Soviet Union at that time. They were not genuine radios, but loudspeakers connected to a central radio somewhere in the building. Our little set was equipped with a dial that allowed us to choose one of two radio stations, "Moscow 1" or "Moscow 2." The volume control on the radio could not be turned all the way down, nor could the radio be turned off. Even when I tried to silence the infernal thing with a pillow we could still hear the voice or music thinly drifting through the room. Every night at midnight both stations played the Soviet national anthem, a stirring and martial piece that the radio engineers had managed to give more volume than normal. Pat and I have burned into our consciousness to this day the memory of this music resonating in our ears. (In December 2000, the same national anthem, earlier discredited for its Soviet spirit, was re-adopted by post-Soviet Russia.)

We shared a toilet and a shower with our "block-mates," a couple of Russian students living with us, a man and a woman who almost never spoke to us. They were obviously nervous about being in such close proximity to American students. While almost all the other students on the floor were friendly and sought us out for conversation, the two who were closest to us spatially never became acquaintances, despite our initial efforts. They were from a rural area of Russia, and they converted the entrance to the room, which was also our entrance, into a root cellar. Boxes there were filled with dirt, and in the dirt were unimpressive carrots, potatoes, and onions, brought from the private plots on the collective farms where our block-mates lived. Our Russian neighbors also made the windows into little refrigerators. Most windows in Moscow were of double glass, to keep out the cold winds sweeping in from Siberia, and between the glass there was space to keep milk, butter, and sour cream (*smetana*)—if you could find any. Both windows could be opened, and occasionally a bottle of *smetana* would catapult down eight floors and explode in a circle of smeared cream all over the main entrance to the dormitory.

As an advanced graduate student, most of my time at Moscow University was spent on research in local libraries, not classwork. Nonetheless, I visited many classes in the university, some in the natural sciences, but also in Russian history and literature. I joined with undergraduates in excursions to historical sites in the city and surrounding countryside. And several times a week I attended an advanced course in the Russian language for students whose native language was not Russian (there were many such students) where we read texts in classical Russian literature, such as Leo Tolstoy and Aleksandr Pushkin, and also had conversational exercises.

No courses in my special area, the history of science, were available at the university when I was there, but in downtown Moscow there was an institute of the Academy of Sciences where the history of science and technology was the center of attention, and I often attended lectures there. The library of that institute was an important location for my research on the history of the Soviet Academy of Sciences, as was the Gorky Library of the university and the Lenin Library, a large public institution.

Virtually all of the Soviet students who lived on the floor of my dormitory were members of the Young Communist League, or Komsomol, whose leader Volodya lived with his wife and daughter in a small room down the hall. Volodya ignored the rules of decorum, but he assigned each of us tasks to help clean the dormitory on the weekends. The division of labor was so incredibly fine that my task consisted in washing the leaves of the rubber plants that grew in the lounge. Performing this forced labor required all of half an hour a week. I was happy to comply. Also on many weekends there were compulsory "*subbotniki*," or work days at local construction spots. A part of Soviet culture was the belief that all citizens should help in the "construction of Soviet socialism," which meant that we were assigned occasionally to work crews. I was asked to help build the "University" station of the Moscow subway, which was being constructed about four or five blocks from my dormitory. My task was to haul bricks in a wheelbarrow. To my pleasant surprise, I found that no one took their assignments very seriously, and I soon adapted myself to the careless work habits of the people around me, spending most of my time talking and resting. But the subway station eventually was completed, and in later years when I frequently went through it I always admired the bricks.

Every two weeks or so a meeting of the Komsomol organization was held in the lounge on my floor of the dormitory, presided over by Volodya. I sometimes attended, although I was not a member of the Komsomol. One meeting, which I remember particularly clearly, consisted of skits performed by the students in which every member of the dormitory came in for some criticism. I was curious to see what sort of criticism would fall on me. Would I be depicted as an alien American capitalist, an ideological foe? When I heard that I was to be the subject of a skit at a forthcoming meeting, I hurried off to observe. One of my floor-mates borrowed my winter coat, stuck my hat on his head, and caricatured me as a bookworm who hurried down the hall toward the library each day with his briefcase, oblivious to the burning social issues of the day.

What were the social issues of the day? Of course, colonialism, imperialism, and capitalism, which we were all expected to criticize. But also, according to my critic, I did not spend enough time at the evening social events and made inadequate contributions to the liquor that was consumed at them, particularly since I had access to foreign vodka sold in hard currency stores that were closed to Russian students. After the skit was finished I was expected to respond, to engage in a little self-criticism. (I was aware of the Communist tradition of criticism and self-criticism, *kritika* and *samokritika*.) I squelched my initial impulse to observe how curious it was for the Komsomol to recommend behavior specifically prohibited by the university rules against alcohol, and instead I expressed my gratitude to my floor-mates for their hospitality and indicated that I would try to return it in fuller measure. They seemed to find my response to be satisfactory and greeted me with warm smiles. I never embraced their "social issues," but after this event I did drop in on the parties more frequently even though my consumption and supply of vodka never met the standards my fellow students expected me to maintain.

Quite a few foreign students studied at Moscow University, and in the course of the year I met many of them. In certain communist families in Italy and France in this period there was a tradition of sending off the young members to the Soviet Union for education. One of them with whom I became particularly friendly was Pietro Longo, the son of one of the top leaders of the Italian Communist Party. Pietro's father Luigi, who was at that time second in command in the Party to Palmiro Togliatti, would in three years become the head of the Party and would hold that position for many years. The father had a very colorful history, fighting in World War I, the Spanish Civil War (in which he was wounded), and World War II. He was imprisoned at various times in Italy, France, and Spain for his radical activities, but he was so highly valued by the Allied armies for his role in the struggle against Hitler that the American army awarded him a Bronze Star for valor. As a young man Luigi Longo studied in the Soviet Union, at the Frunze Military Academy, and when his son Pietro reached the appropriate age he supported his enrollment at Moscow University.

Pietro was a particularly attractive and intellectually curious young man, and he was constantly checking out his immediate perceptions of social reality with what he had been told back in Italy in communist circles. Before he left Western Europe for Moscow he visited Geneva, where, in accord with his usual practice, he sought to examine the worst slums in the city. He insisted to me that the worth of a society could be judged by how it treated its least privileged members. To his surprise, slums seemed not to exist in Switzerland, even though it was a capitalist country. In Moscow he also searched for the poorest living quarters. I went with him in search of the worst slums in the city, and we found some frightful places, apartment buildings without running water or central heating. I remember in particular one brick building that had an enormous crack in the middle that progressively got wider as it proceeded up to the top floor, where it gaped so awesomely that the residents had placed old rugs over it in a futile effort to stop the frigid Moscow winds. Pietro was obviously sobered by the conditions he saw in these places, but he bravely maintained to me that the people who lived in them did not live such morally depressed lives as the miserable poor in Naples and other Italian cities. Looking at the Russian slum buildings Pietro would point at curtains in the windows and say, "You see, those people still have a sense of human dignity living under socialism that the wretched of capitalism do not have."

But Pietro was clearly troubled by the discrepancies between what he saw around him, whether in Switzerland or in the Soviet Union, and what he had been taught as a loyal young communist. The more I talked to him the more I saw that he was beginning to question many things he had been told by his father, whom he revered as a brave man but whose political judgment he doubted. Pietro was particularly upset by the privileges enjoyed by top Soviet bureaucrats and party leaders, such as special stores where scarce vegetables and fresh meat, as well as foreign luxuries, were available even though they could not be found anywhere in Moscow in regular stores.

Pietro was a truth-seeker, and I was not surprised to hear that within a few years after his return to Italy from Moscow he broke completely with the Italian Communist Party. He became the leader of a social democratic party that brought energy and life to Italian politics, even though it never gained a large share of the vote in national elections. Nonetheless, he was very visible in Italian politics because everyone knew his family; his political opposition to his father, at that moment running the largest Communist Party in Europe and a great political force in Italy, naturally attracted the attention of the more conservative elements of Italian society, some of whom began to cheer him on for reasons that Pietro, at least initially, did not share. The American embassy and the CIA station in Rome were eager to support anti-communist organizations in Italy and began funneling money to parties like Longo's in order to counter the communist threat. In 1982 Pietro played a large role in the formation of a new coalition government in Italy, the forty-second postwar government.

Gradually Pietro, the man whom I had so admired for his sincerity and curiosity—both intellectual and social—was worn down and transformed by the tumult and corruption of Italian politics. Eventually he was linked to several financial scandals, and in 1992 he was arrested and jailed for taking bribes. I sadly watched this from afar.

At this time there were many mainland Chinese students studying at Moscow University, including a number on my floor. They stuck together and had nothing to do with the rest of us. They never came to the Komsomol meetings, so it was useless to caricature their behavior, even though it would have been easy to do so. Once I ended up sitting next to one of them at the student cafeteria. I cheerily told him that I was an American from New York City, where I studied at Columbia University, and asked where his home was. He stared at me in amazement as if I had said I was from Mars, wordlessly picked up his tray, and walked away.

The Chinese worked harder than anyone else, even the bookworm American. The Russians regarded them as "curve-raisers" in the classes, and heartily disapproved of their conscientiousness. Every morning before dawn the Chinese assembled outside in front of the dormitory in their blue pants and jackets and performed calisthenics. We would awake to the staccato sounds of their counting out exercise numbers in Chinese.

While I was a student at the university I witnessed the beginning of the Sino–Soviet split, the divorce in relations between the Soviet Union and China that shook the communist world and eventually led to armed clashes on the Yalu River. By the time spring arrived there was not one Chinese student left at the university out of the hundreds who had been there in the fall. Even the restaurant in the Peking Hotel in downtown Moscow, which had been one of the finest eating-places in the city, lost its Chinese chef and staff, and deteriorated to the level of other Soviet restaurants.

The historic Sino–Soviet schism began in 1960 on my floor of the dormitory at Moscow University, although I have never been able to persuade the relevant experts on international relations to take proper note of the events around me that year. It all began one day in the fall when the Chinese students purchased a goose at the local peasant market and decided to prepare it in honor of a feast day. The only kitchen available was the communal one that served our whole floor, so they baked the goose there for several hours. During the last hour the aromatic attractions of the goose wafted through the entire dormitory, causing every student nearby to dream of slicing into that treasure. The Chinese casually drifted in and out of the kitchen, occasionally basting the goose. Finally a group of Russians could withstand the temptation no longer; they quietly slipped into the kitchen when none of the Chinese was around and spirited off the goose. When the Chinese returned and discovered the theft, the hullabaloo that ensued shook the entire building, indeed the world. All the Russians swore that they knew nothing about the incident: "What goose? Don't bother us, we are studying." The rage of the Chinese in our dormitory quickly spread and the international communist movement broke asunder. Within days, not a Chinese could be found in the university, and they also pulled out of the entire country. For years the Chinese and Russians would not speak to each other.

In addition to washing the leaves of the rubber plant and helping to build the Moscow subway, I periodically was assigned duty answering the telephone for the whole floor of the dormitory, at the phone station opposite the elevator. Individual rooms did not have telephones, so the telephone operator had to summon students from their rooms to the central desk. With the phone often ringing, and the frequent trips to fetch students from the rooms, along with the constant conversations with students passing by, it was impossible to do any serious reading while on phone duty, so I often answered correspondence. In November of 1960 I received in the mail an absentee ballot for the American presidential election from the voter's registration office in Lafayette, Indiana, where I was at that time a legal resident. Sitting at the phone booth I studied the absentee ballot, and was soon surrounded by a crowd of Soviet students who wanted to see what an American ballot looked like and who were curious about how elections in the United States worked. I showed them that I had to make a choice between John F. Kennedy and Richard Nixon for president, as well as choices for candidates for other offices; with about a dozen Russians following my every move, I made a large "X" in the bloc opposite Kennedy's name, and then made choices for the other candidates. I sealed the ballot, put it in the envelope, and said it would be mailed the next day. At the same time, I observed that I would like to see how a Soviet election worked. Volodya, the Komsomol leader, promised that he would arrange for me to do so. (I later heard from my in-laws, who lived in Lafayette, Indiana, that the local radio station a few weeks later announced: "An absentee ballot has been received from, of all places, Moscow, and the vote was for John F. Kennedy." So much for the privacy of elections in Indiana. I think the radio station was owned by a Republican.)

A few weeks after I mailed my absentee ballot Volodya came by my room and invited me to come down to the main hall of the university where voting booths were set up for the elections to the City and Supreme Soviets, the local and national legislatures. I went off with Volodya and soon arrived at the voting area. As we left I noticed that a group of Komsomol activists, operating under Volodya's general direction, was going around to each room in the dormitory in order to ensure that every student would vote.

On the ground floor of the central area of the main university tower a voting area had been established, guarded by members of the citizens' militia, *druzhiniki*, wearing red armbands. The voting booth had been arranged with such a strong patriotic style that it was almost like a religious altar. Each student picked up a ballot at a table, where his name was checked off, and then proceeded to an urn that was situated in front of a gold-colored bust of Lenin and below the Soviet flag. At this point the voter had a choice: one option was to simply fold the ballot, making no mark on it of any kind, and drop it in the urn. This action was considered a positive vote for the Communist Party slate. The other option, if the voter desired to take it, was to enter a little curtained voting booth to the side, mark the ballot in some way or another, and then come out and drop the ballot in the urn. I was curious to examine a ballot and asked Volodya if I could see one. He handed me a ballot, and I saw that for each position only one candidate was listed. I remarked to Volodya that this system of election did not seem to leave much choice, and reminded him that when he had helped me with my American ballot, we had chosen among several candidates for each position. Volodya observed that in his opinion all the American candidates were "just the same," so it really did not mean anything that the voters were given what appeared to be a choice. Furthermore, he continued, Soviet voters really do have a choice, since if they wish they can enter the secret voting booth and write something on the ballot. "What would they write?" I asked Volodya. "Oh, they can write anything," he replied, "such as complaints about the way the government works, or the name of any other candidate they might wish to put in. But," he continued, "over 99 percent of the voters here approve the Party slate, which shows how satisfied they are with our system."

I stood with Volodya in front of the voting booth for about fifteen minutes, and I counted the number of students who merely dropped the ballots in the urn, indicating they accepted the Party slate without comment, and those who entered the curtained voting booth. To my surprise, I found that about one quarter of all the students entered the booth. I asked Volodya how this could be, since he had told me that over 99 percent of the students accepted the single choices listed on the ballot. Volodya answered that the students who went inside the booths were writing comments on the ballot, but that most comments were positive ones, praising the Party for its brilliant leadership of the country.

As I stood there I saw a Russian friend of mine enter the curtained booth. He was a student whom I knew to be deeply disaffected from the Soviet regime. He had described to me while we walked in the cold and dark snow around the university late at night how intensely he hated the Communist Party, how unfair and undemocratic he considered the system of government to be. I noticed that he was in the booth only a few seconds, then came out and dropped his ballot in the urn. As he left I stepped up to him, called him by name, and asked what he had done to his ballot. "Why, Loren," he replied with a smile, "I wrote 'Glory to the Great Communist Party' on it."

When I returned to the line of students Volodya pointed to the ballot that I still held in my hand and asked if I would like to vote. With surprise, I replied that I was not a Soviet citizen, was not registered, had shortly before voted in the American elections, and surely could not now vote in a Soviet one. Volodya explained that the Soviet Union was not created as just another nationalistic state, but had been viewed as the beginning of a world communist system. The assumption was that people all over the globe would join in, participating in elections, and creating world communism. Some day the United States and all other countries would be a part of the Soviet Union, which would be a world commonwealth of socialist states. Volodya admitted that hopes for the quick advent of this system had soon diminished when the Russian Revolution of 1917 was not followed by similar revolutions in other countries. Nonetheless, he observed, a vestige of the early hopes remained in Soviet voting regulations, which stated that the citizen of any nation on earth could vote in Soviet elections if he or she wished to do so. Therefore he and all the voting officials would be delighted if I decided to vote in their election.

I looked down at the ballot and for a moment entertained the wild thought of entering the voting booth, writing something zany and definitely un-communist on the ballot, and dropping it in the urn. Then I remembered reading somewhere (was it on my U.S. passport?) that cause for depriving a U.S. citizen of his or her citizenship included serving in foreign armed services and voting in foreign elections. I turned to Volodya and said that I thought I would not actually vote, but that I would very much like to keep the ballot as a souvenir. He replied that the ballots were numbered and that therefore I could not keep it without causing difficulties for the voting clerks. "Why don't you just keep this poster that lists the qualifications of all the candidates?" he asked, handing me a sheet of paper with the pictures and short biographies of each of the names on the ballot. I handed him the ballot, and took the poster, which I still have.

Years later a Soviet émigré who had served as a voting clerk in Moscow regional elections gave a talk at the Russian Institute at Columbia University which I attended. He said that the figures of almost universal approval of the Party candidates were simply fabricated, in the sense that if any ballot contained something other than a positive comment on the official slate, it was simply disallowed as a defaced ballot. To this day, I do not know what the approximately 25 percent of university students who entered the curtained booths were doing, but I think it is safe to assume that quite a few voted for candidates other than the Communist slate, or expressed their dissatisfaction with the regime.

Having conversations with students at Moscow University in Soviet times about what the political sentiments of the Russian population would be if freely expressed was not easy, since any such conversation might be reported to the secret police and become cause for difficulty. I was often advised by one Russian student not to trust another student because "he is a Chekist," or member of the secret police. One never knew whom to trust in such situations, but the result was to put a damper on revealing conversations.

However, one night after quite a bit of drinking a group of five or six of us who had come to know each other quite well and cemented considerable trust gradually moved onto political subjects. My Russian friends made fun of the official elections and said that they revealed nothing about the actual political preferences of the Soviet people. "What do you think these preferences are?" I asked. The students talked together and finally agreed that if free and open elections in Russia could ever be held, they guessed that about a quarter of the electors would vote for the Communists, about a quarter for Western-style parties supporting true democracy, about a quarter for right-wing nationalistic or fascist parties, and about a quarter would be divided up in a plethora of special interest parties such as agrarian and ethnic groups. I was a bit surprised by the strength of the fascist sentiments, but when free elections finally did come to Russia almost thirty years after this conversation the results were not markedly different from what my university friends had predicted.

A few doors away from Pat's and my room lived a slight and morose-looking student named Iurii Dimitiev. Iurii always wore the same outfit: dark and non-descript pants topped by a double-breasted suit coat that looked like it had been inherited from his grandfather. Iurii's hair was always uncombed, and the shoulders and lapels of the suit coat were covered with a blizzard of dandruff. One of his eyes wandered out of synchrony with the other, adding to a composure that can only be described as giving the appearance of dementia.

Iurii began making frequent visits to our room. He wanted to talk, to talk about anything. He was interested in politics, in history, in literature, in philosophy. Smoking constantly, his eyes wandered over the room, inspecting our clothes, our food, but especially the books in the bookshelf. He spied a book on Soviet history that I had brought from the United States, Leonard Schapiro's *The Communist Party of the So-*

viet Union. Published in 1960, this book became a standard work for Western specialists on Russia.

The title fascinated Iurii and he begged to see it. The strength of his interest caused us unease. We had been warned by State Department officials before leaving the United States that one of the standard ways that Soviet secret police agents compromise Americans is by getting them to give Soviet citizens "anti-Soviet literature," an act forbidden by Soviet law. Iurii told us that the reason he wanted to read the book was that he was interested in the "dissident and heretical movements" among the Communists, from Georgi Plekhanov, to Leon Trotsky, to Nikolai Bukharin, to Tito. He thought he would find substantial discussion of such movements in Schapiro's book. From my knowledge of the book I knew that he was correct. But I was afraid to give the book to him, and I refused.

From that point on, Iurii launched a campaign to get his hands on that book. He became such a pest that Pat and I simply stayed away from our room until late at night in order to avoid him. We would come back to the dormitory after 1:00 A.M., walk up eight flights of stairs since the elevator ceased operation at midnight, and silently make our way to our room. We would not be in the room more than five minutes when the slight rap would sound at the door. It would be Iurii, bearing gifts of pineapples and champagne, wanting to talk. Neither Pat nor I had ever seen pineapples for sale in the Soviet Union, and we had no idea where Iurii obtained them. The pineapples were so unusual, in fact, that we dubbed Iurii the "Pineapple Man."

The Pineapple Man used every blandishment he could think of to get the book. He appealed to our political and moral sense, asking, "Are you not Americans, defenders of the freedom of expression? Can you deny such information to a Soviet citizen who shares your values?" He ridiculed our fears, maintaining that nothing bad could happen to anybody if we gave him the book. Leonard Schapiro, who I later came to know, would have been, and subsequently was, surprised and complimented to know what an intense topic of negotiation his book became.

Pat and I discussed whether to give him the book. Iurii's moral arguments were telling. But he was certainly a strange character and we had no idea who he really was. He easily could have been affiliated with the secret police, or eager to gain political advantage by turning in Americans for "anti-Soviet activity." I did not particularly like the fact that he seemed to have an endless supply of pineapples when no one else I knew in Moscow could find even one. But finally I decided that I would give him the book (I saw no difference between a loan and a gift, and giving it away would mean I didn't have to lug it back to the United States) if I could determine to my satisfaction that he was not an agent.

The next time the Pineapple Man showed up at the room with the usual gifts and asked for the book I said that I would give it to him under one condition: he must sign a piece of paper and leave it with me in which he said that he asked for the book, that I had not wanted to give it to him, and did so only after he agreed to take full responsibility for the act. Iurii was shocked and said that he could never sign such a piece of paper. "It would be my neck," he observed, but added that if I gave him the book without the paper I would risk no more than expulsion from the Soviet Union. I stood by my demand.

We did not see any more of the Pineapple Man for several days. Then, late at night, he showed up at the room without pineapple or champagne. "Please give me the book," he asked, adding, "I am ready to sign the paper." I took out a piece of paper, wrote on it in Russian the statement that I demanded, and asked him to sign it. Iurii signed. Then, while he stood there, I took out a match, burned the paper, crushed the ashes, threw them out the window, and gave Iurii the book. What happened then was so melodramatic that even yet, years later, I am affected by the telling. Iurii threw his arms around my neck, buried his face in my shoulder, and sobbed like a child.

Iurii then told us how much he wanted to get out of the Soviet Union, and that he wanted to study in an American university. Would I go to the American Embassy and ask them to get application materials for him to go to an American university? I knew that at that time it was impossible for a Soviet citizen to leave the country to study abroad without the backing of the Communist Party—something Iurii was not likely to get—but I agreed to his request, went to the embassy several days later, and made the contacts for him.

I have never seen Iurii since that time. I know, however, that somehow he got out of the Soviet Union and came to the West. I suspect that he subsequently began to work for American intelligence, since the one time that I heard about him again was several years later when an American FBI agent came to me and asked me what I knew about Iurii Dimitrev. (I have described that episode in another chapter of this book, "Spies and Scholars.")

If Iurii Dimitrev, the Pineapple Man, was an example of a disaffected Soviet student, Viktor Chuprin, another of my floor-mates at Moscow University, was an example of a loyal Soviet citizen, a member of that quarter of the population who would enthusiastically vote for the Communists in the freest circumstances. Viktor was an enormous Siberian law student who talked about Siberia the way expansive Texans in the United States talk about their state. Viktor even had some of the mannerisms of a Texan; he was quick to grab your hand with his massive paw, he chaperoned you everywhere with light touches to your arm, and in a crowd he considered it only natural that he towered above everyone. He didn't know it, but he would have been perfectly at home in a ten-gallon hat and a Cadillac.

Viktor was intensely patriotic in a sublimely unreflective fashion. His grandfather had been killed fighting for the tsar in World War I, and his father had died fighting for the Soviet government in World War II. It was all the same cause as far as Viktor was concerned. He told me that he did not want to die in yet another war, but it was perfectly clear that he was prepared to do so. Once when discussing these sacrifices of his family for motherland Russia, Viktor disclosed that still another member had died in the armed forces; his brother, he said, had been a member of a tank crew who was killed while fighting in Ukraine in 1946. When I expressed surprise about the date, since World War II ended in 1945, Viktor explained that action against anti-Russian Ukrainian partisans continued in Ukraine long after the war. I knew something of these struggles after the war, but I was impressed to hear that domestic resistance to the Soviet government had been on such a scale that tanks were destroyed as late as 1946. Viktor confirmed that large-scale actions occurred in Ukraine at this time, but he did not consider the fact particularly remarkable.

In a charming and personable way, Viktor made it clear that he viewed me as a representative of his ideological enemy, the corrupt and capitalistic West, a social order that he was convinced would soon pass off the political stage. He described this process as an already determined social and economic transition, an inevitable unfolding of history in which individuals played no role. Therefore, he could be on the best of terms with me, and, indeed, displayed great curiosity in me in about the way that an anthropologist might be interested in discovering a member of a passing culture in a remote jungle. Yet the fascination was entirely personal; Viktor never asked political questions, and deflected them when they were asked of him. Even when I tried to appeal to his professional training in the law, asking him about the rights of the accused in Soviet courts, Viktor sailed right through with no display of awareness of truly difficult questions. For me to try to draw him out by admitting that in the United States there were troublesome issues of civil rights such as the current struggles over black rights in America, was totally unsuccessful; to hear that bourgeois scholars worry about their legal system was to Viktor simply what he had known all along, since Western society was riddled with contradictions. It was obvious that Viktor was headed for a successful bureaucratic career in the Soviet Union.

The only remotely critical remark that Viktor would make about the Soviet Union was that the Russians from the European region of the country were too docile, even servile. The reason, he said, was that most of them were descendants of serf families that were released from political and economic bondage only about a century ago. They inherited attitudes of dependence. Siberians like his father's family, on the other hand, had never known serfdom and were therefore truly independent spirits. Yet Viktor gave no examples of how this Siberian freedom had political effects; he saw its expression in the love of Siberians for nature, open spaces (*prostor*), and uncluttered landscapes. He told how, as a boy, he went camping with his friends along Siberian rivers, staying away from home for several weeks and obeying nobody's rules. Waving at the Moscow apartment buildings, he said that the city's residents "have no soul," as indicated by their willingness to live in concrete buildings instead of wooden structures, which Viktor considered much closer to the soil and soul of Mother Russia.

I was afforded a searing insight into the dark side of the Soviet Union during those student years when I witnessed abject terror for the first and only time in my life. A Jewish friend in New York City asked me to deliver a letter to relatives in Moscow with whom he had no contact in forty years. They were an aged couple living in the central city. I went to the address and knocked on the door. When the couple appeared and I told them I was an American with a letter for them from relatives in New York they literally went into shock. For years they had feared a visit from the secret police or a political provocation. I later learned that many of their friends had been arrested and disappeared forever in the camps. Their defense was to try to remain invisible. Now an unknown person stood before them saying he was an American wishing to give them a document which easily could be a fabricated military secret, providing the pretext for their arrests. They began to tremble and threw their arms around each other, their faces drained white. They were petrified by the visit they had so long dreaded. They could not move, only shake. I was so affected by their plight that I reached out, put a hand on the man's shoulder and then closed the door myself. I stood before it for several minutes, their letter still in my hands. What to do? After about five minutes I heard the bolt move forward in the door, locking it. I slipped the letter under the door and left. But the memory of that quaking couple will never leave me.

At the end of the academic year Pat and I, along with the other members of our group of American exchange students at Moscow University, went on a tour of Soviet Central Asia and the Caucasus. This jaunt was a highlight of our year in the Soviet Union. It occurred shortly after the Asian and Caucasian areas had been opened up to foreign tourists and therefore seemed a particularly exciting exploration.

Bokhara and Samarkand are now fairly standard tourist spots, but at that time they were exotic. When we landed at the airport in Bokhara we found that the runway was entirely grass, and cows munched unconcernedly on airport property as we zipped by. The single hotel in the city had no bathrooms, just an outhouse, the detailed description of which should be passed over quickly. Our guide in Bokhara was a young Uzbek who, as he showed us the wonders of medieval Arabic architecture—richly ornamented towers and mosques—rather sarcastically commented, "Our Russian friends tell us that when the Russian Empire took over this area in the late nineteenth century it represented a step upward in culture." This skeptical highly educated young man illustrated both the strengths and weaknesses of Russian colonialism: emphasis on education combined with a condescending attitude toward local cultures.

From Central Asia we went to the rural Caucasus, where our train passed several villages that were completely deserted, with glassless windows in the ruins staring vacantly at us. They had belonged to Caucasian peoples like the Ossetines and Chechens whom Stalin forced out of their homes and to far-away Central Asia, fearing their disloyalty during World War II when the Germans invaded the Caucasus. Fifteen or twenty years after the war some of them were still agitating to return to their homes. Over fifty years after the war, when post-Soviet Russia engaged in an incredibly destructive new war against the restive Chechens who had returned, I would recall these ruined and deserted Chechen villages, remnants of an earlier struggle. The Chechens have for well over a century fought against Russian rule.

On our return to Moscow, Pat and I found an unwelcome surprise. Our room at the dormitory had been stripped of all its possessions. A robber had taken everything, all our clothes, books, and personal possessions. To be absolutely accurate, he had left one or two items of clothing, so few that we could see clearly that he considered these pieces below his standards of taste.

We called the university authorities, who called the police. I knew that in New York such a robbery was so common that the police would not even bother to show up. But a whole party soon arrived, a female police lieutenant and her two male assistants. They crowded into our tiny room and immediately began looking around and asking questions. Soon all our Soviet friends on the eighth floor of the Zone G dormitory were trying to cram into the room, and it became so crowded that Pat and I could hardly move. But the police lieutenant seemed not in the slightest perturbed by the chaos which was making a true investigation impossible.

One of the assistants announced that he thought he should go get a dog that might be able to follow the smell of the intruder. The lieutenant rebuked him, saying that he had read too many detective stories. A dog clearly would not work here, she said, looking at the dozen or so people who were already in the room. The important thing, she said, was to look around the room for a clue to the robber. Perhaps he left something that might permit him to be identified. She began a search of every corner of the room. Under the bed she found that the robber had emptied one of our suitcases but had left the suitcase in place. Opening up the suitcase she extracted a round piece of rubber, and held it to the light. "What is this?" she wanted to know. Pat and I saw simultaneously that it was Pat's contraceptive diaphragm. The lieutenant clearly had never seen anything like it, and neither had her assistants. She carefully examined it, holding it by the edge so that she would not get fingerprints on it. She reached into her bag, extracted a detective's fingerprint set, and sprinkled fingerprint powder on the diaphragm. I thought this was going a little too far, so I mumbled that it belonged to us. The detective lost interest in the diaphragm at this point, and gave it to her assistant. Before I could get my hands on it, the assistant passed it off to one of the students in the room, who stretched it about, peered at it, and then passed it hand-to-hand around the room while Pat slowly turned beet-red.

The detective and her party completed their inspection of the room without success in finding any indication of the robber. As she left she gave us a telephone number and said that we should keep a close eye out, and if we should discover anything in the room that did not belong to us, we should not touch it, but instead call her. It might be something the robber left behind with his fingerprints on it.

The next morning I awoke before Pat. Since I could not get up without dumping her on the floor, I lay there a bit and contemplated the world. From the little blue radio receiver above my head, unsuccessfully turned off, I could barely hear the voice of the morning exercise program. As I looked around the room from bed level, about ten inches off the floor, I spied a little brown object under the bookshelf. It was nothing I had seen before. Perhaps this was the clue the detective was looking for! Forgetting the importance of my prone position, I jumped up and simultaneously deposited Pat on the floor on the other side of the small cot. Holding the object with a handkerchief, I saw it was a round plastic container, a little larger than a pillbox. Ungentlemanly ignoring the first cry of protest from Pat about her undignified treatment, I asked if she had ever seen this object. Without her glasses, she was not sure that she had ever seen me before. Upon repairing her difficulties, she peered at the object, announced that she had not the slightest idea what it was, and crawled back into bed.

I got dressed, left the room, went down the hall to the *pul't,* or control-desk, where the floor telephone was located, and called the police number that the lieutenant had given me. She was not in, sensibly, since it was about 6:30 A.M., but the dispatcher promised to inform her later in the morning.

In several hours the police lieutenant arrived and requested to see the new evidence. I proudly presented the box to her, holding it carefully in my handkerchief. She took it in her hand, looked at it somewhat sheepishly, and announced that it was a part of her fingerprint outfit that she had left behind when she had inspected the room. Quickly recovering, she told me not to give up hope, but to keep an eye out. She felt confident that the thief lived in the dormitory. How would he have gotten all that stuff out past the guard (*dezhurnaia*) at the dormitory door?

Pat and I managed to survive rather well with the clothing and items we had taken with us on the Central Asian trip. Furthermore, we were to be in the Soviet Union only a few more days, so we did not need much clothing. And my notes, the fruit of my year's work, were safe in the embassy. I was even pleased by the thought that when we traveled through Europe on the way home we would not have to lug enormous amounts of luggage. The biggest loss, however, was Pat's jewelry, which, although very inexpensive, had sentimental value. Her Danish relatives had given her some of it when she was a child.

After we left the Soviet Union the police did, in fact, find the thief. He turned out to be Nikolai Kuznetsov, a student on our floor whom I knew. He already owed me ten rubles, which he wormed out of me early in the year when he came to my room and pleaded poverty. My first suspicion about the authenticity of his needs arose when, after taking the ten rubles, he gave me "as security" a ticket in the state lottery, which, of course, was worthless. Other students soon told me that Nikolai was an inveterate gambler and drunk who borrowed from anyone innocent enough to give in to his invented stories of suffering.

Nikolai had not only a room in the dormitory but also an apartment of his own in Moscow, a violation of the housing rules. Students who had apartments in the city, either their own or with their parents, were required to live there and commute to the university, thereby freeing dormitory space for other students. In Nikolai's Moscow apartment the police found an enormous cache of stolen goods, much of it Western, since Nikolai specialized in robbing foreign students. When he came to my room to make his plea for a loan, I am sure he was looking to see what was in the room that might be worth a special trip. He knew that all the Americans were going on a several-week jaunt to Central Asia in early May. He also knew that picking the lock to our room was simplicity itself; in fact, many of the skeleton keys from other rooms would work in the lock on our room.

While we were gone Nikolai went into our room with a roll of brown paper and string. He packed up the clothes and other items in the paper, tied up the bundles, and then dropped them out the window. He then walked out of the dormitory past the guard unencumbered with baggage, went around to the spot under the window where the loot lay, and took it off to his apartment.

The police asked a friend of ours, Lennie Kirsch, to come to the apartment to identify items that might belong to us. Lennie looked over the enormous pile of stuff, and realized that he could not remember what we had in the room. He saw several pieces of Danish jewelry, remembered that Pat came from a Danish family, and identified them as Pat's. They were. He spied several other nice items of clothing and announced that they also belonged to Loren and Pat. One or two of them did.

We were reunited with a few of our belongings when Lennie Kirsch brought them back to the United States many months later. But while he had solved one of our problems, his were just beginning.

CHAPTER FOUR

LENNIE IN THE
WORKERS' PARADISE

THE ONLY OTHER AMERICAN in my dormitory at Moscow University during the 1960–1961 academic year was Lennie Kirsch, a graduate student in economics from Harvard University who lived two floors below me. Lennie came from a worker's family in Pittsburgh with roots in the struggles between capital and labor in the depression, and his political preferences were definitely left. Officials in the United States government had tried to prevent Lennie from coming to the Soviet Union on the new academic exchange program because he had a "file" somewhere, probably in the FBI, which indicated that he had engaged in radical activities.

Over a period of more than thirty years after that time I knew several hundred American students who studied in the USSR but I never saw one who returned to the United States more politically sympathetic with the Soviet government than when he or she left, although most of them returned with a genuine affection for the Russian people. Before our departure, officials from the State Department warned us never to get into romantic or sexual situations with Soviet citizens because we would be photographed, compromised, and enlisted in the services of the KGB. Against this background, it was interesting to observe Lennie's social and political evolution during the year he was in Moscow and afterward.

More than any other American in Moscow, Lennie went native. He was a bachelor and made little preparation for the trip to the Soviet Union. Most foreigners arrived in Moscow (there were very few of them at that time) equipped with clothing and supplies as if they were going to Antarctica, but Lennie came as casually packed as if he were spending the weekend in Paris, and poorly equipped even for that. He intended to buy what he needed in Moscow, and he politely ridiculed the rest of the dozen or so American students for our cultural ethnocentrism. Trying to equip himself with a winter coat, boots, note cards (Lennie was supposed to be researching a doctoral dissertation; he eventually made it to the library), toothpaste, and all the other accouterments necessary for graduate student life in Moscow was Lennie's first introduction to the practical side of the Soviet economy. He found it a daunting task, and for a while I was regularly loaning him toothpaste. Toilet articles and some other items were available at the American Embassy commissary, but Lennie for the first several months refused to patronize this little store, considering it a distasteful cultural compromise. Instead, he scoured the stores of Moscow, spending a good part of his first months there trying to find basic equipment. In the process he soon came to know Moscow as well as his native Pittsburgh.

Lennie spoke Russian atrociously upon his arrival, but his ignorance of the rules of Russian grammar never fazed him. He spoke Russian constantly and easily, and developed a way of swallowing the word endings so one could not quite hear that most of the case endings and other inflections were incorrect. So far as I know, he never attended the language lessons that the Soviet authorities provided free to all of us, preferring to pick up the language his own way. If he had a grammar or dictionary, I never saw it. I spent a lot of time with Lennie, since he was living in my dormitory, but he usually insisted that I speak Russian with him, not English, a fact that immensely amused our Russian friends.

Lennie brought to mind the famous description of the writer Heywood Broun: "he looked like an unmade bed." His rimless glasses were always coated with such a layer of grime that surely his vision operated on the same basis as his language, mostly intuition. In conversation (Lennie knew no other state of existence) he constantly scratched himself, often the calves of his legs, but any other spot, including the most intimate, that made itself known to his sensory perception. His clothing, all Soviet, soon lost what little semblance of style it once had possessed. During the entire year he sent nothing to the cleaners. (Preparing clothing for dry cleaning in those days required removing all buttons and sewing them back on when the clothing returned in several weeks.) The imitation fur collar on his new overcoat soon came half off, and flapped in the wind as Lennie hopped off buses and onto trolley cars all over Moscow.

Traveling around the city with Lennie required special talents and brought its own rewards. In his company one never hurried anywhere, for he had to sample every edible or drinkable ware that was offered on the streets, whether it be fermented mare's milk, the drink made from bread known as *kvas*, or the little stuffed pies called *pirozhki*. Lennie was totally unconcerned that most of the drinks were served to all customers out of one glass or cup, sometimes perfunctorily rinsed in cold water. The people who sold these refreshments were usually chunky little women bundled in brown scarves, soiled white aprons, and felt boots covered with rubbers. The food came off tiny tables set up on the streets, and the drinks came out of portable tanks, sometimes with wheels. Occasionally, soda water could be purchased from automated machines, complete with a glass and a self-rinser; Lennie frowned on the machines, however, since he always wanted to strike up a conversation while making his purchase, and the machines were unresponsive.

On one occasion as Lennie and I made our way down a back street in downtown Moscow he spied a woman setting up a stand with hot *pirozhki*. This was one of Lennie's favorite street foods because it absolutely demanded conversation and negotiation. *Pirozhki* came stuffed with a great variety of different fillings, from cabbage, to sausage, to a rare piece of pork, and identifying what one was getting was part of the game. Lennie hurried up to the woman to make sure that he was first in line, greeted her jauntily, and asked "What's in the *pirozhki* today?" Naturally, he butchered the Russian language, confusing his pronouns, and actually asked "Who's in the *pirozhki* today?" (*pirozhki s kem*, not *pirozhki s chem*). The woman looked at Lennie with amused eyes, and replied, "What are you, a cannibal?" Lennie smiled through his spattered glasses and said that he would take whatever she had.

So long as Lennie did not speak, he was often taken for a Russian. After several months in Moscow his new Soviet outfit acquired the necessary run-down appearance for him to meld with the subway and street crowds imperceptibly. Once Lennie and I were walking along Gorky Street (now Tver Street), in the absolute center of Moscow. I stopped to look in the windows of one of my favorite used-book stores between the Ermolaev Theater and the National Hotel, located in a building that was later torn down in order to build the glassy Intourist Hotel that sat there for years until torn down again in the post-Soviet period and replaced with yet another hotel, the Ritz-Carlton. Lennie walked on ahead, munching on a piece of khalva that he had picked up a block or two back, and soon was at what is probably the main street corner in Moscow, the intersection of Gorky Street and *Okhotnyi Riad* (Hunters' Row, for a time in the late Soviet period, Marx Street), in sight of the Kremlin and Red Square. At this intersection two American tourists popped out of the National Hotel on what was obviously their first day in Moscow. Being confused about their location, one of them spied Lennie, clearly a native, walking down the street. He caught up with Lennie and asked in English, very slowly so that he would be understood, "Can you please tell me where the Bolshoi Theater is?" Lennie replied, "Well, you go underground here across Gorky Street, then you walk straight ahead a block and a half, and then look on your left, and you can't miss it. It dominates the square." The two Americans thanked Lennie and as they moved in the direction he indicated, one of them turned to the other and said, "Did you hear that English? I told you that the Soviet system of education is just vastly superior to the American system."

Lennie was immensely popular with the Russians, especially with the women students. During the fall he had a series of wonderful and passionate romances, violating every rule of behavior the State Department had recommended. I learned to knock and wait outside his dormitory room for an invitation to enter. He was almost never alone, and the women were amazingly unembarrassed about being caught in various states of dress. The Victorian prudishness that we had been told characterized Soviet society was invisible.

In the evenings there was often a party, or *vecherinka*, in Lennie's dormitory room, where ten or twelve of us would crowd into the tiny space. It was at one of Lennie's parties that I learned the technique of opening a bottle of Soviet wine by giving it a sharp slap on the bottom. The cork obligingly pops out the top, and if one does it just right, no wine is spilt, or at least not much wine. I became rather expert at it, but, strangely enough, the method never worked for me outside the Soviet Union. I once made a real mess of a railroad car compartment in East Germany when I tried the technique there. And the wine was a Soviet brand, too.

About halfway through the academic year we noticed that Lennie was spending a great deal of time with one Russian girl, a sensitive and serious young woman named Elena (Lena) Kniazkina. She was a specialist in Portuguese literature with a striking background. Her father had fought against the Bolsheviks as a member of an army under General Anton Denikin, one of the leaders of the White forces during the

Civil War after the Russian Revolution. At the end of the Civil War her father had been arrested and sent to a labor camp near Ukhta, in the Arctic region of Russia. During the decades of the Stalin period he continued to live in the camp, married, and had a child, Lena. Sometime during the process he became a trusty of the camp, and moved into a minor supervisory role. After Stalin's death Khrushchev disbanded this camp, along with many others, and Lena and her parents were free to go. However, they continued to live near Ukhta, and still had a home there, although Lena was now a student at Moscow University.

After my wife Pat joined me in the dormitory in the early spring, we both became close friends with Lennie and Lena. Often we would have breakfast together, with Pat fixing pancakes on a one-burner hot plate in our tiny room. Lena did not speak English, so all conversation was in Russian. This threw Pat into the position that Lennie had been at the beginning of the year, and soon Pat was jabbering away in ungrammatical but perfectly understandable Russian. Since Pat's field was American history, there was no reason for her to learn Russian, but she did. She actually had the best of reasons, pure survival in a totally Russian environment. I was proud of her, but Lennie was even prouder, since he recognized in her his type of Russian language student. He enjoyed teaching her outrageously obscene phrases while pretending that they were the absolutely proper ways to say certain things. Pat did not learn how scatological some of these phrases were until she was expelled the following fall from a Columbia University language class by a very proper émigré Russian language teacher. When the teacher had asked Pat how she was feeling today, Pat had answered with a phrase often used in the Moscow dormitory, which was roughly equivalent to "Fine, and how's your hammer hanging today?"

In the late spring Lennie and Lena announced that they wished to get married. At that time such marriages between American and Soviet citizens were very rare. In fact, Lennie and Lena may have been the first such marriage coming out of the academic exchange program, which had just been established two years earlier. In later years there were many. Pat and I celebrated their decision together over champagne in the Sofia Hotel, together with another couple, Russian and American students also, who were playing with the same idea. But the other couple became discouraged by all the obstacles that such a marriage between citizens of antagonistic countries entailed; they knew, for example, that Robert Tucker, who worked at the American Embassy after World War II, had to wait many years before his Russian wife, Zhenia, was permitted to leave the Soviet Union. Lennie and

Lena were determined, however, to make the attempt, and we knew
that they would not be easily discouraged.

Getting married meant first gaining permission from a Soviet bureaucracy in charge of issuing marriage licenses, ZAGS. That required
weeks of importuning, applying all known methods of getting results
out of Soviet officials. At moments the chances seemed nil. Suddenly,
on May 17, 1961, permission came. Lennie and Lena wanted to get
married the same day they received the license, fearing that it had
been issued as a bureaucratic mistake soon to be corrected. Lennie
called me and asked if I would act as best man (literally, "first witness"), found Lena's parents touring the Tretiakov Art Gallery (they
had come to Moscow from Ukhta in preparation for the hoped-for
wedding), and we all assembled in the Palace of Marriages.

The Palace of Marriages was a yellow stucco building ornately decorated with chandeliers, parquet floors, and oriental carpets. Like others
of its type, it had been created by the Soviet government in a grand
style so that it might compete with Orthodox churches as an impressive place for marriage. Weddings were held here in assembly-line fashion, with each party given twenty or thirty minutes for a ceremony and
a reception, complete with refreshments.

Lennie and Lena's wedding party consisted of about ten or twelve
people: her parents, Pat and me, and a handful of other friends, both
Russians and Americans. We marched in to the wedding ceremony
to music, played on a loudspeaker connected to a tape-recorder. The
music was the Soviet national anthem, already too familiar to us.
Standing in front of us were two women dressed in business suits, one
of them a deputy of the local City Soviet, or governing body. Beside
her was a bust of Lenin, and on the wall behind a Soviet flag. She read
the marriage vows, to which I paid little attention. I noticed that Lennie and Lena, dressed much more simply than the Soviet officials,
paid no attention at all to what was being said. Lena's father and
mother stood on the other side of the bride and groom. They had been
yanked out of the Tretiakov Gallery so abruptly for the ceremony that
her father had not had time to shave that day, and stood there with a
very healthy growth of stubble covering his chin.

The Soviet deputy droned on as I mused. Suddenly, I realized that
she was turning to me. As first witness to this marriage, she said, I had
the responsibility to see that all progeny of this union would be "raised
in the spirit of Marxism-Leninism." Did I agree? Without blanching, I
agreed, resolving inwardly to send each of Lennie and Lena's children
all 62 volumes of Lenin's collected works on their first birthdays. I

could think of no better set of building blocks, although they would have to be warned not to crawl into the houses they built, since those collapsing tomes might do real damage.

After the wedding we repaired to the reception room, where we drank champagne and ate "Gagarin" cookies, named after the Soviet space explorer. As we drank and nibbled, we were aware that the next wedding party was already assembling in the hall, making quite a bit of noise, so there was little chance that we would imbibe too much or tarry too long.

During conversation at the reception Pat and I saw one man in a stylishly cut suit, obviously made in the West, who was unfamiliar to us. He was also eating and drinking and seemed to want to be a part of the wedding. Since we knew most of Lennie and Lena's friends, and surely all of his Western friends, we were curious about his identity. We went over to talk to him, and learned that he was an official from the American Embassy. He said that the embassy wanted to know about all marriages between American and Soviet citizens, since frequently they lead to later diplomatic negotiations about place of residence. In fact, he said that this was the second marriage between an American man and a Soviet woman he had recently attended. This observation greatly surprised us, since we thought we knew all Americans, or at least almost all, in Moscow at that time. The other American he said, was named Oswald, and the marriage took place in Minsk. A little over two years later Pat and I recalled this conversation when the name Lee Harvey Oswald was catapulted onto the front pages of newspapers all over the world.

Twenty-one years after Lennie and Lena's marriage, in the spring of 1982, I chaired a faculty seminar at Harvard University which Priscilla Johnson McMillan, the biographer of Marina Oswald, attended as a guest. Finding myself beside her after the seminar, and trying to make conversation, I told her the story of Lennie and Lena's wedding. I mentioned that after the wedding my wife and I had met an American official who said that he had just recently attended Lee and Marina Oswald's wedding in Minsk. "Are you sure?" she asked. When I replied that I was quite sure, she exclaimed, "Oh dear, I hope the believers in conspiracy never get hold of this." It had never occurred to me that my story would be of more than passing interest to her, so naturally I was curious about her strong reaction. She said that there had been much speculation about contacts between Oswald and American officials while he was in the Soviet Union, but the Warren Report had concluded, after questioning relevant government personnel, that no contacts of any kind had taken place. "Are you certain that the American said that he attended Lee and Marina's wedding?" she repeated. "That was a very small ceremony, as described by Marina to me, and she never said anything about an American official." I said that I was sure, but added that when I got home I would check with my wife.

When I returned home that evening I asked Pat, without any preparation, what she remembered of that long-ago conversation. She told the same story I have told above, including the statement by the official that he had recently attended the wedding of an American named Oswald in Minsk. I then asked her if it was possible that we were mistaken in saying that he had *attended* the wedding of Oswald; maybe he had merely said that he knew of the wedding. Pat said that it was barely possible that he had said the latter, but she, along with me, had no doubt that we had met the man at Lennie's and Lena's wedding, and that he had said that this was the second recent American–Soviet wedding with which he was connected, and the previous wedding had been Oswald's in Minsk.

I have never read the Warren Report and have little interest in the conspiracy theories of John F. Kennedy's death. I have been told that American officials have denied all knowledge of any contact with Oswald during the time he was in the Soviet Union. I am not sure about contact, but I am absolutely certain that at least one American official knew about Oswald's wedding in Minsk in the spring of 1961. I doubt that this fact strengthens conspiracy theories, but I offer it for what it is worth.

With Lennie's and Lena's wedding their struggles had barely begun. Getting permission to get married was one thing; obtaining permission for Lena to leave the Soviet Union was entirely another. Lennie stayed on in Moscow after the other American students studying in the 1960–1961 academic year left. He managed to get his visa extended for a while, and together with Lena they battled the bureaucracy in an effort to get Lena out. Lennie told Lena to practice bending over double touching her toes because if all else failed he said he was going to smuggle her out by putting her in a fold-over garment bag and carrying her onto the plane. During this time in Moscow Lennie met many other Soviet citizens who were fighting officialdom over one issue or another, or who were suffering some sort of persecution. I knew that Lennie's sympathies for the suffering citizens of the Soviet Union were deepening when I heard that he, a convinced atheist, was giving prayer shawls to members of the Moscow Jewish community who were having difficulty finding them. After four or five additional months, Lennie's visa could no longer be extended, and he had to return to the United States, with no garment bag. From Cambridge, Massachusetts, he carried on his campaign, badgering the Soviet Embassy in Washington and anyone else who would listen. The months dragged by.

Lennie knew how to enlist people in his aid. Indeed, anyone who spent five minutes with Lennie, even on the telephone, was his ally. After a long period of frustration, Lennie managed to get Eleanor Roosevelt and Nina Khrushchev in direct communication with one another in his and Lena's behalf. That it would take this sort of contact to unlock the doors was typical of Soviet bureaucracy. Often the reason that a request was not granted was not because of a negative decision on a high level, but simply because without some sort of push from the top, the answer to every request was negative.

Lennie and Lena were reunited. Lennie, Pat, and I met her at Kennedy Airport in New York and brought her to our simple graduate student's apartment on West 111th Street near Columbia. Lena did not notice the dirty streets and cockroaches; she noticed the fresh fruit we served with the late breakfast with which we welcomed her.

Lennie and Lena moved to the Boston area, living at first in a sunny apartment on a hill in Somerville overlooking Harvard in the distance. Later, Lennie wrote quite a good book on Soviet wage policies, based on interviews and research he did in Moscow, and received a tenure appointment at the University of Massachusetts, Boston. They bought a house, moved to suburban Lexington, and soon had a lovely daughter, Lara. To my eternal shame, I did not send Lara the promised collected works of Lenin.

Lennie never quite became a typical American suburbanite. His political views remained left, although now very critical of the Soviet Union. He participated actively in the anti-Vietnam War and peace movements, and was a consultant to the United Auto Workers. He still considered himself a democratic socialist, but I remember being astounded hearing him say in Moscow, shortly after his marriage and following a fruitless trip to a grocery store, "You know, Loren, I am going to go up to the first fat bourgeois supermarket operator I see in the United States and kiss him on the cheek."

In the United States he continued to demand that everybody and everything that he met converse with him. He still sampled everything edible that came his way. His girth grew with his experience, and soon his doctor was advising him to jog, since he had developed a heart condition. Lennie could not jog alone the way other Cantabridgians did; whom could he talk to? He formed a jogging club at the Russian

Research Center at Harvard, and interspersed his puffs with acerbic comments on the state of the world.

On July 5, 1977, at the age of forty-two, Lennie Kirsch died of a heart attack. He was buried in his native Pittsburgh. Lena Kirsch still lives in Lexington.

I have never met anyone who had such an extraordinary mixture of qualities and attributes—and I suspect I never will. Lennie sailed through life navigating without charts and following his own unique, solipsistic compass. Like Don Quixote, he was an errant knight (well, perhaps a very erratic knight), and, in his own way, admirable.

CHAPTER FIVE

RURAL RUSSIA AND
THE FORBIDDEN FISH

THE DIFFICULTIES I ENCOUNTERED when I tried to take Pat and
our daughter, Meg, with me on that first odyssey to Russia stemmed
not from the fact that Pat was somehow *persona non grata* in the eyes
of the Soviet government but that for some reason its officials refused
to give three-year-old Meg an entry visa. We could not abandon our
daughter for a year, so before my departure time we constantly but
fruitlessly pestered the Soviet Embassy in Washington to relent. Finally, at the last moment when a change would have permitted us all
three to be in Russia together, I demanded on the telephone with a
Soviet Embassy official that he either give permission for all three of us
to come, or state the reason for the refusal. The nonplussed consular
officer replied, "Your daughter's entry is considered dangerous to the
Soviet state."

We were flabbergasted at the thought that our sweet little child could
be any kind of threat. We admitted to ourselves that Meg was sometimes very rambunctious, and might occasionally be considered dangerous to a state of composure, but a threat to a mighty political state,
the vanguard of socialism, she was not. We spent many hours speculat-
ing what the actual reason for the refusal might be. Could it be that the
Soviet officials felt that they did not have room for a family of three in
the Moscow University dormitories? Possibly, but when I arrived in
Moscow I found Russian families of three and four living in one room
in the same building as I. Or was it that the Russian officials did not
want to set a precedent for exchange students taking whole families to
the other country out of fear that if Russian families did the same thing

on trips to the United States, the entire family might defect? This theory seemed a bit more likely, but it was also only a speculation. In the end, we never found out why Meg could not come, and simply had to accept the reality of the refusal, whatever the reason.

Thus our decision that I would go to the Soviet Union alone, but that in January Pat and Meg would fly to Europe to live for a while near Danish relatives, and then in the early spring Pat would come to spend the last three months together with me in Moscow. For those three months Meg would stay in the United States with a family of friends that included another little girl her age, one of her nursery school classmates and already her best friend.

When, in the early spring of 1961, Pat was finally able to come to the Soviet Union, I was ecstatic to meet her. She was already in Western Europe and decided to come to Moscow by train from the Hook of Holland. We agreed that it would be wonderful to meet halfway, in Warsaw, Poland, spend the Easter weekend there, and then return on the train to Moscow.

When Ole Mathiesen, an American at Moscow University participating in the same exchange program as I, heard that I was going to Warsaw he asked if I would do a favor for him. Ole was a fisheries specialist from the University of Washington, and he had helped make a documentary film on the breeding habits of the sockeye salmon of the Columbia River. The film, entitled "The Sensitive Sockeye," evidently (I never saw the film although later I wished that I had) depicted the complicated spawning cycle of the sockeye salmon with many sequences taken in the rapids of the Columbia River. A Polish colleague of Ole's in the Institute of Ichthyology of the Academy of Sciences in Warsaw was very eager to show the film to researchers at his institute. The film was 16 mm in size in one large reel, and was contained in a brown plastic case the size of a briefcase. Not having had the experience of crossing Soviet borders that I gained in the following thirty years, it never occurred to me that the film would present difficulties. I instantly agreed to Ole's request.

Going to Warsaw and back by train was not the simple task that one might think, even though both Poland and the Soviet Union were allies in the Warsaw Pact. As a foreigner I was required to obtain permission far in advance, and I also needed an exit and entry visa for the trip, since I would be crossing the Soviet border twice. Straightening out these bureaucratic details required countless trips to the *inotdel* (foreign office) of the university and also multiple visits to the central Soviet office that issued such visas (OVIR), both to foreigners and to So-

viet citizens themselves. The natural instinct of Soviet bureaucrats to
all questions was to delay, to tell you that your request was "being pro-
cessed." By this time I had developed the tactic for conquering the
Soviet bureaucracy which I utilized for many years, namely, to be extremely polite but at the same time to be an enormous bother, showing
up every morning early enough to meet the relevant official as he entered the building, calling frequently, and soaking up the time of all
the personnel in the office while never giving genuine grounds for
irritation. An occasional flower or two for the secretaries definitely
helped, which could then be a preface to a long conversation about
any innocent topic. The goal, of course, was to persuade the bureaucrats that it would be easier for them to give me what I wanted than it
would be to have to spend so much time dealing with me. Such a
tactic would never work on a truly difficult issue, but for fairly simple
ones was quite effective. Eventually my visas were in my hands, and I
left Moscow by train from the Belorusskii station.

The trip itself was revealing for the view of the Russian countryside
that it gave in the early spring, the time of the infamous *rasputitsa*
(season of bad roads). From the train windows every country road appeared to be an impassable bog. The trucks and occasional horse-
drawn sledges tried to avoid the worst ruts by cutting other paths to the
left or right of the main road, having the effect of creating crisscrossed
seas of mud as wide as double lane superhighways. Looking out at this
view of rural Russia I could understand a conversation between the
leader of the Soviet Union Nikita Khrushchev and the American corn
farmer Roswell Garst. Khrushchev vowed to bring Soviet agriculture
up to the level of American agriculture and visited the United States to
inspect personally the ways in which American farms were run. In the
process he became so converted to the idea of corn (not a traditional
Russian crop) that in the Soviet Union some people called him
kukuruzchik ("little corn man"). When Khrushchev visited the Iowa
farm of Garst he asked the American farmer what particular scientific
techniques lay behind the American success in high productivity of
corn, since the same crop did not seem to do as well in the Soviet
Union. Instead of referring to any genetic miracles behind hybrid corn,
or special means of cultivation or fertilization—as Khrushchev obviously expected—Garst told Khrushchev that the first step in creating a
modern agriculture was to build proper roads that allowed farmers to
get their crops to market, as well as to bring in the right equipment and
materials.

The villages and fields that flashed by my train window seemed me-

dieval in appearance. Women swaddled in dark quilted coats and wearing felt boots walked to the village wells carrying wooden yokes over
their shoulders on which hung wooden buckets. The wells were of the
type that had existed for centuries, open holes topped with hand cranks
of wood from which fraying ropes descended. Other women washed
clothing in streams where plates of ice still clung to the riverbanks.
Goats and cows wandered down the streets without obvious destina-
tions or ownership. Everywhere people walked—through the forests,
across the fields, from house to house—creating a thick network of
trails through the snow and mud. The forests and the fields were held
in common, and anyone could go anywhere. The concept of private
property was unknown.

The collective and state farm system preserved a system of agricultural production that was not in physical appearance or functioning
very different from the remnants of the traditional system of serfdom
in pre-Revolutionary Russia, with small one-street villages lined with
wooden huts close together dominating the vista. While in the United
States, farms were isolated and scattered over the countryside, in central Russia all houses, even in the most rural areas, were concentrated
in villages. This form of organization was historically a relic of the
strip-system of cultivation of the middle ages (one could see vestiges of
the same system in a few parts of rural Western Europe, especially
France) but it had been encapsulated and preserved by the collective
farm system of Soviet Russia, and its contemporary form presented
itself to me graphically from the windows of my train car. This Soviet
system of agriculture even contained controls over places of residence,
just as serfdom had. Soviet agriculture was not based on strips of land,
except for the small private plots behind all the village houses, but it
maintained the ancient communal form of cultivation. Everyone in
the village participated in planting and harvesting at the same times. It
was a highly inefficient system, allowing no room for individual initia-
tive, and it resulted in extremely low productivity, at least by Western
standards.

Yet every system has some advantages, I suppose, and as I looked at
the little clumps of people talking over back fences or gathered around
the village wells, I realized that the Soviet system resulted in a great
deal of social intercourse. Everyone had opportunity to exchange
the latest piece of social gossip with the neighbors, and conversation
seemed more common than work. Coming from the farm region of
the Middle West I remembered how isolated the farm families there
were; farm wives with small children on the insular farms of the great

plains often spent the whole working day without a word of conversation with another adult, while their husbands worked out in the fields. Rural Soviet Russia did not have that particular problem, but it had about every other problem one could think of. Many of the villages did not have telephones, and some did not have electricity. Yet four years earlier the Soviet Union had launched a satellite into space, opening the age of space exploration.

Eventually our train arrived at the border station of Brest. Here it was necessary to stop while the axles and wheels under the cars were removed and replaced with those of a smaller size, for Soviet railroads (and Russian railroads of today) were of a wider gauge than those of Western Europe. This system dates back to the nineteenth century, of course, and it is said that the reason for it is that the tsarist government feared that if the Russian railways were of the same size as those of Western Europe it would be too easy for an invader to penetrate the Russian heartland. I later found out that the actual reason for the different size gauge was that the Russians adopted the wider gauge American system over the narrower European one as better suited for their broad expanses of land, but the security argument was probably also present in their minds. Before the Revolution, centralization of power was as prevalent as it was in the later Soviet Union, and policy on everything from railroads to publishing was set by authorities in the capital.

Another story (which may not be true, but is so amusing that one hopes that it is) about Russian railroads and the centralization of power concerns the line from Moscow to St. Petersburg. This railroad runs absolutely straight between the cities except for one small deviation about midway. For generations people have said that when Tsar Nicholas I was asked where he wanted the railroad between the two capital cities to be located he took a ruler and drew a straight line between the cities on a large map. His thumb holding the ruler, however, caused the pencil line to make a small half-circle at the midway point, and that ended up as the only deviation on the Moscow–St. Petersburg line.

After the completion of the change of railroad wheels the train rolled on into the border crossing proper. Here we stopped again at a small station while the border officials moved through the cars, checking passports and asking questions about materials being taken outside the Soviet Union. I knew that Soviet officials were extremely careful about materials being brought into the Soviet Union, but I was less aware at that time of their interest in materials going out. This was my first experience in leaving the country. When the young officer came into my compartment his first request was to see my passport. Learning that I spoke Russian, he asked if I had any letters from "other persons" or any manuscripts. My negative reply seemed to satisfy him, but he asked me to open my suitcase, which I did. His rather cursory examination appeared to be the end of the encounter; he told me to close the suitcase, and he turned to go out of the compartment. At this moment he caught sight of the film case leaning against the wall under the window. "What is that?" he wanted to know. I replied that it was a scientific film about fish that I was taking to the Institute of Ichthyology in Warsaw. He wanted me to open it up, and he peered rather unsuccessfully at the first few frames. "You must come with me," he announced, and out the train we went, together with the film.

The Brest station was small, a little similar to a multitude of train stations in towns in the United States in my childhood, now almost all torn down. It had two stories; we went through the main room downstairs, out the back and across an interior courtyard, up an outside stairway, down a hallway and into the largest room on the second floor, which I recognized as the office of the commandant of the border station. This room was a long, fairly wide hall, with rows of chairs going down either side leading to a large desk at the end. Five or six of the chairs had soldiers sitting in them. Despite the imposing stack of rifles, with bayonets fixed, by the door and the fact that everyone in the room was in uniform, the appearance was not rigidly military. The solders appeared to be kids with broad faces straight out of rural Russia, and they slouched in their chairs. Their uniforms were unpressed and worn, and if their shoes had ever been shined there was no evidence of it. They appeared incredibly bored, and one or two dozed. Sitting behind the desk at the end of the hallway there was a more presentable eminence, the officer in charge.

The customs officer who had come through the train explained the situation to the commandant, took the film out of my hand, and laid it upon the desk. The commandant asked me to explain the origin and the destination of the film, which I did. Without opening the film, he told me that I could not take the film with me, that it would remain in Brest. I politely protested, explaining how disappointed the Polish fisheries experts would be and how this would be a disruption of scientific communication in the newly-initiated exchanges between the countries of the Soviet bloc and those of the West. He replied that he had no way of knowing what the film was about, and that it might contain military secrets.

I recognized that I was not going to change this decision in the few minutes that remained. The train was preparing to leave. There was no time to view the film, nor was there time for me to apply my favorite method for dealing with the Soviet bureaucracy. Fortunately, I would be coming back through Brest on my return to Moscow in a few days, and I could pick up the film in order to return it to Ole. It was too bad that I could not deliver the film to its Polish destination, but the turn of events was not a disaster if I could pick up the film on my return trip and give it back to Ole. So I reconciled myself to the commandant's decision.

However, I was worried that when I returned to Brest in a few days I might meet entirely different customs officers who would profess no knowledge whatsoever of my film and refuse to give it back. So I explained all this to the commandant, and asked for a receipt for the film that I could show the officials on my return. "Nyet," was the immediate response. "Wait a minute," I replied, "I have recently read the Soviet custom rules (they were posted at all border crossings and airports, where I had read them) and these rules specifically state that if customs officials take anything from visitors, they are obliged to give them a receipt." The commandant was unmoved. I asked to see a copy of the customs rules so that I could show him where they state that receipts must be given. Again, the commandant simply replied, "nyet." Seeing that my argument was having no effect whatsoever on the commandant, I turned to the young soldier sitting to the side on the nearest chair and asked if he did not agree with me that when one takes something from another person that a receipt may be requested and should be given. The peasant youth was totally unprepared for this interrogation; his mind had obviously been home in Tomsk or maybe Omsk. He stared at me with amazed and frightened eyes, caught the last half of the question, quickly nodded affirmatively, shot a glance at the disapproving scowl on the face of his commanding officer, turned back to me and wagged his head negatively so vigorously that if his hat had been on his cropped head it would have fallen off.

I resumed my argument with the commandant. I explained that this was a very expensive film, that it did not belong to me, that I was a graduate student with little money, and that I needed something to show in order to regain the film, or at least to give evidence for what had happened to it. The officer refused to converse with me, merely pronouncing the one negative syllable that was obviously the safest part of his vocabulary.

"What is your name?" I demanded of the officer. He remained silent, imperceptibly shaking his head. I repeated the question. Again, no reply. I exclaimed that I realized that he was doing his duty, as he saw it, in taking my film. I disagreed with that decision, but I was willing to live with it if he would give me a receipt, or at least identify himself as the officer who received the film. The same soundless negative reply greeted my beautifully logical argument.

At this point I foolishly lost my temper. Part of the reason was the fact that during several months of struggling with the Soviet bureaucracy and difficult living conditions in Moscow I had previously maintained an amiable disposition, and the accumulated frustrations were bursting their binds. Somehow I now held this silent officer responsible for every difficulty I had experienced in the Soviet Union so far, and there had been many of them. I later learned that one "flame-out" of this sort was common among Westerners living for extended periods in the Soviet Union.

I reached in my pocket and took out a pencil and paper, and began writing and talking at the same time. I sensed a secret delight that finally my facility in the Russian language permitted me to express my anger and disdain. "So you won't tell me your name," I said. "No matter, we will not have much trouble finding out who you are. It is April 1, 1961, and the time is 8:15 A.M. (How appropriate, I thought, that this is April Fools' Day.) You are the senior officer present at the Brest station at this time." Staring intently at him, I observed out loud and wrote down on my notepad that he was about five feet ten inches tall, had dark hair receding on each side of his forehead, a mole on his chin, was about forty years old, and had two stars on his epaulets. I then said that upon my return to Moscow I would take up this matter with "my friend" the American ambassador, ask him to work with Soviet officials to identify the Soviet officer who broke customs rules at Brest by taking property from an American citizen while refusing to give a receipt in return, or even identify himself. Here I exaggerated a bit: it is true that I had met the American ambassador to the USSR, Llewellyn Thompson, several months earlier when he invited me along with other American students to his residence, Spaso House, for Thanksgiving dinner, but he was hardly my friend. I doubt that Ambassador Thompson would remember our conversation. But by now my anger and satisfaction with my approach to the customs officer were out of control.

My attack was successful in unlocking the man's tongue. He turned white, rose to his full height, and spoke so rapidly that I had to strain the catch the weighty words. "*Gospodin* Graham," he blurted, "that

train out there is leaving." He turned to the original customs officer
still standing by my side and told him to go tell the engineer to depart
immediately. The officer left the room and I could hear his rapid steps
down the hall and stair. Turning back to me, the commandant announced, "If you are not on that train when it departs momentarily, I
will take no responsibility whatsoever for your safety. Have you ever
heard of Siberia, *Gospodin* Graham? Do you know what we do with
troublemakers like you? Would you like to spend some time in Siberia?"

Everyone in the room was now standing. The soldiers even looked
military for the first time. The train emitted a short whistle. I recognized defeat. I turned and ran out of the room, down the hall, down
the stair. As I ran across the interior courtyard I realized that I was
picking up speed and was now stretching flat-out. I shot through the
waiting room and out on the platform where I found that the train was
already moving. I grabbed the door handle of one of the last cars,
pulled myself on board, and made my way through the cars until I
found my compartment.

Sitting down in the seat, I stared out the window, and with nothing
else to do, naturally had, for the first time, a real attack of nervous
fright. In fact, I became so nervous that I was several hours into Poland
before I calmed down. Despite my anxiety (or maybe because of it) I
noticed as we crossed the Russian–Polish border that it seemed as
heavily fortified as the famous border between West and East Germany. There were the same double rows of barbed fences interrupted
by watchtowers, separated by wide stretches of raked sand so that any
footprint would be clearly visible. I mused that the fact that both Poland and the Soviet Union were members of the same political bloc
did not seem to have an effect on the appearances of borders.

At the railroad station in Warsaw I was met by an ichthyologist from
the Polish institute awaiting the film on the breeding habits of the
"Sensitive Sockeye." When I told him that the film had been taken at
the border he wanted to know if Soviet or Polish officials had done so.
My reply that the Soviets were responsible disappointed him, since he
thought he could do something about it if the Poles had the film.

A few hours after arriving in Warsaw I was supposed to meet Pat
coming on the train from the other direction, from Western Europe.
In those hours I checked in at the European Hotel, and took a short
tour around the city. I was struck with how much more color there was
in the store windows and in the people's clothing than in Moscow.
And the shops were better supplied with food than the Moscow stores,

although they were still clearly inadequate by West European or American standards. Back in Moscow the constant refrain in the newspapers, on radio, and on television was the call "to catch up and surpass the United States" in economic output. Even my Russian language teacher, a sweet and helpful woman who gave a small group of us free lessons in a small upstairs room in the Zoological Museum on Hertsen Street, had often spoken of how the Soviet Union would surpass the United States in consumer goods. I thought that if I were impolite when I returned I would tell her that a more appropriate slogan might be to overtake Poland in lifestyle. I knew, of course, that I would never say it.

Pat and I had agreed that I would meet her train in Warsaw, and she was eagerly awaiting that moment. During her long ride on the train from the Hook of Holland she had ample opportunity to get to know some of the other West European passengers on the train, and she told them how after months of absence her husband would meet her at the Warsaw train station. As her train pulled in to the station her friends peered from the windows to see what kind of a husband she had and to witness our happy reunion. Unfortunately, I was not waiting for her; I had gone mistakenly to another of the several railway stations in Warsaw. Pat got off the train with her suitcases and bags, and stood disconsolately on the platform, while her friends stared from the train at her apparent abandonment. No doubt they doubted the story Pat had told them about the existence of a faithful husband. Pat called out to them that I would soon arrive, no doubt as much for her own benefit as theirs. The train with its spectators left, and Pat waited. At this moment, her situation was the same as if the customs officer at Brest had truly shipped me off to Siberia.

Eventually I came racing down her platform after having discovered my mistake in the other train station and hastily taking a taxi to the right station. After this bumpy start, we had a glorious weekend in Warsaw. We spent a great deal of time in the Old Town, which had only been recently restored to its pre-war splendor.

After several days of relaxation in Warsaw, we started on the train back to Moscow. Pat had a "soft" (first-class) ticket valid from the Hook of Holland to Moscow, while I was traveling on a cheaper ticket that assigned me to a separate car with hard benches. But the train was mostly empty, and I quickly joined Pat in her sleeping compartment, to the delight of the Russian female conductor, who assumed that we had struck up a friendship on the train that rapidly became very close indeed. We did not disappoint her by telling her that we had been married for six years. More importantly, we had been apart for the previous seven months.

We pulled into the Brest station on the Soviet side of the border at about three o'clock in the morning. Of course I had told Pat of my adventures there a few days earlier, and we were both eager and a bit anxious about our reception. The arrival time made me suspect that only the most junior official would be on duty at such an inconvenient moment, a person without the authority to return a movie film to a suspicious-looking American man. Out the window the station looked very familiar, although now completely dark except for lights on the train platform. None of the offices on the second floor looked open, adding to my pessimistic predictions. A young Soviet customs officer soon came through, one whom I had not seen before. Glancing at my passport, he immediately pronounced my name, with a long guttural "kh" in the middle—"Graakhkhaam"—and said that he had heard about me. I replied that I wished to pick up a film that had been taken from me several days before at this same station. I was relieved to see that he seemed to know what I was talking about, since otherwise it was a fanciful tale.

"Come with me," he said, and I headed out the compartment. To my surprise, Pat came with me. She assured me that if this was the first leg of a trip to Siberia, she was making the journey with me. No more waiting at empty train platforms for her.

We crossed into the station, where the waiting room was so dark that we could hardly follow the officer along the path that I now knew rather well. We stumbled in the dark over several unknown objects and made our way out the back door, across the courtyard, up the stairs, down the hall, and into the commandant's office. It was entirely empty, lighted by one weak bulb. I was pleased that there were no soldiers in the room, a good sign. On the commandant's desk lay my, or rather Ole's, film. The officer picked it up, handed it to me, snapped his heels, and saluted. I thanked him, and together the three of us retraced our steps back toward the train.

When we entered the dark waiting room just before emerging on the platform, the young Russian officer stopped me. "I have something I want to tell you," he said. His intentness once again triggered my anxiety. Maybe this adventure is not yet over, I thought. "You know," he observed, "here at the Brest border station the soldiers don't get to see many movies. This is a lonely post. That film of yours," he continued, "is absolutely wonderful. Those rapids, those jumping fish, the forests and the river, the wonderful colors! Thank you for giving us this pleasure." I shook his hand, managed to say that I was delighted, and Pat and I climbed on the train. We realized that the film I was carrying had been shown over and over again to all the border troops of the region, and that it had been a memorable event in their otherwise boring duties.

Pat and I laughed and talked about the episode as the train rolled on to Moscow. The tension had vanished, and we opened a bottle of Polish wine. And of course when I got to Moscow I forgot all about my promised protest to Ambassador Thompson.

CHAPTER SIX

AN AMERICAN SIT-IN
AND A RUSSIAN RIOT

WHEN I WAS A GRADUATE STUDENT at Moscow University the student protests and sit-in demonstrations that later plagued American universities had not yet occurred. American students were, on the whole, remarkably placid.

Paradoxically, the first student protest I ever witnessed occurred not in the United States, but in the Soviet Union, and my wife and I were participants in it. It arose out of a disagreement between the dozen or so American students studying at Moscow University and the university administration. It was shortly followed by a Russian riot in the streets of Moscow.

During the year that we spent at the university we were in frequent contact with employees and diplomatic officers of the American Embassy in Moscow. At the embassy we picked up information sheets that told us of international events and of American news about which the Soviet press was silent. Several embassy officers, especially the political and cultural attachés, Lee Brady and Tom Tuck, were helpful to us in supporting our requests for archival access and microfilm services at Soviet libraries. We were grateful for these acts of assistance.

In the spring of 1961, after enjoying this help for many months, the American students at the university decided that it would be a friendly act to reciprocate by inviting the embassy staff to a party in our rooms at Moscow University. The members of the embassy staff were at this time strikingly isolated from Soviet society. Several told me that during two or three years of being posted in Moscow they had never been inside a Soviet home or apartment. (Many of the American students, on the contrary, were accustomed to being in such apartments several times a week.) None of the members of the embassy at this time had been inside Moscow University, to which access was given only by presentation of a pass, or *propusk*, which all of us exchange students possessed.

We knew, therefore, that before we could invite the embassy members to our rooms we had to obtain special permission from the administration of Moscow University. Several members of our group went to the Foreign Department of the university, which was responsible for coordinating all exchange programs, and asked if we could have permission to bring embassy personnel into the university on a prearranged date. The head of the Foreign Department, Boris Sergeevich Nikiforov, said that it would be all right so long as we agreed upon a certain time that the embassy people would arrive at the main gate to the university, so he could notify the guard to let them in. The time chosen was 1:00 P.M. the following Saturday, and Nikiforov said he would notify the guard.

Arranging this buffet lunch was no simple matter. We wanted to give the embassy personnel a sampling of Soviet food, not the imported items from Western Europe and America to which they were accustomed. For several days students and mostly student spouses scoured the Soviet groceries and collective farm markets for food. The variety and quality at the official groceries were abominable, so the most attention was given to the farm markets where private enterprise on a strictly regulated scale was permitted. But food there was much more expensive than in the state groceries; on our stipends of fifty rubles a month (about thirty-five dollars) we had little money to spare. Nonetheless, we managed to put together a nice assortment of vegetables, fruit, sausages, a little chicken, and deviled eggs. We agreed that the buffet would be held in one of the larger rooms in which an American couple lived. I may be mistaken, but I believe that it was the room of Roald and Eva Hoffmann; Roald was a graduate student chemist from Harvard University who would later end up as a long-term faculty member at Cornell University and eventually the recipient of a Nobel Prize in chemistry.

The appointed time came. All furniture in the Hoffmanns' room had been put together to form a large table on which sat our assortment of Soviet foods. The display would not, we were sure, impress international diplomats, but we were very proud of it. Several of us went down to the main door to the university to meet the visiting Americans and escort them to the room. The embassy personnel arrived in a bus from the diplomatic motor pool.

The guard at the gate refused to let the American diplomats into the university. We said that we had special permission to bring the Americans to our rooms. The guard, a woman, said she knew nothing about special permission, and knew only that her orders were to let only people with passes through the door. We asked her to call Nikiforov, the head of the Foreign Department, and she would learn that all was arranged. The guard refused, said she had never heard of Nikiforov, and wasn't interested in learning who he was. We tried, without success, to call Nikiforov. We then called the main police office for the university. The man there said it was out of the question to permit a large group of personnel from the American embassy to enter the university. We argued; we said that all had been previously agreed upon, and that Nikiforov knew all about it; we said that surely somewhere in the university there was a responsible official who had the authority to let these people in. We were sure that the police could find Nikiforov if they wanted to. All of our entreaties met the same negative response. The police would not let the Americans in, and they would do nothing for us in trying to make contacts with authorities who would let them in.

We knew that the president of the university was named Ivan Petrovskii, a distinguished mathematician, known for his algebraic geometry and parabolic equations (whose work I studied). We wanted to call him. The police would not give us his number. Moscow had no telephone directories, and we had not the slightest idea how to reach him. The same was true of every high Soviet official we could think of who might conceivably help. We were defeated.

The bus with the embassy personnel waited outside the university until the driver said that if he continued to run the motor so that the heater worked, as was necessary in the bitter cold, he would soon run out of gas. So the bus left, and we returned to our untouched array of hors d'oeuvres.

We were furious. In a group of students that had difficulty agreeing on anything, and among whom there were several people who thought the whole idea of a reception for the American Embassy staff was ridiculous, there was now universal agreement that something had to be done.

We finally found Nikiforov in the Foreign Department. He assured us that he had informed the guard. He was not interested in our request that some sort of apology be addressed to the American Embassy from the university authorities. We doubted that Nikiforov had actually informed the guard, but were sure he would not admit it. From that time on, we referred among ourselves to Nikiforov not by his correct name and patronymic (Boris Sergeevich) but by a slightly different form (Boris Sobakavich) which came close to meaning "Boris, the son of a bitch."

We were not going to get any satisfaction out of Nikiforov. We held a council of war. We decided to go directly to the president of the university, we would sit down in his office, and we would not leave until he gave us some kind of satisfactory answer.

Saturdays were working days in Soviet offices, and we hoped to find the president in his large suite located in the central tower of the university, a place, it turned out, with a grand view of the entire city of Moscow, since the university was on hills dominating the city. All fifteen or twenty of us, students and spouses, went into the vestibule of the office. We told the receptionist that we were American students studying at the university and said we wanted to see the president. She disappeared, reappeared, and told us that the president was not in. We told her that we were going to sit on the floor of the vestibule until he was in and until he would see us. We sat down, took out the books which we had brought for this eventuality, and settled down. We ostentatiously displayed our food supplies (we had plenty from the unsuccessful party) and made it clear that we were camped for as long as need be. We were pretty sure that President Petrovskii was actually inside the inner office, since the receptionist kept going back there for further instructions.

I do not remember now how long we were there, but it must have been several hours. Periodically the receptionist would disappear into the inner office for long periods before reappearing. We later learned that the president was totally surprised by this event, unprecedented in his experience; furthermore, he did not have a toilet in his office and could not hold out forever. Should he call the police and have us forcibly evacuated, perhaps arrested, or what should he do? What would be the effects on Soviet–American relations and the exchange programs between the two countries if all the Americans in Moscow were arrested? He had no idea what our demands were. All he knew was that a bunch of American students were totally disrupting his day.

We checked for outside exits by which the president could escape and found none. One of us thought he knew what Petrovskii looked like, so we were sure we could nail him if he emerged. The face of the receptionist showed clearly that she was distressed, even frightened. Student demonstrations just did not happen in the Soviet Union (although they were common in late imperial Russia).

After a long time, the receptionist said that the president had just arrived by another door and that he would be delighted to see us. We all trooped into his office, where he sat behind a large desk. He jumped up, shook all our hands, escorted us to seats around a large green cloth-covered table, folded his hands, and asked if we were enjoying our year of study in Moscow. How was the Russian language coming? Was our research proceeding nicely? Was there anything he could do to make our stay in the Soviet Union more pleasant?

We had designated as our spokesman one of our people who spoke fluent unaccented Russian. I think it was either Dick Yatzick or Don Lesh. He told President Petrovskii that we were there to obtain a formal letter of apology from the administration of Moscow University for refusing to permit the staff of the American Embassy to come to a luncheon at the university that had been previously cleared with the proper authorities. Petrovskii expressed great surprise, and wanted to hear the details. We gave them to him, everybody now jumping up and talking at once.

President Petrovskii could see that we were greatly agitated. But the idea of writing a formal apology for not allowing a group of American diplomats in these Cold War times to penetrate his university was not something that immediately appealed to him. No doubt classified research was going on in the university, unknown to us. How would Petrovskii's superiors, and the secret police, react to his apology to intrusive American diplomats, some of them connected, doubtlessly, to the CIA? But we were so resolute that Petrovskii realized that he had to do something or we would never go away. He finally managed to smile and said that he "promised" to write a letter. Such an indefinite statement was not satisfactory to us. We demanded that the letter be from him personally, that it be addressed to Ambassador Llewellyn Thompson of the American Embassy, that he write it on the spot so we could help with the details, and that we be given a copy of the letter. At this point I wondered if we were pushing our case too hard. I could see Petrovskii visibly hesitating.

Finally he shrugged, laughed, and said he would dictate the letter on the spot, and he called his secretary. While we waited he dictated a letter to Ambassador Thompson regretting "the misunderstanding" that had occurred at Moscow University that day. President Petrovskii said the letter would be typed immediately in the outside office, and that we would be given a copy. We noticed that in his letter he made no promise to the ambassador to rectify the error by permitting the embassy staff to come to the university on another day, but we decided to let well enough alone. We stood, thanked the president, said we also regretted the incident, and went out into the vestibule. After we received a copy of the letter from the typewriter of the receptionist, we thanked her, and left, letter in hand.

In the days that followed both we and the embassy staff marveled over the incident and were sobered by thoughts that it might have all turned out much worse. But from that time on the embassy staff seemed to treat us unruly students with more respect. Maybe they feared a sit-in by us in the embassy as well.

A few weeks later the political attaché of the embassy, Lee Brady, invited Pat and me to dinner in his apartment. It was our first such personal invitation from embassy personnel, and we were sure it was connected to the earlier event. Neither he nor we had any idea that this social event between the embassy and university exchange students would also turn out badly.

Lee Brady had just married, and his new American wife had recently arrived in the Soviet Union. This evening was, I believe, her first social event in Moscow. She was a southern woman who spoke with the lovely accent of Georgia, and seemed, at first sight, naïve and totally unprepared for Moscow life. But she certainly knew how to put on a formal dinner, complete with lace tablecloth and candles.

The Bradys' apartment was in the main embassy building, up on the fifth or sixth floor. The windows in the dining room looked out on one of the main streets of Moscow, *Sadovoe Kol'tso*, a curving street circling the entire inner core of the city.

About halfway through the dinner we suddenly became aware of some sort of commotion out in the street. Since it was spring, the streets were still light from the late-setting sun. We looked out the windows and saw, approaching the embassy, several columns of people— thousands of people. They were shouting and waving signs and banners and they looked angry. It soon became clear that their destination was the embassy itself. The enormous crowd of people ranged themselves in front of our building and began shouting, in unison, *"Ruki proch' ot Kuby!"* ("Hands off Cuba!").

The news from the Bradys was that on the previous day the American government had supported the Bay of Pigs invasion of Cuba. Some talk of such an invasion had been in the air for several weeks, particularly in the Soviet papers, and I had made a bet with one of my Soviet dormitory friends that the United States would not support such an invasion. I lost the bet.

The crowd became more and more agitated and soon began throwing items at the embassy. At first the favorite objects were ink bottles, filled with the peculiar purple ink then favored in Soviet stationery stores. When the bottles crashed against the wall of the embassy they left lurid purple splotches. Later the crowd began throwing stones and pavement blocks.

As the melee continued, all discipline and order disappeared. People began violently shaking the gates to the embassy, and smashing windows and doors. We could hear the glass of the lower windows of the embassy breaking and crashing to the floors of the rooms and corridors. An actual invasion of the embassy by a mob now seemed likely. Fortunately, the Bradys' windows were too high for the apogee of most of the missiles, and their glass was still intact. Lee called Ambassador Thompson at his home in Spaso House, seven or eight blocks away, and informed him of the situation. Ambassador Thompson ordered the U.S. marine detachment stationed in the embassy to mobilize in the hallways and also requested all embassy personnel to report to their offices to safeguard their property there.

As Lee prepared to leave to go to his office, a small stone, thrown by a particularly hefty demonstrator, crashed through the dining room window and landed right on the table, next to the flowers and on top of the lace table cloth. Mrs. Brady, that innocent Southerner whom I had judged so unprepared for Moscow life, rose, went over to a desk, extracted a mailing tag, tied it around the stone, wrote the date and "Moscow, USSR" on the tag, and placed the stone and tag on the book shelf. She observed that it would be a nice souvenir "back home."

We heard new noises in the street. We looked down and saw dozens of uniformed Russian militiamen approaching on horses. They rode as close to the iron fence separating the embassy from the street as possible, forcing the crowd back from the gates. When the line of horses and riders extended across the entire front of the embassy, facing the crowd, the commander of the militiamen blew on his whistle. The long line of horsemen wheeled in unison so that the rear of the horses now faced the crowd. The commander blew on his whistle again and then each of the horses kicked backward, one leg at a time. As the horse's leg returned to the ground, each of the horses stepped backward one step toward the crowd. At another whistle each horse kicked backward again and repeated the maneuver, dispersing the crowds further at each step.

It was the first time I had ever heard of such a maneuver on horseback. I was certain, however, that this effective and violent method of crowd control had been refined by the Russian police in tsarist times. It worked perfectly. I did not see any injuries. In fact, the demonstrating people turned and ran the moment they saw the horses wheel around. The tsar's Cossacks may have disappeared, but their spirit lingered on.

Pat and I returned to the university by subway after the dinner with the Bradys was over, and after the crowd had dispersed. As we left the embassy, we turned and looked back at the smashed windows and defaced front of the building, which was not fully repaired for weeks. We resumed our normal activities at the university, and, surprisingly, found that we encountered no hostility on our dormitory floor because of the American invasion of Cuba. The Russian students did not hold us responsible for the actions of our government, just as many of them felt no responsibility for their own.

CHAPTER SEVEN

THE FATE OF MY CLOSEST RUSSIAN FRIEND

AMONG ALL MY FRIENDS in the Zone G dormitory on Lenin Hills at Moscow University, the closest one became Vitalii, a specialist in American literature who lived on the same floor as I. When I first met him he was an athletic bachelor who loved tennis, was full of good humor, and smiled quickly and easily. But Vitalii was also a calm, highly reflective young man with an intense curiosity about the world. He wanted to know exactly what Western opinions were on every subject, and his first reaction upon learning some surprising aspect of Western views was pure joy that the world could be so variegated, not either agreement or disagreement. He was not a dissident, and never became one, but he had an entirely open mind on all questions. He devoured foreign literature, especially American, and over the period of fifteen years that we were in almost constant contact, Pat and I gave him what amounted to a small library of American fiction. He loved the English language, and might stop a sentence in midstream in order to analyze the nuances of a certain word or phrase. I felt an immediate close bond with him because of his innate love of words. While his English was almost fluent, he was often exasperated by the intricacies of meaning and usage that prevented him from having absolute mastery of that language.

Trust between an American and a Soviet citizen during the height of the Cold War did not come easily and certainly not instantaneously. It was something that grew slowly over the months and years. Vitalii and I gradually built that confidence to the point that we trusted each other completely and openly. He became as dear a friend as my closest

American friends—maybe even dearer. Because of the nature of Soviet society, where so many subjects that would seem fairly innocent in
the West were intensely serious or inherently dangerous, friendships
often seemed deeper in the Soviet Union than they did in the West;
they were based on the exchange of views that would be highly compromising if they were known to the authorities. In the West it is not
often that the discussion of literature, art, or philosophy would lead
one person to know something about another that could seriously hurt
that person if revealed to yet a third person. That sort of thing was
routine in the Soviet Union.

Vitalii had grown up in Riga, at that the time the capital of the Soviet republic of Latvia. Between World Wars I and II, Latvia, along
with the other Baltic republics of Estonia and Lithuania, had been
independent from the Soviet Union (as they would be again after the
collapse of the USSR). These three areas were taken over by Soviet
troops who pushed the Germans back during World War II. The majority of the Baltic population greatly resented the reinstitution of Russian rule—so much so that some of them even cooperated with the
Germans in their wartime resistance, an act that complicated their
later political situation. The Russians managed to suppress the resistance, and branded all supporters of Baltic independence as "fascist
partisans," a grossly untrue charge, since many Balts opposed the anti-
democratic forces of both fascism and communism.

After the Soviet troops occupied the Baltic states, the Soviet government knew that it had a predominantly anti-Soviet population on
its hands, and it wished to do everything possible to change this situation. The most direct way to accomplish this political shift, the Soviets
thought, was to redistribute the population, to ship many Russian families to the Baltic area in order to introduce loyal elements. This policy
was followed on a wide scale. Russians were brought to the Baltic,
given leading administrative and political posts, and provided with
preferential housing. Vitalii's family, of good Russian stock, was one of
these Russian families. As a small boy he was involuntarily introduced
into a volatile and dangerous political situation. From the earliest age
he learned that the world contains political hatred and cruelty. One of
his first memories was of returning home one afternoon and finding
near his doorstep the body of a Russian soldier, his throat slit by the
local Latvian resistance. Such a traumatic experience could have ruined some children. Vitalii was not severely damaged, but he certainly
was affected; he reacted to the experience by refusing to countenance
violence. He always feared that he would be inducted into the Red

Army and asked to do something similar to what soldiers of his childhood did to Latvia: suppress its freedom and encounter violent resistance as a result. One reason he eventually became a translator and interpreter was to acquire a skill that would exempt him from military service.

It was Vitalii who showed me one of the most pleasant diversions in Moscow in good weather, walking in the forests near the city. The edge of Moscow in Soviet times came abruptly, unlike American cities where the suburbs serve as a sort of transition between urban and rural. Within sight of the last row of six or ten story apartment buildings on the boundary of the city one could find forests interlaced with paths along which people sought mushrooms in the spring and colored leaves in the fall. Without automobiles, most Soviet citizens walked a great deal, and since there was no private property, all the forests and fields were considered appropriate for strolling.

Vitalii and I would take the subway to the end of the line, then perhaps a trolley car to cover the last distance where the subway line had not yet been constructed, and we would then walk for long hours in the forests, talking constantly. Over the years the boundary of the city shifted outward, but it could always be found without any trouble. One of our first walks was around the old tsarist palace of Kolomenskoe, at that time situated among forests and collective farms. The road there was a long and picturesque mud rut, and the villagers obtained their water from open wells with buckets hanging from cranks. In later years, still during the Soviet period, we watched the city swallow Kolomenskoe. It became a subway stop, and not the last one on the line.

Still later, after the fall of the Soviet Union, I watched commercialism, capitalism, and private property erase the line between city and forest that had been so clearly demarcated during the Soviet period. (Although my Russian language was by this time fluent, I did not learn the Russian words for "real estate" [nedvizhimoe] or "discount" [skidka] until after the fall of communism.) In recent years the edges of Moscow have become more and more a suburban area, like one finds near Western cities, and the loss of direct contact with nature on the periphery is palpable. On the outskirts of the city fast food outlets appeared, including McDonald's, and commercial malls proliferated. Further out, the "New Russians" built their suburban homes, sometimes with swimming pools and often surrounded by brick walls. The common space of socialism was fenced off and supplanted by private property. The tiny elite of people who quickly got rich in the post-Soviet period erected country houses and mansions around Moscow, fenced in the land with gates for their Mercedes and BMWs, posted "No Trespassing" signs, and sealed themselves off from the outside world.

Years before these developments, in the sixties and early seventies, Vitalii and I walked frequently on the edges of Moscow and discussed every topic in the world. During these walks I learned that although Vitalii was open-minded on almost all subjects, this tolerance did not obliterate his own opinions. He calmly described the Soviet Union as a police state, and was pessimistic about the chances for changes in a democratic direction in the near future. He objected to the system of privilege based on political influence and status that had developed in the Soviet Union. The most important determinant of status and living standard, he said, was not talent and not even money, but "access" to closed systems of supply and privilege, systems open only to the politically influential. While still a student, and one with a great thirst for intellectual and artistic stimulation, he particularly complained about the difficulty of getting the books he wanted and the fact that students found it almost impossible to get tickets to the best productions of theater, ballet, and opera even if they had the money; the sale of tickets to new and interesting productions at places like the Bolshoi Theater was tightly controlled, with the best ones going to high officials, diplomats, and foreigners. It irritated him that I could get tickets to plays and concerts that he could not, since I could apply through the foreign department of the university or one of the service bureaus of the downtown hotels serving foreigners. Access to the few good restaurants was similarly controlled, the entrance guarded by doormen who sent Soviet citizens away, but let foreigners in. Vitalii and I could crash the gates together if I spoke English to the doorman and showed my U.S. passport, but if Vitalii tried to get us in, we often failed.

Vitalii wrote a paper for one of his university classes in which he complained about the system of selling theater tickets and also about the depressing effect that catering to foreigners had upon the repertoires of Soviet theaters. The same classical productions were staged over and over again because they were what the foreign tourists and high Soviet officials wanted to see. The tourists could not bear the thought of visiting Moscow without seeing Swan Lake or Boris Godunov, and the Soviet officials who controlled artistic life were also known for their conventional tastes. In his school paper Vitalii tried to shift most of the blame for the staleness of the Soviet offerings upon the foreigners (and he believed that the preference for foreigners was at least partially the cause) because he knew that if he referred to the philistine cultural tastes of the Soviet officials his paper would be con-

sidered unacceptable. But he learned that even this moderate criticism was not looked upon positively by his teachers. The paper was
reported to the local Komsomol, and Vitalii was reprimanded, lightly
but tellingly. I believe that this paper was Vitalii's first and last attempt
to make public his private views about some aspect of Soviet society.
From that time on, he kept his views to himself or his close friends, but
they continued to develop.

In our conversations with each other we talked entirely freely about
our respective countries, whether the topic was the economic and political systems, race and ethnic relations, women's rights, the academic
systems, or just the details of life. Some of the things we told each
other at first seemed, in the 1960s, hardly credible to the other. He told
me about the strikes among Soviet workers in factories on the Volga
River which were brutally suppressed by army troops who, on several
occasions, used artillery; about famines or near-famines among peasants in remote villages; about civilian airliners that crashed killing dozens of passengers but never reported in any Soviet news media. I told
him about Harlem, the great slum on whose edge I lived and about
race riots during which I could hear gunfire from our apartment; about
the "flower children" in the universities at the time; about the American Civil Liberties Union that defended the political rights of both
communists and fascists; about celebrations of homosexuals and lesbi-
ans in Central Park in which thousands marched and called for sexual
freedom. My accounts did not seem very remarkable to me, and his
were ordinary to him, but to the other person the stories were novel.
And all of them were true.

I later gained an insight into just how strange the story about homosexual celebrations seemed to Vitalii, living in the Soviet Union where
homosexuality was publicly considered one of the darkest crimes and
severely punished whenever discovered. Melor Storuia, the Soviet correspondent for the government newspaper *Izvestiia*, gave a talk at the
Smithsonian Institution in 1982 which I attended in which he said
that he had written up the story of such a demonstration in Central
Park but that it had been rejected by his editors back in Moscow on the
ground that it would be disbelieved by Soviet readers and rejected as
crude anti-American propaganda.

I cannot help but add the slightly irrelevant comment that Storuia's
first name, Melor, is an acronym standing for "Marx-Engels-Lenin-
October-Revolution." His name originally was "Melsor," but he later
changed it, eliminating the "s" which stood for "Stalin" after that letter

became politically inconvenient. Not only the written work, but even the name of this correspondent changed with the political winds. His early articles were thoroughly Soviet in tone and politics, but he came to the United States after the fall of the Soviet Union and continued his work as a correspondent, with an entirely different approach. One is reminded of Albert Einstein's comment about the Nazi authorities who, in an anti-Semitic campaign, eliminated "Einstein" as a street name in his hometown only a few years after it had been installed because of his fame; Einstein wrote to the authorities that to avoid future such difficulties, he suggested that the street be named "Wind-vane Street."

Vitalii was an example of a Soviet citizen who led a public life that was entirely acceptable to the authorities, although his mind, had they known what was in its recesses, would not have been. He acquired the skills requisite for a career as a translator, a position that paid satisfactorily, did not force him into overt falsehood, and provided some room for diversion. As the years went by I learned that there were quite a few such people in the Soviet Union: intellectuals who worked as translators, archivists, librarians, copy editors—they were members of the service trades of intellectual life who were not required to make independent pronouncements. Many of them in a less repressive environment in which their imaginations could have flowered would have led creative lives.

Vitalii's first marriage lasted only several years. He married again in the late sixties a woman named Natasha, whose lovely face seemed innocent and unsophisticated compared to Vitalii's countenance, with its constant manifestation of intellectual curiosity. Pat and I later learned that Natasha was a remarkable woman, highly talented, and with an inner strength that would later be fully tested. Natasha spoke no English, so our conversations shifted linguistically. Pat and I soon came to know and love Natasha along with Vitalii.

Because of his facility in English, soon after completing his studies at Moscow University Vitalii was sent to Damascus, Syria, where he served as a translator and interpreter for Soviet advisors there. This foreign assignment would never have been given to him if his political record had been considered dubious.

Upon his return to the Soviet Union Vitalii obtained a position in Moscow at the publisher and news agency *Novosti*, where he specialized in translating English technical books into Russian. Here he was able to gain access to foreign publications otherwise unavailable to

him, although few of them were about his favorite subjects of literature
and politics. He gradually settled in to a position where the promotion
possibilities were small, but where the job security was excellent.

Vitalii and Natasha lived in an apartment in one of the oldest districts of Moscow in a building that in the United States would have
been judged from the outside to be a slum dwelling. The yellow brick
structure had been constructed long before the Revolution and was
crumbling at every edge and in the middle as well. Inside, the halls
and stairs were so dark that even in the bright daytime one stumbled
uncontrollably if one did not know the characteristics of each broken
step. One skirted the stair well with its trash at the bottom and felt
one's way to a dark door, covered with brown insulated fabric against
cold and noise, and finally found the one bell button that still worked
out of the five or six old and non-operating ones. Inside the dark door
was an apartment shared by three families, with one communal hallway. The one bathroom and kitchen were also communal, and the
kitchen was primitive in its equipment, although excellent food often
emerged from it. Vitalii and Natasha had at first one room in the apartment, but as time went on and other occupants moved to new apartments on the edge of the city, they expanded. In their room one found
a complete change of mood from the building, the hall, and the
kitchen. While the exterior was grimy and dark, that small room was
immaculate, and illuminated by natural light from the large windows
overlooking the inner court, which had trees that cast pleasant green
shadows in the room during the summer. Around the room were their
few possessions, which gradually grew with time. Vitalii's books always
occupied a central place, and pushed somewhat intolerantly against
everything else.

Crammed in to such small quarters, Vitalii and Natasha made use
of every available space. The utility door in the wall that opened for
access to electrical and plumbing lines had become an extra closet,
with skis and ski poles crammed inside, as well as boots placed there
where they would not soil the floor. A bicycle hung from the ceiling
and winter coats sometimes were draped over the wheels. The better
kitchen utensils that could be left in the communal kitchen only at
considerable risk of loss were stacked inside each other near the door,
where they could be grabbed as one headed out of the room. In the
corridor one was often assailed by a combination of smells, often wonderful when Natasha was preparing something for Pat and me in the
nearby kitchen, frequently disagreeable at other times because of the
equal proximity of the communal toilet.

Usually we spent our time with Vitalii and Natasha in this apartment, or walking around the city. Once, however, they decided to take us to lunch in one of Moscow's newest restaurants, to which, through a friend who worked for Soviet television, they had obtained the necessary tickets. This establishment was called "Seventh Heaven," and was located high atop the new, central television tower that dominated Moscow then, and still does. The tower was a part of the television complex that in 1993 would be the site of the deadliest firefight between supporters and opponents of the old order of the Soviet Union.

Like some other such towers in Europe and America, this one had a rotating restaurant near the top from which one could get a fine view of the city. The Soviet tower differed from the others, however, in having a much higher rate of rotation. It was new at this time and perhaps the engineers had not yet decided that a slower rate would be no less impressive and considerably more convenient, because the restaurant went around so fast that the surface of the wine in the goblets was tilted by centrifugal force, and the waiters had to lean to the side to maintain their balance as they carried trays of food to the tables.

It was about this time, perhaps from Vitalii's abstinence from the tilting wine, that we became aware that he had a problem with his kidneys. That problem rapidly became worse. Soon his kidneys were reduced to only a fraction of their normal function, but he managed to survive, carefully watching his diet.

In 1969 in New York City I received a telegram from Vitalii. It read, "Urgently need Shenter's Shunts from medical supply house." Vitalii was not in the habit of asking me to get things for him, so I knew that the word "urgently" was an understatement. I did not have the slightest idea what "Shenter's Shunts" were, but I was going to find out, and fast. I walked from our apartment on Claremont Avenue to St. Luke's Hospital, near Columbia University where I was teaching. There I found Dr. Alfred Fretz, whom I knew only through the fact that his daughters went to the same school as our daughter. I asked him what "Shenter's Shunts" were. He told me that they were plastic tubes that were used to connect a patient to a dialysis machine. He obtained two in about five minutes and gave them to me, refusing even to listen to my attempt to pay for them. The Shenter's Shunts looked very simple and inexpensive: thin, clear tubes, coiled up in a roll not much larger than a pack of cigarettes.

I later found out the details of Vitalii's plight. His condition had so deteriorated that he needed periodic treatment with a kidney machine. Gaining access to such a machine was no simple matter. At first the Soviet doctors told him that none was available. Vitalii then went through all the predictable and obligatory methods of trying to gain the attention of the hospital authorities. I am certain that an important part of the process was bribes of liquor, candy, and probably more. In the past Vitalii had often criticized the prevalence of such practices in the Soviet Union. Now he was fighting for his life. Finally, he was told that a machine was available but that there were no connecting tubes, so, unfortunately, it could not be used. Vitalii insisted on learning the make and model of the kidney machine, and then he applied the technical expertise that he had gained as a translator of books about foreign technology. He dragged himself to the library, looked up the specifications of the kidney machine, found out that it required "Shenter's Shunts" as connectors, and sent off the telegram to me.

At this time there were no courier services between the United States and the Soviet Union, such as DHL or UPS. The fastest way to get something from one country to the other was air mail, and it usually required two to three weeks to reach its destination because Soviet authorities checked each item. I suspected that several weeks would be too long, so I tried to mail the tubes in a form that would cause the censors the least difficulty. I put the tubes in an unsealed mailing bag that was secured with metal fasteners that could easily be unfastened and fastened again. I sent the package air mail, without any enclosed message, and I wrote on the envelope in both English and Russian: "Attention: Emergency Medical Supplies; Please Hurry." The package was in Vitalii's hands three days later.

When Pat, Meg, and I went to Moscow again in 1970 we found Vitalii in the Moscow City Hospital which was, coincidentally, almost across the street from the Academy of Sciences Hotel on October Square where we were staying. It was easy to visit him in the hospital, and we did frequently. Vitalii had gained much weight around the middle and looked flaccid, but he was able to walk, and, indeed, several times went home. He had frequent dialysis treatment, and each time he brought the plastic tubes to the hospital, and, after treatment, washed them and took them home. It pained him to realize that if he left the tubes with the machine another person's life might be saved or prolonged, but he also knew that the tubes would not be there when he returned.

When visitors entered the hospital they were required to stop at a little changing room close to the door, remove their shoes, put on hospital slippers, and also a white smock that covered the body almost completely. These sanitary requirements seemed incongruous once one entered the hospital itself, where one could see dirt in the corners of the dark hallways. Built long before the Russian Revolution, the hospital had none of the conveniences and improvements of a normal Western hospital. Vitalii was in a room with ten or twelve other people, the iron frame beds crowded closely together.

If he happened to be feeling good, Vitalii would walk with us outside the hospital into the little garden in front of the door, just off busy Lenin Prospect. There, sitting on a park bench, he would tell us about his life and Soviet life. He had obtained access to a kidney machine and his condition, at least temporarily, was stable. In the ward in which he stayed there was nothing to do but talk, and so all the patients talked constantly. Many of them were in more serious condition than Vitalii and were anticipating death. The state of their health unlocked their tongues. Like the patients in Alexander Solzhenitsyn's *Cancer Ward*, they no longer had anything to fear from the authorities, for they could not be punished. So they criticized Soviet life. All of them believed that conditions were steadily growing worse: there was less food in the stores, the economy was stagnating, and the political controls were tightening.

Despite his health problems, Vitalii was often in good humor, and he, Natasha, Pat, Meg, and I often had wonderful times together. He would get sausages and drinks for us that he could not consume himself because of his diet, and he would toast us with his glass of water. We were delighted to see that he and Natasha had expanded in their apartment building and now had two rooms all of their own. He took a great interest in Meg and assured us that soon he and Natasha would have a family of their own.

We returned to the United States. By 1974 I was commuting back and forth between Boston, where Pat had taken a job at Radcliffe and Harvard, and New York City, where I was still teaching at Columbia. One day at our house on Garden Street in Cambridge we received a very long telegram from Vitalii. His condition had suddenly become grave. Just what the reason was I could not tell. With all the attention to detail that was characteristic of him, Vitalii supplied voluminous information about his condition, in fact, his entire medical record: blood pressure, salinity indicators, medication applied, frequency of dialysis, and many other things which I cannot remember. I realized that—although he asked for nothing—he wanted me to show the record to an American specialist, since he was losing confidence in his Soviet doctors.

From the director of the Radcliffe Program in Health Care, Jeanette

Haas, Pat got the name of leading kidney specialists at Deaconess Hospital in Boston, Dr. Robert Schlesinger and Dr. Anthony P. Monaco. I went to see Dr. Schlesinger on the same day we received the telegram, and he studied Vitalii's record. He said that if he or Dr. Monaco were able to treat Vitalii he was certain that they could save his life. In fact, he said that Vitalii's condition was better than many of the patients he was currently treating in Boston and whom he expected to survive. The important thing, he said, was to put Vitalii on a special regime of treatment that involved complex medication, careful control of diet, and intermittent dialysis. The process could not be directed from afar. Vitalii must come to Boston. If he did so, Dr. Schlesinger believed that the chances were good that eventually Vitalii would recover to the extent that he could be taken off the dialysis machine permanently. As a last resort, they could try kidney transplant, but that step did not appear to be necessary.

At this time Soviet authorities kept very strict control over travel by Soviet citizens. For the average person obtaining an exit visa was simply impossible. I feared, for both legal and financial reasons, that we would never be able to get Vitalii out and properly cared for. The treatment was very expensive, and there was no health insurance that would cover him. However, Drs. Schlesinger and Monaco had taken an interest in the case, and, with my encouragement, they decided to make the attempt. They were friends of Senator Edward Kennedy and Paul Tsongas, then a candidate for the U.S. Senate. The physicians would work through them in the effort to get an exit visa out of the Soviet authorities. At the same time they would ask the Board of Trustees of Deaconess Hospital to guarantee free medical care for Vitalii. But there was little time because Vitalii's condition was steadily deteriorating under the present treatment. Drs. Schlesinger and Monaco promised that they would call for a special meeting of the Board of Trustees of the hospital the next day, a Sunday. The meeting was held, and a decision was made to guarantee Vitalii free medical treatment up to $300,000, and a letter stating this guarantee was drawn up at the meeting. The letter was given to me the next morning, just about thirty-six hours after I received the telegram from Vitalii. I was determined somehow to get that letter to Vitalii immediately. At the same time, I realized that Vitalii, should he recover, would with wry humor describe how he was rescued by the personal connections of influential people, the system in the Soviet Union that he had so often decried.

I called Pan American airlines, which at that time made regular flights to Moscow, and explained the situation to them. Could they arrange a special delivery of a letter to a Soviet resident of Moscow? There was no regular courier service, they replied, but they would check to see if anything could be done. In about half an hour a Pan Am pilot called back. He was flying to Moscow that afternoon; after his plane landed in Moscow he would take a taxi directly to Vitalii's apartment and deliver the Deaconess Hospital letter. I quickly added a note to Vitalii telling him to apply for an exit visa immediately, and added that we would work on the situation from this end. I said he should not worry about money; the important thing was to get to Logan Airport in Boston as fast as possible. The letter went off.

We heard nothing for several days. In the meantime the Deaconess Hospital arranged for an ambulance to be ready to meet Vitalii's plane at Logan Airport and bring him directly to the hospital, where Dr. Monaco would meet him. Senator Kennedy and Paul Tsongas appealed to the Soviet ambassador in Washington to facilitate the quick issuance of an emergency exit visa to Vitalii. The Boston newspapers picked up the story and heralded it as an act of mercy between two Cold War adversaries. In all this quick action it was clear that the Deaconess Hospital authorities were aware of the good publicity that would come to them if Vitalii's trip was successfully completed, but I was unconcerned by the political and public relations overtones. Anything that would do the trick was all right with me.

Four or five days after the Deaconess Hospital letter was sent to Moscow, Vitalii called me on the telephone. The Soviet authorities did not consider the letter to be an adequate guarantee that the Soviet government would not be asked to pay for some of the expenses. Who would pay for Vitalii's living costs after he was let out of the hospital? They asked for a letter, signed by me and notarized, that no expenses of any kind would be asked of the Soviet government. We produced such a letter immediately and sent it to Moscow, again getting the instant cooperation of Pan Am airlines.

Vitalii now had all the necessary documentation. He left the hospital to make the obligatory personal application to the Soviet office that granted exit visas, OVIR, returned to the hospital, and waited . . . and waited . . . and waited. As he sank lower and lower, his friends began desperate appeals to every Soviet authority they could get on the telephone. A Soviet diplomat who had known Vitalii in Syria besieged OVIR, pleading for the quick issuance of an exit visa. Vitalii was convinced that it would come. He waited and waited.

The visa never came. After about five weeks of waiting, Vitalii died. His pregnant wife Nastasha cabled us with news of his death.

A few weeks later we received a seven or eight page letter from Natasha describing Vitalii's last days that I translated from Russian to English for Pat as we sat in our living room in Cambridge with tears rolling down our faces. As I write this account, years later, I know that the letter is still down in the basement, in a cardboard box, and I could go get it and quote from it, but even yet my emotions do not permit it. I have never read the letter since that first time. Some time I will read it once more, but not yet.

In later trips to Moscow we heard the story of Vitalii's funeral, attended not only by his friends but also by many others who did not know him but had heard of his unnecessary death and unsuccessful fight with Soviet bureaucracy and wanted to show their sympathy and protest. The sight of Natasha brought tears to the eyes of all, for she was eight months pregnant and enormous. Their child died at birth one month later.

As I reflected on Vitalii's death I saw that it revealed inherent features of Soviet bureaucracy. It would be easy to suppose that the reason the Soviet officials would not permit him to go to the United States was intentional; they did not like for Soviet citizens to leave, whether it was for medical treatment or to emigrate to Israel, and they put up obstacles. However, in Vitalii's case I doubt that the reason was intentional. I think (although I do not know) that the Soviet bureaucracy simply could not be moved more rapidly than its normal glacial pace. The inertia and inefficiency were so enormous that special pleading on humanitarian grounds was insufficient to overcome them. After Vitalii's death the Soviet diplomat who tried to persuade OVIR to act called the office again to see what the officials would say when they learned of the situation. Their reply was that they intended eventually to issue the visa, but the bureaucratic process was still not completed.

During the next twenty years Pat and I lost contact with Natasha. When I was in Moscow I tried on several occasions to find her. She no longer lived in the old apartment building, and the people there did not know what had happened to her. When I visited twenty years after Vitalii's death one young man in their old building said he remembered, as a boy, hearing of the "tragedy long ago of the man in the building whom the Americans wanted to save," but he had no idea what had happened to Natasha. Several other of her old friends told me that she had simply "disappeared." I went to the journal where she had worked as an editor, and there I was told that she had left long ago, and no one knew where she was. Moscow had no telephone directories so I could not hope to find her that way.

The years passed and eventually the Soviet Union collapsed. In 1997 I decided to make one more effort to find Natasha. Many things had changed in Russia, but there were still no phone books. I went to the city authorities and insisted that surely there must be, somewhere, a listing of city residents. They sent me to a reference bureau (*spravochnoe biuro*) on the second floor of an office building in downtown Moscow, on Tver Street (the old Gorky Street). The woman there told me that she could not search for people in her listings unless she had the full name and birth date of the person. I did not know Natasha's maiden name. I was not even sure that I knew her last name, since she might have remarried and changed it. And I had no idea of the date of her birth, although I knew she was considerably younger than Vitalii or I. But I insisted that the woman check her listings and I guessed that her birth year was around 1946. The woman shrugged, checked her listings, handed me a phone number, and asked for ten rubles. I leapt up, gladly paid, and left.

Within minutes I was talking to Natasha. She immediately recognized my voice, before I could identify myself, and asked about Pat and Meg. I told her that Pat was with me in Moscow and suggested that we meet that afternoon. She readily agreed, and soon once again the three of us were walking together in downtown Moscow, where in the post-Soviet times Western stores abounded.

Natasha had not changed very much in physical appearance and was well dressed. She had remarried and had a family. She half-apologetically remarked "I live in a completely different world now than the one you knew me in." She and her husband were members of the small group of "New Russians," the people who were financially benefiting from the new capitalistic economy. Her husband was a contractor, building dachas and mansions on the outskirts of Moscow for other New Russians, erasing the demarcation line of the city and the country that Vitalii and I had so often explored. Natasha and her new husband had their own modern apartment, with European fixtures and accessories, and they drove a luxury German automobile. She acknowledged that years ago, with Vitalii, she had lived a life in which books, art, and music were central, even though there was almost no money. Now there was quite a bit of money, but their concerns were entirely different. It was a commercial world, and one in which corruption was rampant. She did not invite us to meet her new husband.

We sought topics of mutual interest and exchanged photographs of our children. The bond between us was still strong, but we all three realized that the world had changed in such a way that the old relationship could not be reestablished. We exchanged addresses and telephone numbers, and when I go to Moscow again I will call. There has been a great expansion of freedom in Russia, and I rejoiced in that and in Natasha's prosperity. But the oppressive old Soviet Union had nurtured a few friendships between Russians and Americans of unique intensity, giving those friendships a quality that cannot be matched in the contemporary casual world. Many other Americans who have known both the old Soviet order and the new Russian one have told me they have had similar experiences, and that their new friendships, precious as they are, do not equal the intensity of the old ones. Many of the things most cherished in our lives are those realized only through great difficulty or in the face of adversity, and among those are, so often, friendship, love, faith, and hope.

CHAPTER EIGHT

THE VODKA CAPER

DURING THE 1960S AND 1970S I made many research trips to the Soviet Union, usually working in libraries and archives in Moscow, but sometimes in Leningrad and other cities. Frequently my way was paid by research grants from American foundations, but on other occasions I went on my own money, staying at the cheapest hotels and flying by the most economical means, such as Icelandic Air or Freddy Laker's cut-rate runs from New York to London. In the spring of 1966 I went to Moscow on my own money in order to spend a month doing research in the Lenin Library. I traveled under a special inexpensive arrangement called "the businessman's rate" which allowed me to make my own hotel arrangements in Moscow and also gave me little coupons (*talonchiki*) for one meal a day. By taking some powdered oatmeal with me for breakfast, and by eating lunch at the very inexpensive (but awful) cafeteria in the basement of the Lenin Library, I could get by on the one full meal a day at the hotel that my coupons entitled me to, and live very inexpensively.

I knew from previous visits how important it was to be located in one of the hotels in downtown Moscow, within walking distance if possible of the Lenin Library. Several hours a day in transportation time could be saved in that way. Oddly enough, in the 1960s several of the cheapest hotels in Moscow for foreigners were ones that before the Revolution in 1917 and after the fall of the Soviet Union in 1991 were the most expensive: the National and the Metropole, old and wonderfully located hotels. I chose the Metropole, not because it had a good reputation at that time (it did not), but because of its location and history.

Within easy walking distance of everything interesting in downtown Moscow, including Red Square, the Bolshoi Theater, and my research library, it was also a traditional location of romance and intrigue. Only a short walk away was what at that time was my favorite restaurant in Moscow, the Ararat, where one could listen to music played by Armenian musicians on instruments so strange and old they deserved to be in a museum, and feast on pita bread and other Middle Eastern specialties. And, most amazingly, I managed to arrange for a month in the Metropole for the equivalent of $6 a night. True, I was not promised a bath, but I knew that a communal facility would be available nearby. All these arrangements seem incredible today, because the Metropole has once again become a luxury hotel, completely refurbished by a Western hotel chain, and charges around $400 a night. But in the 1960s Moscow was another world.

When one of my friends in New York heard that I was going back to Moscow he came to me with a request. He was Don Mix, an executive in the Madison Avenue advertising agency of Batten, Barton, Durstine and Osborn (BBDO). It seems that he had recently been given the Gilbey's vodka account, and he wondered if I could help him with an advertising campaign he had just conceived. His idea was to run a series of ads that would depict photographs of three bottles of vodka, two of them Soviet, and the third one Gilbey's. Under the ad would run the slogan, "Three of the World's Greatest Vodkas; Gilbey's Is the Only One You Don't Need a Passport to Buy." (This was long before it was possible to buy Soviet vodka like Stolichnaia or "Stoli" in the United States.) Don needed Soviet vodka bottles in order to set up his campaign, and the more variety of bottles the better, since he wanted to choose particularly colorful or picturesque bottles of Soviet vodka for his backdrop to Gilbey's. He said that it was not necessary to bring back full bottles, since he could fill them with water or colored liquid. He continued that if I brought back the bottles his firm would reimburse me on my return for my expenses connected with purchasing the vodka.

I couldn't see anything wrong or illegal about the proposal, and Don was an old friend. Furthermore, BBDO would pay the taxi fares to and from the airports with my heavy luggage. Other than the taxi fares, I would charge BBDO only for the actual costs of the vodka in Moscow, so there was no compensation or honorarium for me, and I would not be converting an academic trip into a commercial one.

In Moscow I was soon ensconced on the third floor of the Metropole Hotel. The Metropole was built near the beginning of the century, before the Revolution, in art nouveau style. The top floors facing the street were covered with glorious paintings and mosaics, some of them by the well-known Russian artist M. A. Vrubel'. Immediately after the Russian Revolution in 1917 the building was taken over by the victorious revolutionaries and made available to various high officials of the government. (I later learned from Anna Larina, the wife of the famous Soviet leader Nikolai Bukharin, that she and her husband lived in room 307 of the Metropole in the 1920s, just one room away—if the numbering system remained the same—from my room in the Metropole in 1966.) In the late thirties, after the purges of Party and government leaders went into full swing, Muscovites often remarked that "many of Stalin's guests who stayed at the Metropole never 'checked out.'"

Inside, in the 1960s, the atmosphere of the Metropole could be described as what the Plaza in New York would be like if a socialist revolution had occurred in the United States forty years earlier, all the millionaires had been run out of the east sixties, and the service in the now state-controlled Plaza had been allowed to go into steady decline over the ensuing decades, with the result that its past glory was visible only to the discerning eye. Just like the Plaza in New York the Metropole had a famous palm court on the first floor. The waiters at the Metropole Palm Court were surly, the menu listed hundreds of items that were never available, but the palm trees in the central, glass-covered courtyard lived on, amidst a pervading air of decadence, once genteel, now socialist. Dining at the tables, drinking their vodka and occasionally dancing among the palms with mysterious women who seemed to come out of nowhere at exactly the appropriate moment, was a collection of corpulent men of uncertain origin, usually sitting alone. It took no imagination at all to know that they were spies, KGB agents, mafia dons, and equally questionable characters.

My room was enormous, complete with a chandelier in the middle of the ceiling that was twelve or fifteen feet above me, but with the exception of a TV set the room had no modern facilities whatsoever. Heat in the room was turned on about four hours a day, and the only available bathroom, far down the hallway from my room, often had no toilet paper and left much to be desired in its cleanliness. All this was typical of the Soviet Metropole, and somehow I wanted it no other way.

On arrival in my room I decided to try the television. It would not turn on, and upon examination I found protruding out the back an unraveling electrical connection, the separated wires hanging in air. There was no phone in my room, so I went down three flights of stairs to the main desk, where I complained to the woman at the desk that the TV set in my room would not work. She grunted in response, and wrote down the number of my room. Each day for the next three days this exercise was repeated, but nothing was done about the television. On the fourth day I visited the woman once again, told her that my TV set had been broken for four days, and that I wanted a new one that worked. She grunted once again, and wrote down my room number. Knowing that nothing would be done, I lost my temper, and gave her a little lecture about hotel service, exclaiming, "You know, a good hotel would be interested in the satisfaction of its customers, and when one of them complained about something broken, would fix it." The woman stared at me without a flicker of emotion and replied, "That's just the point. This is not a good hotel," and returned to her work. There was nothing to be said; I turned away helplessly and went back to my room. The television was never repaired or replaced.

If one were going to make a cold war spy thriller movie in Moscow, only the Metropole would be suitable as a place for filming it. It has always been the home of foreigners engaged in suspicious activities. During World War II the American military advisory group was located in the Metropole, and I have heard stories from some of the veterans of those days of what it was like to live there at that time, when Americans were more admired than before or since, but still considered doubtful characters. Once a German bomb dropped through the glass-covered courtyard, landed in the middle of the Palm Court, but did not explode. Before it was removed the Russian orchestra played and a few hardy souls danced around the bomb.

One of the members of the American military group in the Metropole during World War II was a handsome young naval officer who met and fell in love with one of the most beautiful Soviet film actresses of the time. Some of their most passionate moments were spent in the Metropole. The officer tried but failed to marry the actress and take her out of the country. The Soviet authorities would authorize neither the marriage nor the departure. The actress fell under suspicion for associating with a foreign spy, and her career was ruined. But the two lovers continued to meet in the Metropole and eventually they had a daughter. Upon revelation of this fact, the American officer was forced to leave the Soviet Union, and he never saw the actress again. After the fall of the Soviet Union, fifty years later, the daughter, the product of the romance, came to the United States and met her unknown father. He was an aged and ailing retired admiral, living alone in Miami Beach.

Not far from the fading Palm Court was a foreign currency bar that was the favorite hangout of Moscow prostitutes and Soviet secret police agents. Even before the Revolution, prostitutes and the tsarist secret police, the *okhrana*, had a special affection for the Metropole.

The door to the outside near the bar was attended by an aged uniformed doorman with an enormous square beard, thick as a spongy carpet. I was told that he had worked there almost fifty years, since the Russian Revolution. In later years I noticed to my regret that he had been replaced by a colorless fellow sixty years younger. After the fall of the Soviet Union and the Westernization and modernization of the Metropole, this traditional entrance to the hotel was closed and locked. It was considered too accessible to the disreputable elements of downtown Moscow, now neocapitalist. Access to the Metropole today is through a door in an inside court, where guards survey each person who approaches.

Before the old main door was closed, a rather famous episode in U.S.–USSR relations occurred there. Just several years before my visit, the Yale professor Fred Barghoorn was arrested at that door by the Soviet secret police. As he emerged from the door a Soviet agent secretly inserted an incriminating piece of paper in his pocket, and a few steps beyond, another agent arrested him, pulled out the paper, and accused him of being a spy. President Kennedy went on television and demanded his release, giving his word that Barghoorn had no contacts with the CIA. Barghoorn was eventually released, but Kennedy later learned that there had indeed been some contacts between Barghoorn and American intelligence, but that information had been concealed even from the President.

I went in and out of that door several times every day I was in Moscow on this trip, and, mindful of the unfortunate Professor Barghoorn, I found myself steering clear of all passersby and protecting my pockets.

The elevators in the Metropole at this time were the old, ornate, open-cage type, and an attendant in each elevator noisily clanged the bronze gate closed after the passengers entered, and then rammed forward the control lever. The rumor was that the elevator operators knew everything and could arrange anything. I loved the aesthetic experience of riding with them, but soon found that the wait for their arrival could be as long as five minutes. If I were in a hurry, I would ignore the elevator and head for the stairway. It was fun to take, two at a time, the steps covered with faded oriental carpets held in place on the steps by large metal rings that could break your foot if you stepped incorrectly.

Going up the stairs brought one to a highlight of the Metropole experience: the ancient brass statue that stood on the landing halfway up to the second floor. It was of two naked lovers in an embrace, probably Daphnis and Chloe. The statue had once been shiny, but seventy years of Metropole smoke and gloom had reduced it to a dingy brown —except for one part. Every morning as I descended from my room a cleaning lady was industriously shining, with rag and brass polish, Daphnis' penis. The studied labors of decades of cleaning ladies had given Daphnis a brilliant appendage that could not be missed from the bottom of the stairway. I noticed that each morning the cleaning lady was a different one and that she always laughed deliciously whenever anyone looked at her or commented on her work. It was obvious that there was competition among the cleaning ladies for the task and that each morning a different one had a turn. Many years later, in the spring of 1982, Pat and I returned to the Metropole for a visit, and went to see how Daphnis and Chloe were doing. A new respectability had settled over the Metropole; both figures had been burnished to such a lustre that Daphnis' main feature was only relatively prominent by virtue of its gleam. Obviously the management had decided that this statue reflected on the Metropole's reputation. But someone else, no doubt disappointed by the loss of Daphnis' singularity, had drilled a small hole right through the head of Daphnis' member and inserted a small plastic flower. Returning to the Metropole again in June, 2001, I found the place even more respectable; the plastic flower had been removed and a bit of brass surgery had restored Daphnis' anatomy.

I soon settled down to my routine of working in the Lenin Library. As I made my way to and from the library by foot I noticed that I was being followed. It all seemed so appropriate, to come down the stairs inside the Metropole, see the agent get up from his table at the infamous bar, follow me through the equally infamous door, and then lag behind me as I made my way across Sverdlov Square, past the old Noble's Club, the National Hotel, the ancient buildings of Moscow University, and then on to the Lenin Library. I took secret joy in knowing that I would bore the agent to tears by spending the entire day in the library.

After three weeks of labor in the library, which went very successfully in terms of the book I was writing, I realized that I had only ten days left in the Soviet Union, and that I had still done nothing about Don Mix's vodka request. All right, I resolved, I will go about it. Each afternoon about four o'clock I began leaving the library and frequenting the liquor stores of Moscow. This turned out to be a revealing sociological adventure.

My idea was to buy no two bottles with the same labels, to buy only bottles with attractive labels, and to get as many of them as I could. Soon I became a specialist on Soviet vodka. I was staggered by the variety that existed if one looked far enough, since on previous trips to the Soviet Union I had known only two varieties, *Stolichnaia* (Capital) and *Moskovskaia* (Moscow). My ignorance was partly explained by the fact that I had never paid much attention to vodka, since I do not like it, although a little in orange juice, tonic, or tomato juice is all right. But my Soviet acquaintances drank their vodka in pure form and straight down in gulps. I always found that to be a destructive habit, and indeed it is, as the statistics on life expectancy among Russian men indicated.

My collection soon included such brands as *Iubeleinaia* (Jubilee), *Okhotnichnaia* (Hunter's), *Pertsovka* (Pepper), *Posol'skaia* (Ambassador's), *Kubanskaia* (Kuban), *Stolovaia* (Table), *Krepkaia* (Strong), *Russkaia* (Russian), *Limonnaia* (Lemon), *Petrovka* (Peter), *Gornyi dubniak* (Mountain Oak), *Russkii suvenir* (Russian Souvenir), *Sibirskaia* (Siberian), and, perhaps best of all, *Pshenichnaia* (Wheat). As I gathered all this vodka, and many more the names of which I can no longer remember, I gained a certain reputation among the sales personnel of the liquor stores of downtown Moscow. I found it necessary to come back to the same stores again and again in order to search for new brands. As I would come into the store, I would hear one of the clerks call out to a friend, "Here comes that crazy guy again." They thought I was crazy not because I bought lots of vodka (that was eminently normal) but because I kept saying, "Oh, I've got that one already; don't you have any new ones? I would like to have one with a prettier label."

In the process of making the rounds of Moscow vodka stores I gained many insights into what might be called the Soviet vodka culture. Drunks were often seen lying on the sidewalks, slumped on park benches, and scattered in the doorways. I had often been on the Bowery in New York City, so the sight of a drunk did not shock me, but in Moscow it soon became apparent that many ordinary workers and otherwise respectable bureaucrats went on periodic binges that either prostrated them or gave them what I called "the Moscow lurch." Special work crews gathered up the drunks just as they cleared away the snow and the leaves at appropriate seasons of the year; the crews then took the drunks to state-run drying stations known as *vytrezviteli*. A visit or two to such a station was evidently not a great shame, but if a person ended up there repeatedly he (almost never she) was likely to be photographed in a dissolute state; the local Party organization would then display the photograph at the guilty person's place of work in a futile effort to shame him into sobriety.

My position was problematic because although I was buying quite a bit of vodka, I never drank it, but instead took the full bottles back to my hotel. Neither the sales clerks nor the other patrons could understand this behavior. Most of the other customers opened their bottle while still in the store and took a first quaff at the doorway. Sometimes at the entrance to the liquor store I would meet two men who would motion to me and hold up three fingers. They did not have enough money to buy a bottle, but if I would join them with a little money, they would share the bottle with me. Turning them down, as I did, and then buying vodka on my own was seen as a decidedly unsocial act. Only once did a man break down my defenses. He approached me, spread his arms wide, and gave a speech with full rhetorical flourishes that included the statement: "I appeal to you as a fellow member of the human race to be my co-bottle man." And he extended an open bottle to me. I pretended to take a swig, gave him one of my bottles, and hurriedly made my way out of the shop.

Alcoholism has always been a problem in Russia. A story that Russians love to tell is that when the tenth-century ruler of medieval Kiev, Prince Vladimir, was trying to decide what religion to adopt he hesitated between Islam and Christianity, but turned down Islam because of its strictures against alcohol. One of my professors of Russian history at Columbia University, Michael Florinsky, once told our class that in old rural Russia the state liquor store in the villages was always located a hundred yards or so back from the road. The distance from the store to the road, Professor Florinsky confidently assured us, was carefully calculated so that when the peasants collapsed after consuming their just-purchased vodka their bodies would not block traffic on the road.

In my room back at the Metropole I lined up the vodka bottles on a ledge that ran around my room at window height. The cleaning ladies and the floor ladies soon expressed great interest in what was going on in room 306, but, so far as I know, not a single bottle disappeared while I was away in the library.

A few days before my scheduled departure I realized that I had not yet consumed one glass of vodka, and that in my room I had an enormous amount with which something had to be done. It could not be taken out of the country because of export rules. My first thought was to arrange a few big parties in my room, inviting people whom I met downstairs in the Palm Court while having my evening meal. This turned out to be a major mistake. The people you met in the Metropole Hotel who would come up to your room in response to your invitation for a little vodka happened to be one of the most dubious crowds you could select if you tried in several years of world travels. I remember, in particular, one absolutely mad Georgian who brought tins of Kamchatka crab to the party, which he proceeded to open with his teeth while singing at the same time. He cut his lip rather badly on the ragged edge of a can, but was undeterred, and mixed crab, vodka, and blood in a recipe that he enthusiastically pronounced delectable.

Yet another person who came to several of my parties was a middle-aged merchant of Chinese extraction who had a roll of one hundred dollar bills that seemed to be as large as a roll of toilet paper. It turned out that he was in the Soviet Union buying railroad car loads of deer and elk horns to ship to Hong Kong where they would be ground up in powder to sell as an aphrodisiac. How he managed such massive trading in a country where private trade was illegal, and arranged shipments to Hong Kong on state railroads, requiring the permission of innumerable bureaucrats, was incomprehensible to me. (I had read recently in a Soviet newspaper that the manager of a store in Moscow had just been executed for private trade, labeled "speculation.") No doubt the huge roll of hundred dollar bills helped my Chinese acquaintance avoid such problems.

It soon became clear to me that if I continued to hold such parties in my room my reputation would soon be associated with those who accepted my invitations. I knew that KGB agents were following me, and they were no doubt already aware of my parties. Probably they were attending them. If for some reason the KGB wanted to attack me, or try to blackmail me, I was providing them with ammunition. I decided not to hold any more parties.

The next morning I announced to the floor lady (*dezhurnaia*), who by this time knew me well and had even been present at one of the parties, that there would be no more evening celebrations in my room. I went into the room and counted the ten or fifteen full bottles of vodka still remaining. I knew that airport regulations permitted only one bottle to be taken out of the country. I chuckled at the thought that such regulations would be no problem for my Chinese acquaintance, but recognized my much more limited talents in this area. Besides, I was trying to live by the law, even though I was temporarily living in a country where no one had a very clear conception of what the law was. There were only two alternatives: I had either to throw away the vodka or give it to someone. Both drinking it and selling it were out of the question. I called one of my Columbia graduate stu-

dents who was spending the year at Moscow University and asked him
to bring some containers for vodka, if he liked the stuff. He replied that
he would be happy to have some vodka, but wanted to know why he
had to bring containers. Didn't vodka already come in bottles? I had
to explain that I wanted the empty bottles, feeling more and more
that Don Mix and BBDO had gotten me into more complications
and strained explanations than I cared for. The student arrived with a
couple of glass milk bottles and we filled them with vodka. I then gave
away some more to the floor lady, asking her to provide her own containers as I had the student. She was delighted and arrived with pots
from the hotel kitchen.

The morning of my departure from Moscow one full bottle remained. Although I was entitled to take that bottle with me, I didn't
want to have any more to do with vodka. I poured it down the communal toilet, and flushed it. I then called a taxi to take me to the airport.

The empty bottles completely filled my largest suitcase, a cheap and
ugly gray plastic container I had purchased from Sears. Even though I
wrapped each of the bottles in a sheet of Pravda, as I walked down the
hallway toward the front door the suitcase emitted a constant "clink,
clink, clink." At the door I got in the waiting cab and off we went.

The cab went by way of Dzerzhinskii Square, on which sits the most
infamous jail in Moscow, the Lubianka. In its basements the secret
police shot a whole generation of old Bolsheviks, including such lumi-
naries as Bukharin, Karl Radek, and Gregory Zinoviev. The Lubianka
was also the first stopping point, and interrogation center, for people
who were sent to the labor camps. As my cab turned off the circle
around Dzerzhinskii's statue and went along the Lubianka wall toward
a gate that obviously led into the interior of the jail, I thought how
simple it would be for the secret police to arrange for my taxi driver to
pick me up at the hotel as earlier scheduled and drive me right into the
heart of Lubianka. No fuss at all. It would be the easiest matter in the
world to slip incriminating evidence into my luggage and then arrest
me for espionage. All this business about thrusting notes into your
pocket at the Metropole door and then arresting you in front of everybody showed how crude the police were. The whole operation could
be carried out so much more deftly, if the secret police were a bit more
clever. And once I was in the hands of the KGB in Lubianka, it would
be simplicity itself to manufacture stories about me that would con-
demn me in the minds of newspaper readers. This American professor
was not only an intelligence agent who was trying to take out of the

Soviet Union the military secrets found in his luggage, he was also a moral degenerate who staged late-night vodka parties in his Metropole room attended by the dregs of society. The article in *Pravda* could feature a picture of dozens of empty vodka bottles found in the American agent's hotel room. My imagination was in overdrive. Only when the taxi drove right by the Lubianka side entrance and took me uneventfully to the airport did I relax.

As we approached the airport I suddenly realized that I had not even considered, until this moment, how the Soviet customs officials would react to my vodka bottles. Surely those suspicious characters would find something wrong with a suitcase that had nothing in it but row upon row of empty vodka bottles. My only hope was that they would let me pass without opening the suitcase. Occasionally this had happened to me before, although another time they had searched me so thoroughly that I was required to open up a small bottle of opaque cough syrup so that the guard could insert a stirrer and ascertain that nothing (diamonds? dope?) was inside. I brought my suitcase before the uniformed guard and waited for his permission to pass. He pointed straight at the gray suitcase and said, "Open it up." My heart fell as I obeyed. He looked at the vodka bottles with bored eyes and said, "Pass." I closed the suitcase, went through the rest of the departure procedure, and took off for home.

At Kennedy Airport in New York I expected a quick customs procedure since I was not arriving at a peak moment, and my plane was not full. I came to customs, where the inspector asked me to open my suitcase. I did so. He glanced at the vodka bottles, looked again, and then studied them carefully. "What are these?" he wanted to know. I told him they were empty vodka bottles. "Where did they come from?" was his next question. "The Soviet Union" was my reply.

The official seemed perplexed. "Hey, Joe," he called to his colleague at the next counter, "Come look at this." The two conversed about my bottles. Finally the first man turned to me and asked, "How do we know that you are not going to fill these bottles with some cheap American vodka and sell it as expensive imported Russian stuff?"

I know very little about law, and nothing about commercial law, but on the plane en route to Kennedy for lack of anything else to do I had read a long magazine article that explained the legal principle "every dog gets one free bite." It seems that if your neighbor has an absolutely ferocious dog that runs menacingly at you every time you come home, acting as if it was preparing to tear your leg off, you cannot take legal action until that mutt actually sets its teeth in you. After this "free bite" the dog is defined as a vicious animal, and the law knows how to handle such things, so I was given to understand.

This analogy seemed perfectly appropriate for my situation as I stood there, so I responded to the guard, "How do you know that I am not going to murder my wife next week? If I do so, arrest me. And if I sell cheap vodka under foreign labels, arrest me. But until I do so, it seems that you must let me go through since I have not broken any laws or regulations." My legal argument did not seem to allay my inspector's anxieties. He responded, "I'm not quite sure what you are up to, Mister, but with all these vodka bottles, something strange is going on all right, and I would like to know what it is."

As he talked, a debate raged in my head. Should I just tell him the truth, the whole story about Don Mix, BBDO, and vodka ads? Wasn't honesty the best policy? On the other hand, the truth had a commercial ring to it that might not set too well with my inspector, and, besides, it was rather complicated and improbable. I chose the mendacious way out. "Well, you see," I said, "I collect vodka bottles. Some people collect matchbook covers or beer cans. I collect vodka bottles."

"Oh, so you're one of those crazy collectors, eh? Well, you've got a nice collection there. OK, you can go."

I went through, grabbed a cab, and, since it was during the working day, went straight to BBDO on Madison Avenue, where Don Mix expressed appreciation for the bottles. And for the next several years I would periodically admire my vodka bottles in the ads that ran on the back cover of The New Yorker and other publications, emblazoned, "Three of the World's Greatest Vodkas; Gilbey's Is the Only One You Don't Need a Passport to Buy."

PART III

RESEARCH IN THE USSR

CHAPTER NINE

THE MEANING OF
SCIENCE IN RUSSIA

MY RESEARCH FIELD is the history and philosophy of science, especially in Russia. My first book was on the Soviet Academy of Sciences —Russia's premier institution in fundamental science—and my second was on Soviet philosophy of science, a book that was a finalist for a National Book Award in the United States. In subsequent books—all told, about twelve—I have explored the history of science in Russia from the time of Peter the Great to the present. What has been intriguing to me has been the ways in which science in Russia differed from science in the West. Russia has had a different economic system and a distinct religious and philosophical background than most countries in the West, and those differences have influenced Russian science. Most of my work has been on fundamental science in Russia, but I also wrote a book on one of the great Russian engineers—Peter Palchinsky—showing how his approach to technology differed from many other engineers.

I would love to live long enough to have an experience that I am fairly confident will come someday: the moment we Earthlings make meaningful contact with an extraterrestrial civilization. That will be a moment for the ultimate test of the questions I have dealt with on a much more modest level with Russia. How different is their science from ours? How difficult will it be for us to understand their science? To compare Russian science to that in an extraterrestrial civilization is of course extreme; scientists in Russia are in almost constant contact with scientists elsewhere on Earth, at least through publications. Nonetheless, enough different nuances exist in Russian science from that in the West to make me think that science in an extraterrestrial civilization, cut off from all previous contact with Earth, would be different indeed from our science. In the case of extraterrestrials, not only will their social histories be different from ours, but their biological evolution as well. Their brains will probably be different from ours, and they may think differently. Russians' brains are the same as ours, but their social history is different, and I have been able to find distinctions in their science that can be related to that different history.

When I was a beginning graduate student at Columbia University I became interested in Soviet philosophy of science, especially the way in which it was developed and used by scientists of the first rank. The difference between my approach and the few previous Western scholars who had studied the subject was that I believed that Soviet philosophy of science was inherently interesting, not simply a rigid dogma derived from Marxist–Leninist ideology. Of course, plenty of examples of dogma and repression could be found during the Stalinist period and even afterward, especially in biology, but some Soviet scholars continued to work on genuine philosophy of science even during the worst political times. In fact, I found that Soviet scientists and philosophers of science had participated in all the great debates over the meaning of science that had gripped Western authors in the twentieth century—such as the interpretation of relativity theory, quantum mechanics, biological reductionism, and the meaning and structure of the universe—but Western scholars were almost completely unaware of their work. Furthermore, some of the Soviet published work was quite interesting and distinct from that of Western authors. I wanted to make this Soviet research known to the West.

I wrote my master's essay at Columbia on Soviet philosophy of chemistry, especially structural chemistry. I then proposed a doctoral dissertation on the development of Soviet philosophy of science as a whole, including the debates in all scientific fields, from biology, to physics, to astronomy. The proposal was rejected by my major professor, quite correctly, on the grounds that it was impossibly broad, and would require me to remain a graduate student forever while slaving away on an endless topic.

Recovering from this blow to my pride, I resolved to find a topic that was tidy and restricted, one that I could finish in two years or less. I needed, after several years of financial bleakness, to find a job that actually paid a salary. I hoped to publish my dissertation and then return to the big project on Soviet philosophy of science that still engaged my attention, even if my professors warned me away from it.

The perfect topic for a dissertation seemed to be the history of the Soviet Academy of Sciences in the period in which it was converted from a tsarist institution to a Soviet one, the late 1920s and early 1930s. Here was a subject that was restricted to about five years (1927–1932), but was nonetheless significant (the Soviet Academy of Sciences was a sort of National Science Foundation, Harvard, Berkeley, Michigan, Indiana, Stanford, and Columbia all rolled into one).

My good Columbia professors agreed that the topic was an excellent one, but they observed that it would be necessary to go to the Soviet Union to do it properly, and they doubted the Soviet authorities would permit me to come. Academic exchanges between the United States and the Soviet Union were just getting underway, and no one yet knew how well they would work, or what kind of reception American scholars would have in that country. Furthermore, my subject—the Academy of Sciences—was controversial, despite the scholarly and seemingly innocent name of this institution. Members of the Academy in the years in which I proposed to study it had been subjected to political repression and some had been purged (fired or even imprisoned) in a process directed by the secret police and the Communist Party. Surely the Soviet authorities would not be eager for me to delve into this episode. Nonetheless, I decided to take my chances.

I applied to the exchange program in its second year of existence and was accepted by both the American and Soviet authorities. In retrospect, I think that the Soviet administrators did not fully grasp the potential ramifications of my topic, although I described it accurately. The history of the Soviet Academy of Sciences, an institution about which they were intensely proud, apparently seemed innocuous to them.

Upon arriving at Moscow University I was assigned as an advisor a professor of history named Bessonova who, as far as I could tell, knew not one word of English. Her office was located in the history faculty in the old university downtown. When I entered the building for the first time I saw that this was a history department like none I had seen before. The walls were decorated with patriotic red banners and flags, busts of Soviet leaders, and slogans calling for vigilance on the "ideological front." On a bulletin board was a report of a recent visit by a Party "control commission" which revealed examples of ideological laxness among historians and several instances of wastage of state property such as paper and pencils. Another notice criticized the history students for drunkenness at parties, and a photograph graphically displayed one of the graduate students passed out on a sofa, with a warning to him to correct his behavior. Yet another announcement said that all history faculty and students would be expected to leave the city for the countryside in several weeks to help bring in the potato harvest. And attached to the wall was a poster describing the academic work plans of the professors and researchers, listing each project currently underway and its expected completion date. The thought of my professors at Columbia being regulated by annual and five-year work plans was novel, not to mention their harvesting potatoes.

Professor Bessonova was a motherly type, gray-haired and obviously intelligent. Although a senior historian, she did not have an office of her own but instead interviewed me in the "reading hall" of the department, shooing out several students so that we would have privacy. After introducing herself, she asked me to describe my research project, although I could see that she had on her desk the proposal that I had made when I applied for the exchange program. The tone of her voice made me suspect that she was somewhat nervous about having an American graduate student. I described my research in almost exactly the same words contained in the written proposal. Professor Bessonova nodded, and made a few comments about my research that clearly indicated that she knew almost nothing about the subject. She then said that she had a homework assignment to give me that I should prepare before our next meeting two weeks hence. I was a bit surprised, since I was twenty-seven years old, an advanced graduate student, and at a stage usually considered to be beyond homework assignments. Nonetheless, I said that I would be happy to write it down, and got out paper and pen. She then assigned me several hundred pages to read from the collected works of Marx and Engels. I later checked the references and found that they had nothing whatsoever to do with my research. My research time in Moscow was too precious to spend doing this reading, so I decided to ignore the homework and see what would happen at our next meeting.

Two weeks later I was again in front of Professor Bessonova in the reading hall. After pleasant greetings, she asked me to tell her what I had been doing since our last meeting. I described accurately my work in the libraries and uttered not one word about the homework assignment. She again nodded, said that she had another reading assignment for me, and dictated references to several hundred more pages out of the collected works of Marx, Engels, and, this time, Lenin as well. I dutifully wrote the assignment down and again ignored it.

We continued in this fashion for nine months. I never mentioned the homework, and she never asked me why I avoided it. Each time I met her I described what I had, in fact, been doing, and each time she gave me another batch of reading. There was an implicit understanding that each was acting according to his or her own lights. If a superior ever hassled her about her American student, she could describe me as a slothful fellow who did not follow orders. But she was an honorable person who would never voluntarily put me in that sort of difficult position. We gradually developed a collegial relationship and for many years afterwards we occasionally corresponded and exchanged reprints of articles from professional journals.

Meanwhile, I was finding plenty to do in the libraries, especially the Lenin Library, an unusual institution that demands some description. Founded long before the Russian Revolution as a part of the "Rumiantsev Museum," the main building was designed in the 1920s when Soviet architecture was under heavy, modern European influence, and consequently from the outside it displayed clean, functional lines of gray stone. It was completed after Stalinist tastes had been imposed upon all the Soviet arts; signs of the encroaching orthodoxy could be seen in the heroic statues surmounting the roof edges and the massive brass and glass chandeliers inside. Engraved in the exterior stones were the names of the world's great scholars; here next to Plato, Aristotle, and Newton one could find Timiriazev and Michurin. The latter names may not have been well known to Westerners, but every Soviet schoolchild knew them well.

Located practically under the Kremlin walls, the Lenin Library was described by its administrators as the largest library in the world. The librarians of the British Museum, the Bibliothèque Nationale, and the Library of Congress did not agree with this description; they said that the Soviet librarians counted as books items such as manuscripts and even sheet music. But whatever the truth about relative size, the Lenin Library was certainly a massive repository of information.

Finding that information was not always easy. When I visited the library the first time the central card catalog on the second floor was divided into two sections: "Books from the Socialist Countries" and "Books from the Non-Socialist Countries." Yugoslavia under Tito had by the time I came to the library rebelled against Soviet rule, but still claimed to be socialist; the librarians in the Lenin Library were therefore somewhat baffled by the question of where to put the catalog of books in Serbo-Croatian. They solved the dilemma by placing the troublesome catalog in the aisle between the two sections. But this solution broke down during my first year in the library when China cut off relations with the Soviet Union. Where to put the enormous

catalog of Chinese books? Eventually the librarians gave up their political categories and re-divided the main catalog into "Books in the
Russian Language" and "Books in the Non-Russian Languages."

The new system was not the end of political considerations for library catalogers. The card catalog did not contain cards for books that
were considered anti-Soviet. Almost none of the books on the Soviet
Union by Western authors were listed in either of the two main catalogs. I tested the system by looking for references to that heretic of all
Soviet heretics, Leon Trotsky. My heart leapt when I found the fateful
name on several cards, but they turned out to be references to the
works of an automotive engineer specializing in brakes who had the
misfortune of having the name "Trotsky." I was struck by the delightful
thought that the engineer might be a descendant of the Odessa jailor
of the young revolutionary Lev Bronshtein (Trotsky's real name) who
jokingly took his captor's name as a pseudonym.

Missing from the main catalogs of the Lenin Library were not only
the standard Western works on the Soviet Union, but also the writings
of Soviet exiles and dissidents, and books deemed pornographic or otherwise objectionable. Of course, these books were in the library, but
they were preserved in the *spetskhran*, or special collections. In order
to find out that they existed one had to use the special closed catalog
on one of the higher floors of the library. I was never permitted to
utilize this catalog, but once in the 1970s stumbled onto it while wan-
dering through the halls, and realized where I was when I saw the
militiaman guarding the long rows of trays. No doubt he was guarding
references to some of my own works, but they were too dangerous for
me to see.

Even materials that were listed in the card catalog were sometimes
restricted. I had a reminder of these controls in the spring of 1982
when, working in the Lenin Library, I found an article in one of the
main Soviet journals, *Problems of Philosophy*, which discussed the ethical implications of genetic engineering. The author cited another Soviet source, the journal of the Moscow Patriarchate, to show that the
leaders of the Orthodox Church, like many of the Marxist philosophers, were concerned about genetic engineering. Since the journal
of the Moscow Patriarchate was a current Soviet periodical, I knew
that it would have to be listed in the card catalog. Sure enough it was,
but when I ordered it, a senior librarian came out and wanted to know
why it was necessary for me to read a "religious journal." Only when I
convinced her that I was not a Soviet citizen and that the journal was
necessary for my scholarly research was I able to receive it.

All foreign scholars who came to the Lenin Library were assigned desks in "Reading Hall Number One," the best place to work. At any given time its occupants seemed to be a curious mixture of elderly Soviet scholars with academic skullcaps and young graduate students from Western Europe and America, with a sprinkling of foreign professors. And then there was the occasional aged member of the political elite, writing his memoirs. I spotted both Vyacheslav Molotov, Stalin's infamous foreign minister, and Lazar Kaganovich, another former high official equally opposed to Khrushchev's de-Stalinization program. I once badly banged my head on a card catalog drawer that Molotov had pulled out above me when I suddenly straightened up after studying a lower drawer. It was obviously my fault, but I would not have minded an "excuse me" from this alleged master of diplomacy.

Each scholar in Reading Hall Number One had an individual desk, there were some reference books, and even one or two potted palms. Out the windows one could see the golden domes of the Kremlin and the "Palace of the Soviets," the modern theater in which the top Party leaders met at their periodic congresses. In the middle of the winter the reading room began to grow dark by about three P.M., but there was a strange protocol about turning on the green-shaded reading lamps on the desks. Perhaps in order to observe the signs on the wall calling for the conservation of electricity, no one would turn on a reading lamp until the most senior scholar present had done so; when this octogenarian switched on his light, one could hear the clicks follow all over the hall as we less-distinguished individuals concluded it was now permissible to cast a bit of light on our darkening pages.

The rather grand atmosphere of Hall Number One was somewhat diminished by the fact that its entrance was directly two floors above the filthy toilets, and as one swept into the hall with thoughts of footnotes and metaphysics, one often brought in at the same time the fetid smell of the lower reaches. Standard equipment for the most distinguished scholar in the library was a small roll of toilet paper tucked away in a pocket, for the toilets contained none. It was said that all attempts to supply the toilets with paper failed, for this perennially scarce item in Moscow was systematically stolen by anyone fortunate enough to find a fully equipped toilet. Toilet paper in Moscow was so scarce, in fact, that it was not unusual to see a person in the subway festooned with rolls of toilet paper tied to long strings of twine, perhaps thirty rolls on one person, making him look like a version of the Michelin tire man, all bulky and balloony. That lucky person had blundered on to a recent shipment of toilet paper in a store, and he was not going to miss the opportunity to lay in a year's supply or sell some privately. When some years later McDonald's was permitted to establish its first fast-food outlet in Moscow a crisis arose over toilet paper. McDonald's management prided itself on its clean and well-equipped toilets, but as quickly as they replenished toilet paper it was filched by customers trying to supply their home bathrooms. Eventually, guards had to be posted at the doors to check bags for illegal toilet paper.

In the Lenin Library the full kit bag for the international scholar spending long days at research would include the toilet seat as well, for those also were missing. I never saw anyone so equipped in Moscow, but in Leningrad some students and professors actually carried toilet seats with them around the dormitories and libraries, which, like so many Soviet institutions, lacked this amenity.

Despite such impediments, I found a rather rich collection of material in the Lenin Library on the Soviet Academy of Sciences. Particularly valuable were local and "wall" newspapers. Wall newspapers were a Soviet institution; since sales of newspapers were not important to ensure their survival, many of them were posted on walls for passersby to read. The Soviet Academy of Sciences in the 1920s and 1930s had several institutional wall newspapers which were not held by any Western libraries, and they were a great aid to my research.

Even more important were Soviet dissertations on topics related to mine, especially one on Soviet scientific institutions in the twenties written by a man named V. T. Ermakov. Although this source was an enormous boost to my research, I had to use it with caution. Ermakov had altered his account to fit political constraints, and those constraints shifted while he was writing. He had written his dissertation and had it typed while Stalin was still in favor, but before his defense of the dissertation Khrushchev condemned Stalin at a meeting of Party leaders. Such events could, and did, play havoc with the work of Soviet researchers like poor Ermakov. Before his defense, he hurriedly went through the dissertation, erased all references to Stalin, and then typed over them. By holding the pages of the dissertation up to the light I could read both versions. And I knew that even in the first version of the dissertation Ermakov had eliminated all references to other disgraced Party leaders, including Nikolai Bukharin, who played a rather significant role in the events I needed to describe and analyze in my thesis.

In later years on return visits to Moscow I noticed that gaining access to these important sources to my earlier research—local wall newspapers and dissertations—was vastly more difficult. Perhaps the Soviet authorities noticed how useful they were to foreign scholars like me who wanted to learn more about Soviet history and politics, because they erected a new system of barriers. The newspapers were moved out of the Lenin Library to the suburb of Khimki, which was off-limits to foreigners. Sometimes newspapers from there could be ordered from the central library, but the system was very cumbersome. The dissertation catalog was also transferred from the main building of the Lenin Library to an adjoining one, and foreigners were restricted to seeing a small number.

After I finished my book on the Soviet Academy of Sciences, I went on to the larger work on the history and philosophy of natural science in Russia, and I spent many years on this subject, writing a series of articles and books, including one large one, *Science and Philosophy in the Soviet Union*, that was published in both English and Russian, as well as several other languages. I found to my pleasant surprise that the work of the very best of Russian scientists, including world-class physicists and mathematicians, could often be related to their social and political environment. Most scientists in the world do not like to think that their work is affected by their social context; they prefer to believe that science is truth recognized everywhere, and that the social environment has nothing to do with that truth. However, it became clear to me that even the equations used by mathematicians and theoretical physicists, not only in Russia but elsewhere, were sometimes affected by the cultural context in which these scientists worked. For example, one of the Soviet Union's great physicists, Vladimir Fock, used equations different from Einstein's—even though most of the practical results were the same as Einstein's—that could be related to his commitment to philosophical materialism. And several of the founders of the Moscow School of Functions (a great movement in twentieth century mathematics) used an approach to set theory that was related to their secret commitment to religion, carefully concealed from the Soviet authorities. Philosophical ideas and metaphysical commitments play a far greater role in science than usually is admitted.

Mathematics is a field in which Russians have excelled, but I soon saw that Russian mathematics from the late nineteenth century through the entire Soviet period was beset by controversies and polemics that affected the most abstract and complex work, sometimes in innovative ways. These debates set defenders of religion and Marxism against each other, and advocates of free will and determinism. The development of discontinuous functions—a field in which the Moscow School of Mathematics is world famous—was in part an effort by religious mathematicians like D. F. Egorov and N. N. Luzin covertly to rebel against Marxist mathematicians who preferred deterministic continuous functions. And one of the greatest mathematicians of the twentieth century—the Russian probabilist A. N. Kolmogorov—also was deeply involved in these polemics, taking a Marxist position against his teachers. Many people in the West already knew that simple Marxist-Leninists had trouble accepting the probabilistic approach of quantum mechanics, which seemed to undermine determinism, but few people knew that the questions involved here were not just about crude ideology but instead very sophisticated problems of interpretation that sometimes affected science of the highest order. It helps to remember that not only did many Marxist-Leninists have trouble accepting quantum mechanics; so did Einstein, who remarked that "Nature does not play dice."

I wrote about these social effects on mathematics and physics in many publications, and in the millennial year of 2000 I summed up my attitudes on this question in an article entitled "Do Mathematical Equations Express Social Attributes?" that appeared in the mathematics journal *The Mathematical Intelligencer*. Six years later I wrote, with the French mathematician Jean-Michel Kantor as my co-author, an article entitled "A Comparison of Two Cultural Approaches to Mathematics: France and Russia, 1890–1930" for the history of science journal *Isis*. In both of these articles I maintained that even the most abstract mathematics is influenced by cultural currents, in the first article, by Marxism, in the second article, by religion.

It was a significant event to foreign specialists on the Soviet Union when, in the late seventies, the Academy of Sciences opened a new, modern library on the outskirts of Moscow where access was much better. This library, the Institute of Scientific Information on the Social Sciences (INION), was the only one I ever saw in the Soviet Union where foreign sources on Soviet politics were not only listed in the card catalog, but also available for order. It was not a public library, however; entrance was restricted to graduate students and researchers of the Academy of Sciences of the USSR, as well as foreign scholars associated with the Academy. It was a clean and efficient facility in which microfilming and photocopying resources were far superior to those in the Lenin Library, where the photocopiers were kept under tight security control.

Even at the relatively liberal INION library, however, political considerations were not far away. In April of 1982 one of my microfilm orders there was refused. When I inquired about the cause, it became clear that one of the books from which I ordered microfilm, a record of the trial of some Soviet engineers in the early thirties who were accused of sabotage, was considered politically too sensitive even though the trial had occurred a half-century earlier. Several days later, when I checked the card catalog again to get a full citation of the book in order to look for it elsewhere, I saw that the card was missing from the catalog. Visible at the bottom of the tray was a little bit of torn paper showing that the card had been ripped out of the catalog after I had looked at it a week previously. Evidently my microfilm order had alerted a vigilant librarian to the fact that the card catalog contained a reference that should not have been there.

CHAPTER TEN

THE AMERICAN COLONY
IN THE SOVIET UNION

WHEN I FIRST WENT TO MOSCOW, in 1960, it seemed to me that I soon came to know every American in the city. Contact between Americans and Soviet citizens had been sharply restricted for years, and tourism between the two countries was nearly non-existent. Of course, I was incorrect—there were a few Americans there I did not meet in the course of a year. But the American colony in Moscow over forty years ago was very small, and it was made up of just a few categories of people. There was the small diplomatic contingent that lived a cloistered life, dependent for their supplies and groceries on a special commissary within the American Embassy. They were so isolated from the Soviet economy that they even sent their dry cleaning to Finland. Then there were the news correspondents for American newspapers and television networks, another minuscule group. Most of them lived in a special building assigned them by the Soviet government and were closely watched (and regularly bugged) like the diplomats. And of course, there were a few—less than twenty—American exchange students like me, living in university dormitories with Russians and dependent on the Soviet economy for their needs.

Among the foreign correspondents in Moscow at that time there was one—Henry Shapiro, bureau chief for UPI—who stood out among all the others. Shapiro had been the UPI correspondent in Moscow for twenty-three years (and he would be for another thirteen years). While most foreign correspondents in Russia at that time did not speak Russian, Shapiro did, and he had a Russian wife, Ludmilla Nikitina. Together they were seen everywhere that foreigners congregated in the city—at receptions and theater events, at official occasions for foreigners arranged by the Soviet government, and at private parties. His connections with the Soviet bureaucracy were excellent, and other correspondents often tried to check their stories with him, if they were willing to admit his superior knowledge. He and his wife, however, often refused to see the full dimensions of Soviet repression. He was not as egregious in this respect as Walter Duranty had been when he was correspondent for *The New York Times* in the early thirties, but the way Shapiro avoided being expelled from the Soviet Union was by relying primarily on official sources.

Diplomats, correspondents, and students were the obvious categories of Americans in Moscow in 1960, and we soon all came to know each other. Beyond these groups, however, there were other shadowy categories of Americans in the Soviet Union who often avoided, or were denied, contacts with those of us who were there with official permission from the State Department. Some of them were American radicals who had come to the Soviet Union many years earlier, often in the thirties, in the belief that a new utopian socialist society was being created there. When the Ford Motor Company built a new auto plant in the early thirties in the Soviet city of Gorky (Nizhny Novgorod in tsarist times), the Ford management actually encouraged the more radical workers in their U.S. plants to make the trip; in that way they got rid of people they considered trouble-makers in Detroit while at the same time they fulfilled their contract with the Soviet government to get the plant up and operating. About 300 families moved from Detroit to Gorky. The American workers included Walter and Victor Reuther, later famous in the American labor movement. The Reuthers returned to the U.S., like most of the American workers, but a number of Americans stayed on and became Russified. (A few descendants were still in Gorky—by then again Nizhny Novgorod—when I visited it in 2003.)

The son of one of these workers, a man I eventually met named Victor Herman, had a fascinating and tragic personal history. His father, Samuel Herman, had been a Ford worker and a dedicated socialist who came to the Soviet Union in 1931 with his family. Victor, who had American citizenship because he was born in Detroit of American parents, attended school and later taught in Gorky. His ability in the Russian language was such that he was often taken for a Russian. He excelled in athletics and soon also became a participant in the amateur aviation contests sponsored by the government. From flying he progressed to parachute jumping, especially "deadfall" parachuting in which he would jump from a high altitude and fall freely, opening his chute only at the last safe moment.

At this time in a number of countries in the world, parachutists were trying to establish records for various types of jumps. The record for a deadfall jump at this time was 16,000 feet, held by a jumper in the United States. Victor offered to break that record on September 6, 1934, at an air show outside of Moscow that was attended by high-ranking officers in the Soviet military and a few government officials. The plane which Victor planned to use had a maximum altitude rating of 15,000 feet. In order to coax the plane higher, Victor and the pilot retooled the craft by using a different prop, stripping out all extra equipment, and juicing up the fuel. The ascent to 15,000 feet went rather quickly, but the last part seemed interminable. After two hours of straining the pilot managed to lift the lightened and specially-rigged plane to the incredible altitude of 24,000 feet where Victor stripped off his oxygen mask and jumped out, planning to free fall until he could breathe again. At about 1,300 feet he opened his chute. According to Victor the entire fall lasted 142 seconds. When the exuberant crowd, together with reporters from the leading Soviet newspapers, rushed up to him, Victor was standing on the field eating an apple, which he had taken out of his pocket and started munching on the way down. The reporters went wild, and their papers announced the next day that a Soviet airman of incredible braveness and coolness had established the world's record for free-fall parachute jumping.

The catch came the following day, when officials asked Victor to sign the World Records document. The form contained a blank for citizenship, and Victor wrote in "U.S.A." The astounded Russians said that they understood that he was a Russian from Gorky and asked him where he was born. Victor replied "Detroit, Michigan, USA." The Russians then demanded that he sign as a Soviet citizen anyway, promising him a Soviet passport and Soviet citizenship. Victor refused, saying he had only one citizenship, American. The Russians tore up the documents in front of him, and at that moment Victor Herman made an instantaneous transition from hero to outcast. Eventually, after many other difficulties, he was arrested in 1938 and sent to the labor camps, where he spent the next eighteen years. He managed to survive in terrible conditions while doing forced labor in Siberia. In 1956 he was released from prison, but for many years still could not get permission to return to the United States. That homeward trip came only in 1976. Nine years later, after writing a book about his experiences, he died in a suburb of "Detroit, Michigan, USA."

Other American expatriates living in Moscow when I first went there were veterans of the Spanish Civil War who had fought Franco, often alongside Russians, and who decided after that unsuccessful struggle not to return home where they feared their political sympathies would be unwelcome. Muscovite Americans also included a few American blacks who fled racial discrimination in the United States and also a sprinkling of American scientists, artists, and intellectuals of left-wing persuasion who escaped the persecution of the McCarthy period by moving to the Soviet Union. I also heard rumors of Americans involuntarily in the Soviet Union in labor camps in far-off Siberia, prisoners taken by the North Koreans during the Korean War in the early fifties. Only many years later would Boris Yeltsin confirm the earlier existence of such prisoners. Another American prisoner in the Soviet Union when I first went there was Francis Gary Powers, the pilot of the U2 spy plane shot down in the summer of 1960 and exchanged in 1962 for convicted Soviet spy Rudolph Abel. And, of course, Lee Harvey Oswald was living and working in Minsk at the time I first came to Moscow, and I heard stories about him as well.

I first became aware of unusual expatriate Americans in the Soviet Union when I was sitting in a Moscow movie theater. Behind me I heard two people speaking perfect American English to each other. Turning, I saw a man and a woman in their sixties or seventies, to whom I said "You are Americans, aren't you?" They confirmed my guess, but clearly did not want to talk and did not want to explain why they were living in Moscow. I never did learn who they were but I felt certain they belonged to the group of Americans who had emigrated to the Soviet Union to show sympathy and to participate in the socialist experiment. In later months I learned that Moscow contained a little colony of such Americans. They often met each other at certain theatrical or artistic occasions attractive to Americans, such as the frequent concerts in Moscow given by the gifted black American singer Paul Robeson, a fellow supporter of socialism.

Robeson, son of a runaway slave, was valedictorian of his class at Rutgers College (now University). A man of extraordinary talent, he became world-famous for his acting and singing abilities. Disillusioned by racism in America, he found in the USSR a society which he considered superior. He first came to the Soviet Union in 1934, was befriended there by the film director Sergei Eisenstein and many other Soviet artists and intellectuals, and became a strong advocate of Soviet socialism. As a result he was blacklisted by many concert managers in the United States, and in 1950 the State Department revoked his passport, making it impossible for him to continue his popular visits to the USSR. However, in 1958 the passport was restored, and Robeson resumed his visits there. In 1961 he was planning trips to Russia, China, and Cuba, and in March he arrived in Moscow, at a time when I was there as a student. I read about his extraordinary local success in Soviet newspapers. However, on the evening of March 27, 1961, something very strange happened at the Metropole Hotel, where he was staying, which—as far as I know—has never been satisfactorily explained. After what was described as a "wild party" Robeson was found in his room with his wrists slashed. His son, Paul Robeson Jr., a fluent speaker of Russian as a result of his own Soviet education, later said that his father was under intense surveillance by the CIA, which was concerned about his planned visit to Cuba at about the time of the Bay of Pigs invasion; the son implied, without much evidence, that his father had been drugged by American agents in Moscow in a way that would make him self-destructive. Robeson survived, but spent the remaining years of his life in poor health.

One of the most striking Americans who was frequently in Moscow in the early sixties was Filipp Staros, a much talked-about figure who avoided contact with other Americans. A fuller picture of him did not emerge until later years, when I spoke to people who knew him in Leningrad, Moscow, and Vladivostok, all places where he worked as an electrical engineer. And Staros was no ordinary electrical engineer; he was a very creative scientist who later was widely called the "father of Soviet microelectronics." It was Staros, in fact, who introduced the very word "microelectronics" (*mikroelektronika*) into the Russian language. The story of how this American created an entire field in the Soviet Union, and actually built one of the first Soviet computers, is tightly tied to the politics of the Cold War.

Filipp Staros was born in New York City with the name Alfred Sarant. He graduated from Cooper Union in 1941 with a degree in electrical engineering and worked successively at Bell Laboratories in New Jersey and at Cornell University. He was a radical in politics and in the early forties was a member of the American Communist Party, and a friend of Julius and Ethel Rosenberg, later executed by American authorities for atomic espionage. After the arrest of the Rosenbergs in 1950 Sarant was questioned by the FBI, and he obviously feared that he would be detained by the American authorities. He also had difficulties in his personal life—he was in love with a neighbor's wife in Ithaca. In the summer of 1950 he went to Mexico with his girlfriend, leaving his own wife and children back in Ithaca, and then escaped behind the Iron Curtain to Czechoslovakia, where he lived and worked for several years, doing research in computer science. Still fearing the FBI and American intelligence agents, he tried to hide by taking the name of Filipp Staros.

In the late fifties Staros moved to the USSR, where, because of his obvious abilities as a computer scientist, he came to the attention of the highest authorities, including the head of the Soviet government, Nikita Khrushchev. Khrushchev wanted to catch up with the Americans in computers, and he asked Staros to head the effort. Staros was given a laboratory in Leningrad and then was made the head of an entire science establishment in a suburb of Moscow, Zelenograd, which eventually became known as "the Russian Silicon Valley."

For a few years Staros enjoyed almost unlimited access to money and materials. He surrounded himself with bright researchers, hiring Jews and non-members of the Communist Party whenever they seemed to be the best people available, at the same time making enemies among members of the Soviet scientific establishment, who disagreed with his free-wheeling policies and resented his independence. Some of them saw the installation of an American at the head of the Soviet computer effort as an insult. Staros insisted that all his subordinates be thoroughly up to date on the latest computer literature from the West and frequently quizzed them on their knowledge of the literature. He was widely regarded as an outstanding pioneer in his field.

To Staros' misfortune, however, his very success was his downfall. Once he had brought Russian researchers up to his level in computer science, the Russians thought the Zelenograd center could go forward on its own without the guiding hand of its American founder. Eventually the Soviet authorities demoted him to a subordinate status. It was simply too embarrassing for the Soviet computer establishment to be headed by an American, just as it had been considered embarrassing for an American to establish parachute records in the USSR. For a while Staros lived and worked in far-away Vladivostok, exploring artificial intelligence, but political intrigues followed him even there. I heard many stories about him when I visited research establishments in Vladivostok in later years. In 1970 Staros died of a heart attack while visiting in Moscow, an event probably brought on by the pressures of political infighting. Although a few publications about him have appeared in the West, it is still not widely appreciated—either in Russia or the United States—that the founder of microelectronics in Russia, and one of its leading computer designers, was an American who fled the political difficulties of the McCarthy period only to land in somewhat similar problems in the Soviet Union. As a communist, he was not trusted in America; as an American he was not trusted in communist Russia.

CHAPTER ELEVEN

THE BIGGEST FRAUD
IN BIOLOGY

THE MOST INFAMOUS SCIENTIST of the twentieth century was undoubtedly Trofim Denisovich Lysenko, an agricultural specialist of the
Soviet Union who, despite his humble beginnings, became the autocratic ruler of biology in that country (see "Biographical Notes" at the
end of this book). For forty years Lysenko preached a form of biology
that ignored the achievements of modern genetics revolutionizing the
field in the rest of the world. During the last half of this period the
Communist Party enforced Lysenko's fraudulent theories upon all Soviet biologists. Those geneticists who understood the falseness of his
views and resisted were sent to labor camps or executed. Dozens, if not
hundreds, of outstanding Soviet biologists perished in this way, and
Soviet biology went into decline. Even as late as the 1960s, when Soviet space science was impressing the world with its achievements, Soviet biology was still under the thrall of this man who refused to recognize the existence of genes or the significance of DNA.

Lysenko believed in the inheritance of acquired characteristics, a
viewpoint often called "Lamarckism" that incorporates the principle
that changes that occur in the lifetime of an organism can then become inheritable. This approach is rejected by contemporary biologists who emphasize that evolution occurs on the basis of selection out
of genetic variations.

Because of Lysenko's commitment to the inheritance of acquired
characteristics many Westerners have assumed that he preached that
under socialism desirable traits inculcated under the proper social conditions could be bred into human beings, creating "A New Soviet

Man." However, Lysenko sharply rejected all application of his biological views to human beings, calling this viewpoint a form of "bourgeois eugenics." Instead, he applied his views exclusively to plants and animals. In the process he did great damage to Soviet agriculture both through the direct effects of his mistaken methods and also by preventing Soviet agriculture from benefitting from the host of improvements sweeping Western agriculture that came from modern knowledge of plant and animal genetics.

As a historian of science I wanted to describe and analyze this bizarre history, as well as the histories of the brighter pages of Russian science. Usually I based my work on both the published works of the scientists I was interested in and on personal interviews with them. During the Cold War, scientists in Russia often were reluctant to meet with an American, but I developed an approach that usually opened their doors. I would write up a chapter, article, or book on the work of a certain scientist and then, before publishing my research, I would visit Russia and leave off a draft copy of my work at the laboratory of the scientist, with a note attached saying that my description of his or her work was soon to be published in the United States; I added, however, that time still remained for the scientist to influence the account if he or she would agree to meet with me and discuss my interpretations. Prominent scientists usually have large egos, and most of them could not resist the temptation to leave their stamps on publications in the West about them. After meeting with them my obligation, obviously, was to decide which of their comments were valid and should be accepted and which were not.

Lysenko resisted my efforts to see him. I first tried to meet with him in 1961, when I was a graduate student at Moscow University. At that time Lysenko ran a collective farm a short distance from the university, and I could see some of the buildings of his farm from the central skyscraper of the university. However, Lysenko never answered my letters or phone calls, and I was unable to meet with him.

Ten years later, in 1971, I had almost finished several chapters about Lysenko and his supporters in a book I was writing, and I decided once again to try to interview him. By this time he had lost his position as the dictator of Soviet biology but he was still a full member of the Academy of Sciences, a prestigious position that brought with it a good salary and many perquisites, and he was still living in Moscow. I went to his office and left my chapters there, with my usual note saying that these writings would soon be published and inviting him to comment on them before publication so that I might correct any errors that he saw. I gave my telephone number at the Academy of Sciences hotel where I was staying. As I feared, there was no answer. Lysenko was not interested in talking to me. I therefore decided—mistakenly, it turned out—that I would never meet the man, and turned my attention to some of Lysenko's supporters among the other Soviet biologists, a number of whom I interviewed.

My opportunity to meet and talk with Lysenko came several weeks later by accident. As a participant in an official U.S.–USSR scientific exchange I had a pass to use the lunchrooms and recreational facilities of the Academy of Sciences. One of my favorite spots for lunch was the "House of Scientists" near the center of Moscow, a sort of faculty club. This building had been the home of a nobleman before the Russian Revolution and was still ornately decorated with statues and chandeliers. I particularly liked the soups served there, usually borshch or solyanka.

One day toward the end of my stay in 1971 I entered the palatial dining room of the House of Scientists after spending the morning working in the Lenin Library, not far away. At the back of the room, sitting alone at a table, was a gaunt and homely man. I immediately recognized Lysenko. In the Soviet Union it was not unusual for strangers to sit at the same lunch table so I sat down beside Lysenko, ordered a bowl of borshch from the waitress, and began my lunch.

After a while I turned to Lysenko and said "I know that you are Trofim Denisovich Lysenko. I am Loren Graham, an American historian of science, and I have written quite a bit about you. Several times I have sent you my work."

Lysenko replied, "I recognize your name. I have read what you wrote about me. You know a lot about Russian science, but you have made several serious mistakes in describing me and my work."

I immediately inquired what my mistakes were. "The most important mistake," said Lysenko, "was that you accuse me of being responsible for the deaths of many Russian biologists, such as the well-known geneticist Nikolai Vavilov. I disagreed with Vavilov on biological issues but I had nothing to do with his death in a labor camp. You know, I have never even been a member of the Communist Party, and I am not responsible for what either the Party or the secret police did in biology."

I knew that Lysenko was correct in saying that he was not a member of the Communist Party, a fact that I had cited in my descriptions of his political activities. But he was grossly in error in saying that he bore no responsibility for the deaths and imprisonment of prominent Soviet geneticists. His method of behavior was to describe these scientists as traitors to the Soviet cause and in that way to attract the attention of the Soviet secret police to his critics. In Soviet times this method of dealing with enemies was called a "denunciation" (*donos*), and it was well known that such a denunciation was usually followed by the arrest of the person being denounced. Lysenko had denounced many Russian geneticists, including the internationally famous Nikolai Vavilov, who was shortly thereafter arrested while he was on a biological field trip, imprisoned in a labor camp, and died in prison of starvation in 1943. After the fall of the Soviet Union both Western and Russian scholars published accounts of the practice of denunciation. It was often used by people who wanted to get rid of a rival, whether in professional activity, love triangles, or political struggles.

I sat silently for a while, wondering how far I should go in showing Lysenko my knowledge of his nefarious and deadly activity. I decided that since I had initiated the encounter, it would be best if I stayed absolutely calm. But, finally, I said, "You know, I know that you are correct in saying that you were never a member of the Communist Party. But you frequently criticized Vavilov and other Russian scientists in ways that were certain to attract the attention of the secret police. For example, at a meeting in 1935 at which Stalin was present you said that just as there were 'wreckers' in Soviet industry (people accused of purposely slowing down industrial production and subsequently imprisoned or executed for this alleged sabotage) so also there were 'wreckers' in Soviet biology, and you named Vavilov as one of these traitors. Yet I know that, far from being a traitor, Vavilov was dedicated to the Soviet cause and did everything that he could to improve Soviet agriculture. But Vavilov recognized the importance of modern genetics in that effort, which you opposed. So you criticized him in the presence of Stalin, and that criticism had fateful consequences. He died in the custody of the secret police."

Lysenko abruptly stood up and left the table. I was not afraid that he would try to use the Soviet system against me, as he had done with his other critics, because I knew that he had lost his power. Six years earlier, in 1965, the Russian scientists who fully understood the error of his views took advantage of the more permissive political situation and rose up against him, initiated an investigation of his claims of agricultural success, and found that he had falsified the records. Rather than helping Soviet agriculture, Lysenko had done great damage to it. He especially hurt agriculture by ruining the genetic lines of pedigreed agricultural animals. Lysenko did not believe in purebred stock, and allowed herds that had been carefully preserved over generations to be ruined in a few years by interbreeding with non-pedigreed animals.

I sat alone at the table eating my soup. After about ten minutes, to my astonishment, Lysenko returned and sat down beside me. "You are a mistaken man in your understanding of me," he assured me. "You think that I am a part of the Soviet oppressive system. But I have always been an outsider. I came from a simple peasant family, and in my professional development I soon encountered the prejudices of the upper classes. Vavilov came from a wealthy family and knew many foreign languages. When I was a boy I worked barefoot in the fields and I never had the advantage of a proper education. Most of the prominent geneticists of the 1920s were like Vavilov. They did not want to make room for a simple peasant like me. I had to fight to be recognized. My knowledge came from working in the fields. Their knowledge came from books, and was often mistaken."

"And, once again," he continued, "I am now an outsider. Why do you think I was sitting alone here at this table when you came up? No one will sit with me. All the other scientists have ostracized me."

And then Lysenko said an amazing thing to me. "I sympathize with the Jewish refuseniks," he said. "They are scientists who have been ostracized by the Soviet establishment because they applied to emigrate to Israel, were turned down by the Soviet authorities, and now they have no jobs and no place to turn. They are alone like me."

Lysenko was, pathetically, making an attempt to win my sympathy. It is true that Jewish refuseniks at this time were ostracized by the Soviet scientific establishment. But Lysenko was still a member of the Academy of Sciences, with a good salary, an office, and many privileges, including access to special grocery and clothing stores. In contrast, the refuseniks had no salaries and often could not support their families. Lysenko had lost his position of influence in Soviet biology—and that was a very good development for Soviet science—but his attempt to compare his position to that of the Jewish refuseniks was grotesque.

Nonetheless, in his self-serving description of himself I recognized a certain truth about Soviet history: the savage consequences of class hatred when it was linked to state power. Lysenko undoubtedly saw himself as a peasant fighting aristocrats. He also, at least originally, probably believed in his simple agricultural nostrums. He thought, for example, that what counted in obtaining more milk from cows was not the genetic constitution of those cows, but the care that humans gave them. (My grandfather on his Indiana farm thought the same thing.) Lysenko took very good care of his cows, fed them copiously, and even made sure that their stalls were clean. He was certain that they would return his favors by giving lots of milk. He could not understand why purebred cows should give more milk just because they had advantaged ancestors, anymore than why Vavilov and the privileged scientists he fought against should be better scientists than he. Later, when Lysenko saw that the Soviet system gave him weapons against his enemies like Vavilov, such as the ability to get rid of them by denouncing them to the secret police and the Soviet authorities, he eagerly picked up these formidable weapons. The simple peasant, nursing grievances against those he viewed and resented as his social betters, became a vicious tyrant who sent dozens of people to their deaths. The leaders of the Soviet Union of his time—Stalin and Khrushchev—knew little about modern genetics and could not see the error of Lysenko's scientific views. They saw only that Lysenko praised them, their rule, and the class enmity they promoted. Both of them had humble backgrounds like Lysenko and rebelled against the privileged Western world. After this conversation with Lysenko, I did not sympathize any more with him than before—indeed my horror at his methods was intensified—but somehow I better understood the nature of and the motives behind his tyranny.

Almost twenty-five years later, after Lysenko's death in 1976 and after the fall of the Soviet Union, I was back in the same dining room of the House of Scientists with George Soros, the wealthy philanthropist who was helping Russian science after the end of Soviet power. Soros sympathized with the geneticists in Russia who had suffered under Lysenko's rule and who had been imprisoned. He suggested a banquet for all the surviving geneticists who had been fired or imprisoned because of Lysenko. Accompanying Soros and me at the banquet was Valery Soyfer, a geneticist who had written a history of Lysenkoism while still living in the Soviet Union and who then emigrated to the United States. Soyfer organized the occasion in the House of Scientists. As we sat there at this poignant reunion of persecuted geneticists, I stared over at the corner of the room where, many years before, I had listened to Lysenko's description of these scientists as aristocratic traitors to the Soviet cause. Soros asked each of the aged geneticists to describe what had happened. They certainly did not look like aristocrats. Many of them wore frayed clothing, and they were bent over from their sufferings in labor camps. They told the story of the destruction of genetics in the Soviet Union in the forties and fifties, and of their personal fates in prison. They said that Russian biology was now recovering from Lysenkoism, but added that it would still be many years before it occupied the position it had in the 1920s, when Vavilov, Aleksandr Serebrovskii, Nikolai Kol'tsov, and Theodosius Dobzhanskii (who escaped to the West), and many other Russian geneticists had been world leaders in the field.

Although Lysenkoism has been discredited in Russia for thirty-five years, occasionally in my travels around the country in more recent years I have encountered a few vestiges of this doctrine. In 1986 I visited a farm in Novosibirsk, Siberia, where wild foxes have been domesticated over a period of many years and many fox generations. These normally fierce animals have been bred in this particular place to be almost as friendly as domestic dogs or cats. The geneticist directing the experiment explained his success entirely in terms of genetic principles agreed upon worldwide: in each fox litter the one innately "most friendly" is selected out for further breeding, and as a result of such selective breeding over generations the foxes remaining in the farm are strikingly affectionate with humans.

However, the woman who was in actual charge of the care of the foxes had a different Lysenkoite explanation. According to her, the reason the foxes were friendly had nothing to do with genes; their amiability came from the fact that she "loved" them, took excellent care of them, and in return the foxes returned her love, and this love became inheritable. It was the same explanation and recommendation that Lysenko gave for how to get cows to give lots of milk; ignore the pedigree, just take good care of the cows.

When I asked the Novosibirsk geneticist if he knew that he had a Lysenkoite on his staff, he smiled and replied, "Yes, I know, but it is not accurate to call her a Lysenkoite. She simply believes in the inheritance of acquired characteristics. The Lysenkoites had the power of the state and the Party behind them, and the results were disastrous. In her case, it is just her personal opinion, mistaken but harmless. Her false belief may actually cause her to take better care of the foxes than I would, since she attributes to that care a greater significance than I do."

Perhaps the most incredible instance of latter-day Lysenkoism in Russia occurred in October 2003, when I was visiting Samara State Aeronautical and Astronautics University, a place where some of the Soviet Union's rocket engineers were educated. In a visit to a laboratory of optics there I met a graduate student (*aspirant*) who had posted on the wall near his desk a photograph of Lysenko. Amazed that I should see this photo in a scientific laboratory almost forty years after Lysenko's fall from power, I asked the student why the photo was there. "Because he is my scientific hero," the student replied.

The author feeds a domesticated fox at a
farm in Novosibirsk, Siberia, 1986.

"Why is he your hero?" I asked.

"Because he stood for what he believed," was the reply.

"But what he believed turned out to be entirely incorrect and is rejected by biologists all over the world," I responded. "Furthermore, he caused the deaths and imprisonment of Russia's finest biologists."

"That is all malicious and false propaganda," the student shot back.

"What is your scientific field?" I asked.

"Optics," was the reply.

"Thank goodness," I said, "that it is not biology. But I would say that your optics suffers from several aberrations. Would you like to read some books written by outstanding Russian scientists portraying Lysenko's errors and misdeeds?"

The student was not interested in my recommended reading, assuring me that he knew all the facts of the case.

This little episode is a rare exception in Russian science today. It had been over fifteen years since I had encountered a defender of Lysenkoism during my many visits to Russian universities and research institutions. Nonetheless, the episode causes worry that the past of Russian science, both its glorious and inglorious moments, is not sufficiently known, not only abroad, but also in Russia itself.

CHAPTER TWELVE

PETER KAPITSA, A MAN
OF MANY PARTS

PETER KAPITSA (1894–1984) was one of the most famous scientists in the Soviet Union (see "Biographical Notes" at the end of this book). Winner of the Nobel Prize in 1976 for his work in physics, Kapitsa was the developer of a process for liquefying helium. His personal biography was gripping. Although he had been born in Russia, all through the 1920s and early 1930s Kapitsa lived not in the Soviet Union but in Cambridge, England, where he became director of the illustrious Mond Laboratory at Cambridge University. The Russian physicist became an integral part of Cambridge scientific life, a student and then close friend of Ernest Rutherford, and a member of the highly prestigious Royal Society. Kapitsa and his wife and two sons had a house in Cambridge, and put down roots in English society. Nobody expected them to return to Russia, especially at a time when Stalin's ruthless policies were becoming more and more apparent. Each year, however, Kapitsa made a visit to Russia to see old friends and family members, and in September 1934 he made his usual trip. While he was there that month the police informed the forty-year-old physicist that on Stalin's orders he was not to be permitted to return to England. Henceforth, he would do all his scientific research in the Soviet Union.

Kapitsa informed his captors that it was impossible for him to do the same sort of high-quality research in Moscow that he did in Cambridge, since both the scientific and living conditions in Cambridge were far superior. His laboratory in Cambridge, for example, contained equipment that was absolutely unobtainable in the Soviet Union. Stalin decided that the only chance that he had of getting the

cooperation of Kapitsa was to give him everything that he wanted ma-
terially—but not his freedom. As a result of Stalin's decision all the
equipment in the Mond Laboratory in Cambridge was purchased by
the Soviet government and brought to Moscow for Kapitsa's personal
use. Even Kapitsa's most skilled instrument-maker was brought to Moscow to help him. An institute was established in a small wooded area
near the Moscow River where the quiet conditions would be condu-
cive for delicate experiments. And since Kapitsa had become very fond
of the private house and garden that he had enjoyed as a Cambridge
don, Stalin gave Kapitsa a Cambridge-style home next to his institute.
This setting was an unprecedented perquisite for a Soviet scientist.
Although Kapitsa was at first depressed and angry about his captivity,
he soon responded scientifically to the favored conditions he was offered in Moscow. Within three years of his detainment, at the peak of
Stalin's horrific purges, Kapitsa did the most important work of his
scientific career, research for which he later received the Nobel Prize.

I had always been fascinated by these details of Kapitsa's life. Most
Americans believe that freedom and democracy are necessary conditions for creative scientific work, but Kapitsa had excelled under coercion. Indeed, the most productive period of Soviet physics coincided
with the most repressive period of Soviet politics. Eight Nobel Prizes
were awarded to Soviet physicists for work done in the 1930s, 1940s,
and early 1950s, a period of tyranny and terror. One of the physicists
who won a Nobel Prize for work done in these years was Lev Landau,
who was held in prison for a year in 1938, but whose most productive
years as a physicist bracketed his imprisonment. The creativity of these
Soviet scientists did not seem to be depressed by the appalling political
conditions under which they worked, and I have always been curious
to know how this could be.

Although Kapitsa, the proverbial bird in the golden cage, conducted
important research in the 1930s and 1940s, and reconciled himself to
Moscow life, relations between him and Stalin never became smooth.
In fact, they rapidly deteriorated after the war when Stalin asked Kapitsa to be a leader in the atomic bomb project, and Kapitsa refused.
Such insubordination to Stalin was unprecedented, and, according to
all expectations, should have led to Kapitsa's immediate execution or
assignment to a labor camp. Stalin's wrath was obvious, but he gave
Kapitsa a curious form of protected punishment. Instead of having him
arrested by the secret police, and turned over to the KGB prosecutors,
Stalin removed the physicist from the directorship of his institute and
for many years kept him under house arrest at his country dacha. Only

after the death of Stalin in 1953 was Kapitsa allowed to return to his former position. Still, the fact that he had survived at all was striking.

I had known these basic facts of Kapitsa's biography for many years but had never had a chance, before 1982, to talk to Kapitsa himself about them. In that year I had an opportunity to do so. A mutual friend of Peter Kapitsa's and mine, Paul Doty, a professor of biochemistry at Harvard, told me that he had recently visited Kapitsa, had told him of my work on the history of Russian science, and had suggested that the two of us talk. Paul said that he would write a letter of introduction to Kapitsa that I could take on my next trip to Moscow. I was grateful to Paul for his help and delighted at the prospect of meeting the physicist about whom I had heard so much.

Upon arrival in Moscow in the spring of 1982 I mailed off the letter to Kapitsa, along with a note from myself saying how much I would like to meet him. Within a day or two, his secretary called and said that Academician Peter Kapitsa and his wife Anna would like to have me to lunch at their house the following week.

An hour or so before the appointed time I took the subway to the Lenin Prospect stop, got off and crossed the broad thoroughfare, walked a short distance along Kosygin Boulevard, and soon I stood before the famous "Institute of Physical Problems" founded and still directed by the eighty-eight year old Kapitsa. Off to the left of the institute proper, back in the woods overlooking the Moscow River and the entire city in the distance, was Academician Kapitsa's house, where I was soon expected for lunch.

As I stood in front of the institute and looked at the grounds I noticed that they were much neater than the ill-kempt trashy areas around most Soviet institutes I had previously visited. There was, I thought, almost a Cambridge-style tidiness to the place. Then I remembered another story about Kapitsa. It seems that once, not long after the founding of his institute, Kapitsa came into the grounds and was dismayed by the litter around the main building. He asked who was responsible for keeping the area clean and was told that there was a crew of three men who kept their tools in a shed behind the institute. Kapitsa went to shed and found the three men lounging at a table, drinking tea, and playing cards. He asked the three men what their salaries were, and learned that each earned about sixty rubles a month. "All right," said Kapitsa, pointing to the two men on right side of the table, "You two are fired. And you," pointing to the man on the left, "will now receive the combined salaries of all three, one hundred eighty rubles a month. So long as the grounds are neat, you may keep that salary. The minute they become messy again, I will hire back the other two and you will all return to your old salaries." From that time on, so the story goes, the grounds were neat. Kapitsa had found a solution to his problem without raising the institute budget one ruble. It was, of course, a wildly illegal solution.

I looked at my watch and saw that I had arrived at the institute a half hour early. I was supposed to be met at the gate but no one was in sight. I could see Kapitsa's house off to the left, and knew the lunch would be there, but did not want to arrive early. I was curious about the institute itself, so I decided to walk into the main building. Such a direct approach to a Soviet institution was unusual; foreigners, indeed, all outsiders, were normally required to wait outside until an official ushered them in. But I had an excuse; I was there on invitation of the director and his wife, and a visiting American scholar could be pardoned for mistaking the main building for the director's home. So I walked right into the main entrance of the institute and walked straight ahead, past the woman in the coat checkroom who paid no attention to me. I saw a sign pointing up the stairs to the director's office, and went up the stairs. The long hallway on the second floor was lined on both sides with original paintings of modern art. I recalled that all during the Stalin period Kapitsa's institute had been known for its support of heretical artists. Even long after Stalin's death the Soviet regime prevented modern art from being displayed, and in the early eighties, as I was walking down this hallway, still frowned upon it. A few scientific institutes like Kapitsa's provided unorthodox artists with refuges where their art could be publicly shown. Such cooperation between physicists and artists in the Soviet Union was one of the many reasons why the members of the "creative intelligentsia" of the Soviet Union, even when they came from quite different fields, felt so many close bonds. I noticed that one of the paintings had the Star of David worked into the background. Displaying this painting at a time when Soviet television and radio were railing against Israel and Zionism was, in itself, a statement of independence.

The door to the director's office was shut, and not even a secretary sat in front. I went down another stairway and found myself alone in a laboratory. No one was visible, and it struck me that the lab seemed more a museum than a place of work. I looked around at the ancient instruments and realized that I was in the original Mond Laboratory of Cambridge, England, transported lock, stock, and barrel from England to the USSR almost fifty years earlier! There on the wall was a clock with its English brand name proudly emblazoned on the face. The dials for the instruments were encased in dark brown Bakelite, indicating their 1930s origins. The electrical switches had heavy wooden handles that required all of one hand and perhaps two to throw. Even the broom in the corner was of obvious English make, not the bound twigs still common in the Soviet Union. Hanging around the room were photographs of the Mond Laboratory in England; one snapshot of the exterior showed the famous "crocodile" on the outside wall, a symbol known to all historians of early-twentieth-century physics; a photograph of the interior showed on the wall of the laboratory in England the very clock that now hung before me in Moscow, situated in the same place relative to the instruments that it had been in Cambridge.

Feeling that I was trespassing where I had not been invited, I quickly retreated and made my way back to the entrance of the institute. I went to the outside gate and stood there for a few minutes until a man appeared who said that he had been asked to escort me to Academician Kapitsa's house. He was Pavel Rubinin, Peter Kapitsa's research assistant and a man whom I knew to be interested in the history of physics.

We walked off through the woods together. Soon we arrived at the door of Academician Kapitsa's residence. Unless one had lived in the Soviet Union and knew that private homes of the Western type just did not exist there, it would have been difficult to understand how strange this place, just off the subway in Moscow, seemed to me. The front hallway with coat closet on the left, the large living room with oriental carpets and pictures of Cambridge in the 1920s, the formal dining room overlooking the river on the right, the heavy English furniture, the book-lined library—all this would have been perfectly normal in England or America, but here it made the deepest impression. I was escorted into the living room where I met Peter Kapitsa and his wife Anna, their son Andrei, and another researcher from Kapitsa's institute. The conversation immediately began, continued over a delicious lunch in the sunlit dining room, and resumed, without break, back in the living room. We shifted back and forth between Russian and English so effortlessly that I cannot remember now what things were said in what language, but I remember clearly the subjects of our conversation.

Peter Kapitsa looked very old indeed. With sunken eyes and poor hearing, he did not participate actively in the conversation. Occasionally his eyes closed, and I wondered if he were asleep. Yet every now and then he uttered a few words, and when he did, they were absolutely on target. The brain was running at its customary level.

I commented on the pictures of Cambridge and asked if they had been back there recently. Mrs. Kapitsa, a forthright intellectual who was the daughter of one of Russia's most famous pre-Revolutionary scientists, replied that for years they were not permitted to travel, but that they had just recently gone back to Cambridge; unfortunately, she said, almost all their old friends were dead or gone. The embryologist and historian of Chinese science Joseph Needham remained, but they had not known him well. But one event on her recent return trip to Cambridge University was important and fresh in her mind. When her husband was forcibly detained in the Soviet Union in 1934 his colleagues at his college in Cambridge had left his academic gown on its peg near high table; the gown hung there for over forty years and when Peter Kapitsa finally returned he was told before going to dinner that he could wear his old gown, which was in its accustomed place.

I mentioned that many scientists in the West admired the courage of Peter Kapitsa for refusing to work on atomic weapons during and after World War II, sympathized greatly with him when he was put under house arrest, and were surprised that he had not been treated even more severely by Stalin's secret police. Peter Kapitsa smiled and said, "Most of my admirers do not understand the situation. I did not refuse to work on atomic weapons because of principled opposition to such weapons. I am not and never have been a pacifist. I refused to work on those weapons because the man who was in charge of the weapons project—the secret police chief Lavrentii Beria (see "Biographical Notes" at the end of this book)—had no respect for scientists. I could not work for such a person." Kapitsa's statement explained why he abstained from working on the Soviet atomic bomb, but it still did not solve the mystery of why he was not more severely punished for doing so. The answer to this second question would not come until many years later.

Although the discussion at the table was rather free, the Soviet Union was still very much in existence at this time, and there were some serious problems in the wings that could affect our conversations. The Soviet war in Afghanistan was on, and relations between the United States and the Soviet Union were strained. At the moment we were sitting in the Kapitsas' dining room together, the even-more famous Soviet physicist Andrei Sakharov (see "Biographical Notes" at the end of this book) was under house arrest in the city of Gorky, forbidden to have contact with anybody but his family and the secret police. I suspected that the Kapitsas' house was also monitored by the police, and had been for decades. The Kapitsas' son Andrei, sitting at the table, was the assistant scientific secretary of the Soviet Academy of Sciences, and was involved in the administration of scientific exchanges with other countries, including the very exchange on which I had come on this trip to Moscow. As an ambitious administrator of the Soviet scientific system, it soon became apparent that he felt a need to defend that system in a way in which his parents did not. I knew that his career had been a bit checkered; earlier he had been at a scientific center in Vladivostok, had gotten involved in some sort of academic battle in which he had been accused of administrative irregularities, and had been transferred back to Moscow.

Andrei began criticizing the position of American scientists and the American government on the issue of scientific exchanges between the U.S. and USSR. He said that after World War II under Stalin there had been a cold war between the United States and the Soviet Union for which the Soviet Union was responsible; now, he said, a new cold war was developing and the United States was responsible. It was the Americans, he said, who were terminating exchange agreements, cutting off trade, refusing credits to the Soviet Union, and gradually bringing Soviet–American relations to the lowest point in many years. The person responsible, he continued, was Reagan, who was using events in Afghanistan and Eastern Europe as pretexts for renewing the Cold War. The American government was pressuring American scientists, he said, not to participate in exchanges with the Soviet Union. As a result, contacts between American and Russian scientists were diminishing.

I regretted that the contacts were, at that time, diminishing. I also said that I had not voted for Reagan and had many disagreements with his policies. However, I said that if we look specifically at scientific exchanges, the main reason for their decline was not pressure from the American government but resistance to exchanges from members of the American scientific community itself, who were angered at the Soviet treatment of dissident scientists, such as Andrei Sakharov, and at the anti-Semitism evident in Soviet scientific circles. I pointed to the example of American mathematicians, who were, in principle, very eager to have contacts with Soviet mathematicians because of the high quality of Soviet work in the field; nonetheless, many of them were refusing to participate in exchanges because they noticed that whenever they invited a group of Soviet mathematicians to the United States the ones who were Jews were not permitted to come. They had also noticed that Jewish scientists were being systematically excluded from publication in major Soviet mathematics journals, and that the editor of one of these journals, Academician Pontryagin, was a notorious anti-Semite. Many American scientists believed that under these conditions, exchanges with the Soviet Union were unequal affairs, and therefore they declined to participate, and sometimes even refused to receive Soviet scientists in their universities. I pointed out that several dozen American Nobel-laureates had recently signed petitions asking for cessation of scientific exchanges with official Soviet scientific organizations until Andrei Sakharov was released from house arrest. I had wondered myself if I should come to the Soviet Union on an official exchange at the moment Sakharov was under police detention. I concluded by saying that the fact that I had come once again on an exchange indicated that I had not yet agreed with those of my American colleagues who called for an end to the exchanges until improvements could be made; nonetheless, I thought that it was important for Russian scientists to understand the arguments about the exchanges that were going on back in America and which were dividing American scientists.

I had calculated that the Kapitsas, with their reputation for frankness, would not be offended by my outspoken views. Furthermore, I had noticed months earlier that Peter Kapitsa had been one of the few members of the Academy of Sciences to refuse to sign petitions condemning Sakharov for his dissident views, even when put under heavy pressure to do so. But, as I looked at Andrei, who slightly reddened as he listened to my critical remarks, I was not certain that my calculation that the Kapitsas would sympathize with my views was correct. Andrei emphasized with some force that it was wrong for Americans to try to tell Soviets what their politics and policies should be. Scientific exchanges, he said, have to be based on noninterference in each other's policies. I said that I understood his point and added that I had no attention of offending; I was merely trying to reproduce the current American debate.

At this point, old Peter Kapitsa roused himself from what I had assumed was a slumber and forcefully entered the discussion. He disagreed with his son Andrei's position, who lapsed into silence on his father's entry into the discussion. Peter Kapitsa said that he entirely agreed with the American scientists who objected to what the Soviet government had done to Andrei Sakharov. Furthermore, he agreed that Academician Pontryagin, with his blatant anti-Semitism, was doing enormous damage to Soviet science. The old academician further said that he could well understand why American mathematicians did not want to have anything to do with people like Pontryagin. "You should hear how we give Pontryagin a roasting at the meetings of the Academy of Sciences," he added. "Those meetings are closed to news reporters. But we scientists are trying to correct this blight on the honor of Soviet science."

I told Peter Kapitsa that I had heard that he had also defended Academician Sakharov at those meetings. With watery eyes that still managed to twinkle, he asked what I had heard. He warned that one should not trust rumors.

I told a story about him that I had recently heard from a friend in Moscow. Several years ago a campaign was launched to expel Sakharov from his membership in the Soviet Academy of Sciences. This membership was Sakharov's last link to established Soviet society, and provided him with salary and medical care. A meeting of the Academy was held with the expulsion of Sakharov on the agenda. Many members spoke in favor of expelling the dissident scientist, but a few bravely spoke in his defense. One of the defenders said that to expel a member from a scientific society for political reasons was "unprecedented" and should not be permitted. At this point, my informant told me, Academician Kapitsa asked for the floor. He said that he agreed with the previous speaker that the expulsion of Academician Sakharov should not be permitted, but he wanted to add that the speaker was incorrect in calling such action "unprecedented." The Prussian Academy of Sciences under Nazi Germany had expelled Albert Einstein for political reasons, and if the Soviet Academy of Sciences wanted to follow the example of fascism, it could expel Andrei Sakharov from membership. After making this statement, Kapitsa sat down. The vote to expel Sakharov failed.

As I related this story to Kapitsa I could tell that he was fascinated that somehow it had gotten out to an American. When I had finished, he merely smiled at me, and neither confirmed nor denied it.

Andrei Kapitsa remarked that one should not believe everything that one hears, and wondered if the Americans would like it if the Soviets canceled exchange agreements because Angela Davis and the Black Panthers had been politically persecuted in the United States. I said that Andrei Sakharov was a scientist, and a foreign member of the National Academy of Sciences in America; members of that academy who protested his treatment felt that they were raising an issue that was highly relevant to the scientific community and to their professional organization. But I admitted that these questions were difficult ones, and I expressed the hope that we could continue contacts, especially conversations like these.

Mrs. Kapitsa smiled and urged American scientists, including me, not to lose patience. "Political progress in the Soviet Union comes very slowly," she said. "Remember," she continued, "under Stalin it would have been impossible to have you here in our house for a conversation like this. Even to have met you outside in the city would have been dangerous. Of course," she added, "I can understand why foreigners sometimes become irritated at the Soviet government. We are often irritated ourselves, but we can say much less. Our newspapers and television report only the bad news about the West, never anything positive. For example," she said, "a few days ago your space shuttle Columbia experienced some difficulties with some of its instruments while in space, and that was promptly reported both in the Soviet newspapers and on television. But yesterday when the shuttle landed after a successful flight, there was not one word about the event in any of our news media. So I want to tell you," she concluded, "your shuttle is safe." And once again she warmly smiled.

The conversation continued like this for several hours. The Kapitsas obviously enjoyed it, even, or maybe even especially, the differences of opinion. It was an interesting and impressive experience. I felt drawn to them.

Even Andrei became warmer in the conversation. A few weeks later he came to a reception for me held at the American Embassy and was very cordial.

Two years later Peter Kapitsa died. After his death his research assistant, Pavel Rubinin, who had worked with Kapitsa for many years, discovered in his mentor's personal archive something he had never before known to exist. It was an amazing correspondence between Kapitsa and the top leaders of the Soviet Union, starting with Stalin. There were forty-five letters to Stalin, seventy-one to Molotov, sixty-three to Malenkov, and twenty-six to Khrushchev. In these letters Kapitsa spoke to the tyrants of Soviet society in the most direct and unsparing fashion, scorning the "swinish" attitudes of the government toward scientists, excoriating the secret police for arresting scientists, and practically challenging the police to arrest him. When the secret police arrested his colleagues Vladimir Fock and Lev Landau, very distinguished physicists, Kapitsa energetically defended them, demanded their release, and—most striking of all—seems to have succeeded. Both men were released. He did the same for the great mathematician Nikolai Luzin when it appeared that he was to be arrested.

There is no known case of another Soviet intellectual who was able to take such an outspoken stand against the government over such a long period—for almost fifty years. Of course, there were other very brave dissidents, Alexander Solzhenitsyn and many others. But Solzhenitsyn had been arrested and thrown into the labor camps for many, many years merely for telling a joke about Stalin in a letter to another person. Kapitsa challenged Stalin to his face.

It would be mistaken to think that the reason Kapitsa was able to escape execution or the labor camps was because, as a scientist, he was too valuable to the regime. Many other scientists equally valuable were arrested. The head of the Soviet space program, the developer of the Soviet hydrogen bomb, the designer of the Soviet Union's most famous war planes, and three Soviet Nobel-prizewinning physicists were all arrested, yet Kapitsa escaped with house arrest in his dacha. No, there was something about Kapitsa that intrigued Stalin and caused him to protect him. He probably recognized that he was a truth-teller who was, ultimately, harmless to the regime because he kept his complaints confidential. He did not organize resistance or appeal to others to join him in his campaigns. Kapitsa did not reveal his correspondence with Stalin to others, and that correspondence did not become publicly known until after Kapitsa's death. The secret police did know of Kapitsa's letters and beliefs, and its head, Lavrentii Beria, intended to arrest Kapitsa and send him to the camps. Stalin sent Beria a message saying "I'll take care of him personally. Don't you touch him." Kapitsa was a man whom Stalin wanted to keep alive, perhaps to play with, but also to savor. Stalin recognized that he was unique.

CHAPTER THIRTEEN

I BREAK INTO THE
AMBASSADOR'S HOUSE

Spaso House is a pre-Revolutionary mansion in downtown Moscow that serves as the residence of the American ambassador. In the spring of 1984 I was invited to stay there by Ambassador Arthur Hartman as a part of a government program called "AMPARTS" (American Participants) under which American specialists in various fields meet with colleagues in other countries. I was asked to come to Moscow to meet with Soviet historians of science and administrators of science policy.

Although I had in earlier years attended a number of receptions and dinners at Spaso House, I had never stayed there. I looked forward both to the official program and to the experience of living a few days in the ambassador's residence. However, this invitation came at an especially difficult moment in the political and scholarly relations of the Soviet Union and the United States. The prominent dissident scientist Andrei Sakharov (see "Biographical Notes" at the end of this book), for whom I had great respect and whom I had met on several occasions, was on a hunger strike aimed at obtaining permission for his wife to go abroad for medical treatment. Furthermore, he was under virtual house arrest in exile in the city of Gorky. Should I boycott the Soviet Union to show my sympathy with Sakharov?

Before deciding I had conversations about this issue with several science administrators in the United States, including Frank Press and Walter Rosenblith, president and foreign secretary, respectively, of the National Academy of Sciences, and with William Carey, executive officer of the American Association for the Advancement of Science.

Together we made the decision that it would be acceptable for me to go to the Soviet Union if I personally delivered letters of protest about Sakharov addressed to A. P. Aleksandrov, president of the Soviet Academy of Sciences. I also added two letters of my own addressed to Peter Kapitsa's sons Andrei and Sergei. From my previous meeting with Kapitsa I knew that he had been willing to speak out in Sakharov's defense; I was pretty sure that the sons sympathized with Sakharov as well. In my letter to the Kapitsa brothers I enclosed copies of the letters of Press and Carey to Aleksandrov, so that they would know that leading members of the scientific community in the U.S. were concerned about Sakharov. I also resolved to meet with my refusenik friend Alek Ioffe and give him mathematics journals sent by his American colleagues who knew that he was not permitted to receive such journals or use libraries.

I was met at the Moscow airport by an official from the American Embassy and taken directly to Spaso House. It was after eleven P.M. when I entered the large and silent residence and found Ambassador Hartman there to meet me in pajamas and bare feet. My room on the second floor was excellent in every respect, and I enjoyed my entire stay at Spaso House. The room turned out to be a trove of archaeological treasures left by past inhabitants. It seems that every guest of the ambassador in past decades had wanted to leave a sign of his or her presence. Stuck in the mirror was a small ID photograph of my old friend and fellow historian Fred Starr, at that moment president of Oberlin College, and in the bedside table drawer was the schedule of Vice President George Bush's agenda at Leonid Brezhnev's funeral. In the bookcase were works by many American authors with their autographs on the title pages, indications that they had once stayed in that room and wanted to leave their marks. I remember that George Kennan, Stephen Cohen, Zbigniew Brzezinski, and Walter Rostow were all represented. Feeling bound to maintain the tradition, I reached into my suitcase, took out one of my books, signed my name on the title page, and put it in the bookcase. I suppose it is still there, gathering dust along with the others.

There was something a little spooky about Spaso House. I knew, of course, that the KGB had infested it with listening devices and agent-servants. The servants were particularly disconcerting. They were almost never visible, but very much present. When I took a shower in the morning in my room, I threw my pajamas on the floor next to the shower on top of my underwear from the night before. When I emerged from the shower a few minutes later, the pajamas and underwear were gone. How had the laundry person gotten in? I had bolted the door to the room. When I returned to the room after breakfast, only an hour later, the clean pajamas and underwear were already on my bed. I stayed in that room for four days and never saw my silent servant, but she, or he, left constant reminders of frequent visits to the room, sometimes when I was in it, either in the bathroom or asleep.

Each day I participated in the official schedule that my Soviet hosts had arranged for me, but I found a moment to break away and take a taxi to the Presidium building of the Academy of Sciences of the USSR, where I intended to deliver my letters about Sakharov. I went directly to President Aleksandrov's office, which I knew from previous visits, and asked his secretary if I could see Aleksandrov, since I had letters to him from the president of the National Academy of Sciences and the executive officer of the American Association for the Advancement of Science, both in Washington, D.C. As I expected, she said, "Unfortunately, he is out of the city," but added that she would be happy to take the letters. I gave the ones from Press and Carey to her, but did not give her the ones to the Kapitsa brothers. I feared that she would simply throw them in the wastebasket when she found out what they were about. But I felt more secure in giving her the letters from Press and Carey, since the latter two were in frequent cable contact with Aleksandrov, and would eventually learn what happened to their letters. (I later found out that the letters were delivered.)

I wanted to deliver personally the letters to the Kapitsas if I could find a way to reach them. I could go to their offices, where I had been in earlier years, but I wanted to meet personally with them rather than go through another secretary. When Greg Guroff, an officer at the embassy, invited me to a lunch at his apartment and suggested that I give him the names of one or two Russian friends who might also be invited, I saw my opportunity. I suggested he invite Sergei and Andrei Kapitsa, and Greg quickly agreed. We both were curious to see if the Kapitsas would come, since in recent weeks Soviet officials had often avoided contacts with American embassy officials. It was a tense moment in Soviet—American relations.

Only Sergei, the more outspoken of the two brothers, came to the luncheon (see "Biographical Notes" at end of this book). Sergei was (and still is) host of the most popular science show on Russian television. In his shows he avoided political commentary, sticking to discussions of the latest scientific developments. I asked Sergei how his

mother, Anna, was doing in the present difficult period after her husband Peter's death, and he replied that she had spent some time in a
sanatorium but was now back home and was "all right."

We discussed many topics, including the present state of U.S.–USSR
relations. Sergei was gloomy but personally friendly, saying that he
feared that a downward spiral in relations had developed that would be
difficult to halt. He talked rather freely on all subjects except Sakharov.
When the Americans present discussed Sakharov, Sergei just dropped
his head, stared at the table, and occasionally sadly nodded. He knew,
and we knew, that the Guroff apartment, along with all other embassy
officers' apartments, was bugged, and he did not utter one word about
Sakharov; nonetheless, his demeanor remained subdued and completely noncombative as the Americans objected to the Soviet treatment of Sakharov. It was clear that Sergei supported the man, but was
not prepared to express his support, at least not in a gathering such as
this.

I decided not to give him the letters from me and from Bill Carey
(both of which were in my pocket) while we were in the apartment, for
it might force him to say something when he obviously did not want to
do so. Furthermore, he had been the only Soviet person invited to the
luncheon who had actually come, and it seemed a little ungracious to
impose on him at that moment. That afternoon I went to Sergei's apartment on Lenin Prospect and, acting as a mailman, deposited the letters in his mailbox in the foyer, with a note from me saying why I had
not given the letters to him at the Guroffs.

On the evening a day or two later when I went to the apartment of
Alek Ioffe, the refusenik mathematician, the conversations went on
long into the night, and I did not get back to Spaso House, by taxi,
until after two in the morning. This late arrival led to the most memorable event during this short stay in Moscow.

Arriving in front of the dark mansion I gave a brief greeting to the
Soviet militiaman in his little guardhouse at the entrance to the driveway and walked up to the front door, which I found locked. Next to the
door was a doorbell button. I pressed it and was reassured when I heard
the bell resound in the front hallway. Considering the lateness of the
hour, I was not too surprised when there was no response to my first
few pushes of the button. Gradually, however, as the minutes passed, I
began to wonder what I would do if I could not raise someone. I was
not eager to sound insistent at the American ambassador's door, so at
first I pressed the button only once every minute or so. After about

fifteen minutes of standing there, however, I threw diplomacy to the winds and leaned on the button. There was no answer, and, after about half an hour, it became clear that nothing I could do with that doorbell was going to raise anybody. Still, I was not too concerned, since a twenty-four-hour-a-day militia post was at the entrance to the ambassador's house, and surely the policeman there could help me. I walked out the driveway to the guard post where the Soviet militiaman stood, showed him my American passport and the key to my room in Spaso House, said I was a guest of the Ambassador, and asked that he call the Ambassador's home on the telephone and tell the person who answered that their guest was waiting at the front door.

To my amazement he replied that he had no way of calling either Spaso House or the American Embassy. I could not believe that the policeman permanently assigned to watch embassy property had no way of contacting it, and I expressed my incredulity to the policeman, who said nothing. I then asked if he could call the police (or even his bosses at the KGB), tell them my situation, and ask them to call Spaso House on the phone. He refused, saying the problem was mine, not his.

Shaking my head in disbelief, I walked back up the driveway to the mansion, with the militiaman watching me. Was there an alternative entrance? Spaso House, built in 1914, is a grand yellow and white merchant's residence. In front, facing the lawn, are a dozen or so white Ionic columns that I could make out in the darkness. On the far side is a gigantic ballroom, and on the side where I stood at the main entrance is a driveway leading through a portico to the back. I walked through the portico, looking at the base of the house for some kind of entrance. Suddenly I remembered a story that Ambassador Lewellyn Thompson told me in 1960. He said that some American children playing in Spaso House (I believe they were his children or grandchildren, but I am not certain) had gone into the basement and found a passageway leading out under the square at the front of the house. It seems that the pre-Revolutionary merchant who built the house, Nikolai Vtorov, had already taken notice of the revolutionary unrest that was filling the main streets of Moscow only a few blocks from his house, and he had provided an escape route for him and his family when the revolution arrived at his front door. His plans did not work out, however; Vtorov was shot and killed by a revolutionary upstairs in the house before he could make it to the escape route. I decided to stay away from this particular entrance into the house.

In the back of the house was a long row of garages or stables. I stared in the dark at these buildings, wondering whether in 1914 they were built to hold autos or carriages. Staring at the narrow entrances I decided they were built for horses, not internal combustion engines.

Turning back to the house, whose rear now faced me, I saw a stairway leading down to a basement entrance. Surely it will be locked, I thought. I went down the stairs, tried the doorknob, and, behold, the door opened! I entered a totally dark space, absolutely black. I walked around the basement a bit, stumbling over what seemed to be boxes of various kinds. Suddenly, the disturbing thought occurred to me that I might be taken for an intruder. The guard outside knew that I had disappeared in the gloom surrounding the house; had he notified the police? Do the U.S. marines guard Spaso House the way they guard the embassy? I did not want to meet either a marine or a Soviet policeman in that impenetrably dark basement. So I started speaking in both English and Russian, in a loud voice, saying "It's me, Loren Graham, a guest at Spaso House, trying to find my way back to my room." I collided into something large with a bang. Then I remembered that I had in my over-the-shoulder bag a small flashlight that my wife had given me at Christmas. I turned it on the object I had struck and saw that it was a large lectern bearing the seal of the Vice President of the United States. "Oh, yes," I thought, "George Bush was just here for Brezhnev's funeral, and, considering the frail health of Brezhnev's successor, Konstantin Chernenko, they want to keep the lectern ready."

With the flashlight now a great help, I found my way to a stairway and went up into what was probably the ambassador's pantry. Making my way out of that, I went through several anterooms and arrived at the main hall, an enormous room with a domed ceiling and a gigantic chandelier. The space was dimly lit, from a small light bulb somewhere, and here and there on the tables could be seen wine glasses, some half-full, left over from the previous night's festivities. Obviously a big party had just been held. After the ambassador and the official guests had gone to bed, the staff had undoubtedly consumed much of the remaining liquor, and now all Spaso House was sleeping off the effects of the celebration and certainly not answering door bells in the middle of the night.

I was now in familiar territory and made my way up to my room by the stairway, skipping the elevator. I arrived at my bed about three in the morning, apparently not having disturbed anyone. I left a card outside my door requesting breakfast in my room, and it arrived the next morning while I was in the shower. The breakfast came in, and the bathroom laundry departed in one invisible smooth operation. Not only had I not seen anyone the night before, I did not see anyone until I left the front door at nine in the morning and gave my greetings to Galya, the nice woman in charge of the staff. I said nothing about my previous evening's adventure in the basement.

CHAPTER FOURTEEN

THE BRAVERY OF BUKHARIN'S WIDOW

NIKOLAI BUKHARIN WAS ONE of the greatest leaders of the Russian Revolution (see "Biographical Notes" at the end of this book). Lenin called him "the favorite of the whole Party." After serving in a series of distinguished government and Party positions in the new Soviet Union, Bukharin was falsely accused by Stalin of betraying the Revolution. In 1938 Bukharin was hauled before one of the most famous show trials of the Great Purges and then shot in the basements of the infamous Lubianka prison.

Perhaps because he had such strong interests in scholarship and science, I have always been fascinated by Bukharin's writings. His works have an authenticity and appeal for me that far surpass that of any other Russian revolutionary leader. He was the most attractive to me of all the leaders of the Revolution.

I knew in 1982 that Bukharin's wife, Anna Mikhailovna Larina, was still alive, and I often in the past had wanted to visit her. Now I had a reason to call on her, for Bukharin's American biographer, Stephen Cohen—a good friend of mine—had asked that I give Anna Mikhailovna a small gift, an attractive calendar with nature photos. Steve could not deliver the gift himself because he had been denied an entry visa to the Soviet Union the last two times he had applied, undoubtedly because of his close friendships with people like Anna Mikhailovna. Steve's biography of Bukharin, which described the young Soviet leader's preference for a much less-repressive Soviet Union, had been read by Mikhail Gorbachev, and it played an important role in converting him to the idea of reform, or *perestroika*. After the fall of the

Soviet Union Gorbachev and Cohen would become friends. But my first visit with Bukharin's wife would come while the Soviet Union was still very much in existence.

I called Anna Mikhailovna from a pay telephone, knowing as I did so that while I was evading the tap on my hotel telephone, I was almost certainly being listened to through the tap on her telephone. When she answered I introduced myself as "a friend of Steve's" and said that I had greetings and a small gift from him. Without hesitation she replied that I must come immediately. She did not give me instructions on how to find her apartment, certain that I had been told by Steve how to get there.

It was fortunate that Steve had given me such full instructions, for the apartment was hidden away in a complex of rather new buildings not far from the "Trade Union" (*Profsoiuznaia*) subway stop. In the dimly lit courtyard in the center of the buildings it was almost impossible to make out the apartment numbers, but I finally found my way. Anna Mikhailovna opened the door and ushered me to a small table that was laden with sliced sausage, bread, and wine.

Anna Mikhailovna was a big surprise. Although I knew she was considerably younger than Bukharin I had supposed that she would by now be very old, probably senile. After all, it was sixty-five years after the Revolution in which her husband had played such an important role. Instead I found myself facing an attractive and energetic woman of sixty-eight years—but not looking much over fifty-five, with dancing eyes and dark hair that was only streaked with gray. The beauty that attracted Bukharin, the youngest of the Bolshevik leaders, was clearly visible. In contrast to most Soviet women, who because of unbalanced diets heavy in carbohydrates and fatty meats, lost their figures by thirty-five or forty, Anna Mikhailovna was diminutive and pretty, despite the fact that she had spent many years in prison.

As I gave her Steve's greetings and calendar, and sampled the wine, I looked around the apartment. At first there did not appear to be a single sign that this woman had once been married to a man at the pinnacle of Soviet power, with an apartment in the Kremlin itself. Her present apartment consisted of basically two rooms, the one in which we sat, and another behind me that was obviously her bedroom. Three people evidently lived here, Anna Mikhailovna, her stepdaughter Nina, and Nina's small child. The furniture was standard and somewhat shabby; the walls and floors were drab. I saw all this and doubted that Anna Mikhailovna had been able to keep anything from her life preceding her many years in the labor camps. Then I saw one or two items that distinguished the apartment from dozens of others that I had visited in Moscow. Over the partition in the main room that hid Nina and her child's sleeping place hung a fine oriental rug, probably one given Anna Mikhailovna by friends after her return from prison. On the walls were a few oil paintings of obvious good quality.

I let Anna Mikhailovna take the lead in determining the topics of conversation, not knowing what to expect. I soon learned that this remarkable woman would talk about anything, without fear. After exchanging news of Steve and a few other American friends, she launched into a discussion of the current situation in the Soviet Union. She said that she had hoped the recent accession to power of Iurii Andropov (see "Biographical Notes" at end of this book) would result in an improvement in the material and political conditions of Soviet society, but that she could already tell that the opposite was happening. The food situation was particularly bad, she said. In the city of Kazan' the situation was so terrible, she maintained, that the system of rationing in force there did not help, since the stores were empty and there was nothing to ration.

Meanwhile, she observed, the authorities were making police sweeps in Moscow and other cities to enforce labor discipline. The government was concerned about the fact that many workers, particularly in ministerial offices, would leave their desks during the working day and spend hours seeking scarce consumer items in the stores, returning to their places of work just in time to clean up their desks before departing at the end of the day. Andropov ordered the KGB to make sweeps of the stores and pick up all citizens who could not prove that they had the right to be there. I knew that Anna Mikhailovna was correct on this point because just a few days earlier I had spied the blue KGB buses outside one of the largest book stores in Moscow, where I was shopping; I quickly retreated out a back door of the store just as the police agents came in the front. I knew that as a foreigner I had the right to be in the store during the working day, but I did not want to have to try to prove my case to an impatient KGB policeman.

Anna Mikhailovna insisted that despite the police sweeps she did not fear going out on the streets during working hours; if the police stopped her she would tell them she was on pension and did not have to work.

Anna Mikhailovna maintained that the top Soviet leadership of the country had long ago become completely corrupt; they were all, she asserted, "a bunch of thugs" (razboiniki). What this country needs, she added, were reforms of the type that her husband favored in the 1920s: decentralization, opening up of controlled private markets, greater free-

dom. (And, indeed, these are changes Gorbachev would later implement, influenced by his knowledge of Bukharin's policies. But instead
of strengthening the Soviet Union, these reforms would destroy it.)

I asked her if her sharp criticism of the Soviet Union meant that she
had changed her mind about the validity of the Russian Revolution.
"Not at all," she assured me. "You must understand that I come from
families totally dedicated to social revolution. Both my father and my
husband were revolutionary leaders, and I supported them completely.
I still believe that the Revolution could have created a humane socialist society if it had not been betrayed by Stalin and his followers."

I reminded her that her husband had been at the time of the Revolution one of its most radical leaders and that even for several years after
1917 had often been associated with the "left communists" favoring
radical and centralized economic policies, not the type of reforms she
now was praising, ones that aimed for decentralization and partial pri-
vatization. She proudly agreed, and added that at the time of the Revolution Bukharin was, compared to the other top leaders, younger, more
radical, and more attractive to Soviet youth. But Bukharin changed,
she continued, when he saw the suffering that came to the Soviet population as a result of dogmatic economic policies. He was a kind man,
she said, who would not continue stubbornly to favor an ideologically
left policy when it became apparent that it was causing great suffering.
He began to alter his views, she continued, in the early twenties, but it
was collectivization at the end of the decade—with its horrible violence and millions of casualties—that convinced him that Stalin's policies were the antithesis of humane socialism.

I asked if Bukharin did not suspect by the mid-thirties that he would
eventually be imprisoned or executed, since by that time so many
other Old Bolsheviks had met similar fates. She insisted that Bukharin
did not suspect this outcome at all. She reminded me that she had
gone with Bukharin to Paris in 1936 where they could easily have remained, safe from Stalin's vengeance. But they returned to the Soviet
Union together and never discussed the possibility that they would be
killed or imprisoned. I observed that some Western scholars have reported conversations with Bukharin in Paris at that time that indicated that Bukharin was intensely worried both about the fate of the Soviet Union and all his associates except Stalin; I hinted that perhaps
Bukharin had protected his young wife from his worst fears. Anna
Mikhailovna's eyes flashed, and she assured me that her husband kept
no secrets from her, and did not know what was about to happen.

Anna Mikhailovna was firm in her opinions, but she took no offense at my most direct questions; in fact, she obviously wanted to talk about these events. I asked the question that has so troubled Western scholars studying the purges: Why at the trial did her husband confess to crimes he did not commit? Was it "to perform one last service for the Party and the Revolution, which can do no wrong," as described by Arthur Koestler in *Darkness at Noon*, the book in which the main character is widely assumed to be Bukharin? She thought both my question and Koestler's thesis were naïve and replied that the true explanation was "simple coercion." I asked if she agreed with Stephen Cohen in his biography of her husband that in editorials before his trial and at the trial itself, Bukharin spoke in Aesopian language, trying to get a message out to his followers. Anna Mikhailovna replied that while she thought that Steve's biography of Bukharin was a splendid work and accurate in almost all respects, she disagreed with him on this point; her husband, she said, was absolutely honest and sincere, never spoke or wrote with "double meanings," and when he made false statements at his trial, they were coerced fabrications for which he was not responsible. I countered that I did not think it would be dishonest to try to speak in Aesopian language at a moment when that was the only way to express one's real feelings; I added that I had read Bukharin's editorials just before his arrest, and I tended to agree with Steve that they contained such double meanings, which were a traditional means of Russian expression in times of censorship. Anna Mikhailovna smiled and said that I imagined too much.

She had evidently noticed that while we were talking I had been looking around the room for signs that she had been the wife of one of the Soviet Union's top two or three leaders; she suddenly stood and said, "Come with me." I followed her into the small bedroom. On the left was her single bed, and over it on the opposite wall was a large photograph of Bukharin—the only photograph of Bukharin I had ever seen in the Soviet Union up to that time, outside of old publications buried in libraries. Above her bed were two oil paintings of scenes in the Crimea, which she said Bukharin had painted as a teenager. Looking further around the room, I saw that it was a shrine to Bukharin. Above the dresser were old newspaper clippings with photographs showing Bukharin on Red Square, talking to other top leaders, meeting with foreigners. Pinned to a scarf hanging over the dresser were many ribbons and medallions obviously dating from state ceremonies now long forgotten, events in which Bukharin was a central player. One photograph showed Bukharin at his desk as editor-in-chief of the main government newspaper *Izvestiia*.

Anna Mikhailovna noted bitterly that if you go to the building of the newspaper today you will find a sign indicating several of the past editors, but no mention of her husband, who was editor longer than any of those mentioned. She turned to me, and, for the first time, asked a question: "Do you think that some day Moscow, which contains so many historical monuments and plaques, will display markers appropriately indicating the role of my husband in the Revolution and Soviet history?" Without hesitating I replied that I was sure that this day would come, that "history will win out." I reminded her that her husband had once said, shortly before his death, that "history will wash all this dirt off my head." I also observed that in Paris today one can find markers for all the main participants in the French Revolution—Robespierre, Danton, Marat, Condorcet, Lafayette, and many others—even though they belonged to very different factions and most of them died violently, often under the guillotine. She looked at me with eyes that wanted to believe, and replied, "You may be right. But I will never see the day." I did not argue.

I soon found that her memory and knowledge about Soviet politics and history of the thirties were either dim or incomplete. Dates, in particular, were jumbled in her mind. I sometimes knew the chronology of her husband's life more accurately than she. But certain impressions were still absolutely vivid. Her husband gave her shortly before his arrest a letter-testament entitled "To a Future Generation of Party Leaders" and asked her to memorize it and reveal it at an appropriate time. She committed it to memory and murmured it to herself for two decades as she lived in the labor camps. Only in 1961, after de-Stalinization was well underway, did she feel safe enough to write it down and deliver it to the Central Committee of the Communist Party. Yet it did not appear in the public press of the Soviet Union for another twenty-seven years, when Gorbachev promoted its publication in 1988.

During the more than a year between the time her husband was arrested (February 1937) and the time he was executed (March 1938) she heard nothing from him. She told me that she was certain that he had tried to write her, but that the prison authorities had prevented the letters from being delivered. On the other hand, she had been told the exact moment of her husband's death, but her friends (she was already in a labor camp herself) had not been permitted to pick up his remains, despite repeated requests. She supposed that the secret police simply "threw them away."

When she was sent to the labor camps, as the wife of an "enemy of the people," she found herself imprisoned together with the wives of many other famous Soviet leaders, army generals, intellectuals, and bureaucrats. They included the wives of the old revolutionaries Aleksandr Shliapnikov and Bela Kun, as well as the wife of the Soviet Union's most brilliant general, Mikhail Tukhachevskii. One of her best friends in the camps was Sarra Lazarevna Yakira, the wife of another famous general.

After Stalin's death she was released from the camps. She appealed to Khrushchev, she said, to rehabilitate her husband and to publish his collected works. Although Khrushchev mentioned in his famous "Secret Speech" of 1956 that a monument should be erected to the wronged Old Bolsheviks, nothing was ever done, and Anna Mikhailovna never received a reply to her letter to Khrushchev. After Khrushchev's fall from power, Anna Mikhailovna wrote another letter to Leonid Brezhnev, again asking for Bukharin's rehabilitation. This time she received a phone call in her apartment from a member of the Central Committee staff, who informed her that her request would not be granted because there was "no basis for reconsideration."

I asked her if she ever felt that she was still considered to be politically dangerous. Was there fear that some dissident faction in the Communist Party might try to use her as a rallying symbol? She replied that she knew the rules of the game and that if she obeyed them she had nothing to fear. For example, she continued, even though she was convinced that the USSR needed reforms of the type her husband favored during NEP (Lenin's New Economic Policy in the twenties), she would never say this publicly, and would not do anything that might sound as if she favored the creation of a political fraction or party based on her husband's policies. Doing that, she said, would guarantee that she would get into trouble.

Only last year, she added, she had a brush with the secret police that proved that they were willing to let her alone, even were a bit in awe of her. She had gone to visit the apartment of Anton Antonov-Ovseyenko, one of the most outspoken of the Soviet Union's dissidents. Antonov-Ovseyenko was the son of another Old Bolshevik, Vladimir Antonov-Ovseyenko, who led the famous assault on the Winter Palace during the Revolution and who was purged along with many of his associates in the thirties. Anton became a bitter anti-Stalinist and wrote one of the most excoriating treatments of Stalin, published in the West as *The Time of Stalin*. As a result of Anton's anti-Stalinist writings he was closely followed by the secret police.

When Anna Mikhailovna arrived at Anton's apartment in the spring of 1982 she found the secret police in his absence conducting a thorough search of all his belongings and research materials. The police immediately recognized her and politely insisted that now that she had discovered them she must remain in the apartment until they had finished with their business, to prevent her from telling other people before they were done. So Anna Mikhailovna sat down with several cups of tea and observed the secret police as they ransacked her friend's apartment. At five P.M., the end of the working day, the secret police said good-bye to Anna Mikhailovna, and left, taking with them a number of items, including the book of my American friend Alexander Rabinowitch entitled *The Bolsheviks Come to Power: The Revolution of 1917 in Petrograd.* Anna Mikhailovna then made her way home and called some friends to tell them what had happened.

Anna Mikhailovna added that she had not changed her behavior in any way because of this event. Only yesterday, she noted, she had visited another famous dissident, Roy Medvedev, who was also under close police surveillance.

As my visit drew near its end, Anna Mikhailovna expressed some interest in my research, and I told her that I specialized in the history of science. It turned out that she did not know that her husband had headed the Institute of the History of Science of the Russian Academy of Sciences, and was not aware of the great impact on Western historians of science that a delegation of Soviet scholars, headed by her husband, had made when they gave papers at a history of science congress in London in 1931. She said that she hoped that we could talk about these things someday. She added that she enjoyed talking to Americans, but believed that I might be the first American she had ever talked to who was evidently not Jewish.

As I rose I gave her a small book with New England scenes. She said she enjoyed such things, grasped my arm warmly with both hands, and led me to the door.

This tragic story continued to develop. In 1987–88 Gorbachev rehabilitated Bukharin, and the country became aware of their mutually compatible views. After the fall of the Soviet Union Anna Mikhailovna's statement to me that her husband must have tried to write her from prison before his execution proved to be correct. In June 1992, fifty-four years after her husband's death, the authorities delivered to her in Moscow, where she still lived, a letter to her written by Bukharin in his prison cell in January 1938. Can anyone imagine the emotions that must have run through this woman's mind and body as she heard from her husband once again, more than a half-century after his execution? I reproduce below a few lines of this remarkable letter:

Dear Sweet Annushka, My Darling!

I write to you on the eve of the trial, and I write to you with a definite purpose, which I emphasize three times over: No matter what you read, no matter what you hear, no matter how horrible these things may be, no matter what might be said to me or what I might say—endure everything courageously and calmly. Prepare the family. Help all of them. I fear for you and the others, but most of all for you. Don't feel malice about anything. Remember that the great cause of the USSR lives on, and this is the most important thing. Personal fates are transitory and wretched by comparison. . . .

It is not appropriate for me to say more about my feelings right now. But you can read between these lines how much and how deeply I love you. Help me by fulfilling my first request during what will be for me a very difficult time. Regardless of what happens and no matter what the outcome of the trial, I will see you afterward and be able to kiss your hands.

Good-by, my darling,
Your Kolka
January 15, 1938

I met Anna Mikhailovna one more time, after the fall of the Soviet Union and after the publication of the above letter. She came to the United States and visited several of the leading Russian Studies centers here, including the Davis Center for Russian and Eurasian Studies at Harvard University, where I was a member of the executive committee. Seven or eight of the senior scholars there, including me, took her to dinner at the Harvard Faculty Club. She had aged considerably in the more than a decade since I had seen her before; her hair was now mostly gray and her face much more lined. Meeting her at Harvard with a group of historians of Russia was an odd moment; several of us had spent good parts of our lives researching the history of the Russian Revolution in which her husband played such an important role, but we had never thought that we would meet the wife of Bukharin, much less in the Harvard Faculty Club.

We discussed with her several of the same questions I had asked before; she was steadfast that the only reason Bukharin confessed was coercion, not any effort to perform a last service for the Revolution to which he had devoted himself. Several of us gently pointed out that in the above letter which she received in 1992 Bukharin did speak of the "great cause" of the USSR to which he was willing to sacrifice himself, an attitude which might have led him to confess to crimes he did not commit in order to continue support of the cause. She dismissed this argument, saying that this letter, important as it was, was not truly private; her husband knew, she said, that it would pass through the hands of the KGB, and if he told why he was forced to confess the letter would never arrive at its destination. We noted that it took quite a few years for it to reach its addressee. "Yes," she said, looking at me, "but I was right when I told you long ago that such a letter existed. I just did not know whether I would live long enough to receive it."

CHAPTER FIFTEEN

FILMING REFUSENIKS AND DISSIDENTS IN MOSCOW

IN THE LATE FALL and early winter of 1986 I spent eight weeks in the Soviet Union with a film crew from the science program *NOVA*, a production of the public television station WGBH in Boston. The title of the program we were making was "How Good Is Soviet Science?" Our crew consisted of five people, the producer and director Martin Smith, the photographer Jean De Segonzac, assistant photographer Maryse Best Alberti, and sound man David Thomas; I was the "correspondent" and "narrator."

In order to obtain permission to make the film we had to agree with the Soviet authorities to take an official guide and interpreter with us everywhere, and we were told that we could not visit any institutions or film any people without official permission from our host, the State Radio and Television Committee. Within those restrictions we were told that we were free to ask any questions we wished.

From the very beginning of our effort several of us, including the producer of *NOVA*, Paula Apsell, had serious worries about these restrictions. I told Paula that I thought that if we presented to American viewers a story that purported to be an objective picture of Soviet science that it would be necessary for us to interview people and record events that the Soviet authorities would never approve, such as Soviet dissident scientists and refuseniks and their difficult lives; there were at this time in Moscow alone thousands of these unfortunate people, a number of whom were my good friends. They had been dismissed from their academic jobs because they had applied to emigrate to Israel, and they were constantly harassed. Many of them were anxious to publicize their plight in order to attract Western help for their efforts to leave the Soviet Union. I did not see how we could ignore their pleas. But even if we managed to get rid of our Soviet guide long enough to film these beleaguered people, we would very likely be expelled from the country; we might even cause the arrest of some of the dissidents and refuseniks, harming the people with whom we sympathized. Paula agreed entirely that we faced this dilemma, but advised us to go ahead and first film the authorized people and places, and then let her know, back in Boston, how the situation was shaping up with regard to filming the more difficult episodes. If the situation was impossible, the film could always be canceled. On that basis we proceeded.

The Soviet Union that we went to film in 1986 was in turmoil. Mikhail Gorbachev had just become the head of the Party and government, and he was engaging in an enormous, and eventually unsuccessful, gamble. Although he was very critical of many traditional Soviet restrictive policies, he still believed in the system. He thought that Soviet communism could be reformed in such a way that the citizens of the country would come to support it. His byword was "*glasnost*" (openness) and, in the first years of his tenure, 1986–88, he put great emphasis on science, technology, and modernization as the way to reform the Soviet Union. He summed up this emphasis on modernization by the word "*uskorenie*," or "acceleration." He knew that the Soviet Union was falling behind the West further and further in modern technology, especially in the computer revolution that was gaining speed every month.

When we arrived in the Soviet Union we found that computers were in the center of a great debate, a discussion in which I was a participant. Two years earlier, on March 11, 1984, I had published a long article in *The Washington Post* entitled "The Soviet Union is Missing Out on the Computer Revolution" which had been picked up in speeches given by Secretary of State Dean Rusk. A rebuttal to my article had been written by an attaché from the Soviet Embassy in Washington, who rejected my basic thesis. My argument had been that the shift from major emphasis on large mainframe computers to personal ones presented the Soviet Union with a challenge that it was having great difficulty handling. The Soviet Union had been comfortable with mainframe computers because they were controlled institutionally and were believed to improve the ability of the Soviet government to plan a centralized economy. That government was still firmly in control of information so long as computers were the property of large institutions. But the advent of personal computers meant that individuals would control information, and they would do with it what they pleased. The government would lose control.

When the NOVA film crew and I arrived in the Soviet Union in the late fall of 1986 we found the Soviet government totally perplexed about what to do with the new personal computers, which were still virtually unavailable to Soviet citizens, but which were spreading rapidly in the West. Should the government ban them or permit them to spread? Banning them would cause the Soviet Union to slip further and further behind the modern world. Permitting them would mean that the careful control over information that they had exercised for decades would be lost.

This dilemma came out in many of our interviews. Perhaps the moment when I saw the Soviet problem most clearly was at the "science city" of Akademgorodok in Novosibirsk in Siberia. The science city there was an enormous operation, a division of the Academy of Sciences, employing approximately 40,000 scientists in sixty different research institutes. When we arrived in the late fall of 1986 computers had become the center of attention of many of these scientists. They were locked in a debate with the Party and police leaders over the degree to which the new computers were to be controlled; the scientists called for a loosening of the restrictions and the Party and police administrators defended the old controls.

We arranged a filmed interview on the topic with Andrei Ershov, one of the leading computer scientists of Novosibirsk State University. Ershov admitted that the advent of personal computers had caught the Soviet leadership by surprise. I asked if he agreed with commentators in the West, like me, who said that the desire of the Communist Party to keep control over information was hindering the development of computers in the Soviet Union. He replied, "I will not dispute your premise," and he added,

> Our leaders have not yet decided whether a computer is most like a printing press, a typewriter, or a telephone, and much will depend on their decision. If they decide that computers are like printing presses they will wish to continue controls, just as they do over all printing presses at the present time. Individuals will not be able to own them, only institutions. If, on the other hand, our leaders decide that computers are like typewriters, individuals will be able to own them and the authorities will not try to control the actual machines, although they may try to control the distribution of the information produced by them. If, lastly, our

leaders decide that computers are like telephones, most individuals will have them, and they will be able to do with computers
what they wish, but their on-line transmissions will occasionally
be monitored.

This statement was a surprisingly frank interview on camera, with an
official of the State Radio and Television Committee—surely a person
reporting to the KGB—sitting with us. Ershov had taken Gorbachev's
call for "openness" at face value, as many other Soviet citizens were
beginning to do.

Ershov then told us that he was almost certain that eventually the
Soviet government would have to permit personal computers to be
owned and controlled by individuals. Furthermore, he said, it would
become obvious that personal computers were not like any previous
communications technologies—not like printing presses, nor typewrit-
ers, nor telephones. Instead, he said, they are a totally new type of
technology. "You know," he added, "the time is coming very soon when
any individual anywhere in the world will be able to communicate
almost instantaneously with any other individual anywhere in the
world. That will be a revolution—not only for the Soviet Union, but
for you too. But its effects will be greatest here."

As I left Ershov's office at Novosibirsk State University I noticed a
newspaper stand, or kiosk, in the large hallway outside. I knew I would
not find any of my favorite Western papers at the newsstand, but I still
wanted to find some news, since I had not yet read any papers at all
that day, nor had I heard any news broadcasts on the radio or TV.

I walked up to the stand, picked out four or five papers, handed my
money to the salesman, and made some innocent comment about the
wintry weather. He replied courteously, matching my weather comments with his own. I noticed that his Russian was accented and asked
where he was born. He replied that he was born in Berlin.

"How did you end up here in Siberia?" I inquired.

"I was a soldier in the German army during World War II," he replied, "and I fought my way with the *Wehrmacht* all the way to Moscow. When the German army retreated I was captured by the Soviet
forces after a particularly difficult battle. The Soviet police sent me to
a labor camp in Siberia not far from here where I lived under terrible
conditions for many years. After de-Stalinization in the late fifties I
heard that it was possible for German prisoners of war to return to
Germany, and I therefore applied for repatriation, but my requests
were always turned down. Finally, in 1960, I was released from the

labor camp, but the authorities still prohibited me to return to Germany. I was restricted to my place of residence near my former camp, and I still am."

Here it was 1986, forty-one years after the end of World War II, and this former German soldier was still not able to return home! I protested, "But surely it would be possible now. Have you tried recently?"

"I have given up trying," he replied. "I married a Russian woman, learned the Russian language, and have 'Russified'."

"Do you have a good life?" I asked

"Of course not," he answered. "Can you imagine what I make selling newspapers at a small newsstand in a university? But it is too late to do anything. I am sixty-five, I have had three heart attacks."

"But would you not like to at least visit your homeland again? After all, East Germany, including much of Berlin, is an ally of the Soviet Union, a part of the Soviet bloc. Surely the authorities would let you visit. Would you like me to inquire for you?"

"Please do not make a noise about me," he urged. "It will just cause trouble. It is too late to help me."

"Does anyone in Germany know that you are here?" I asked. "Do you have family back there? Do they know you are still alive?"

"I have had no contact with any of my relatives since I was captured over forty years ago. I think they are all dead. The only possibility for a living relative would be my brother Herman Engelbert, who moved to Chicago before World War II. I have no idea if he is still alive."

"When I return to the United States I could check to see if a Herman Engelbert is listed in the Chicago phone directory and call if you wish."

"That would be good. If you reach him, just tell him I am still alive. Do not burden him with the details, which you really do not know anyway."

"If you give me your address and phone number, I will pass them on to him if I reach him."

"Thank you, but I do not have a telephone, and contact now would just lead to grief. Just tell him I am alive in Siberia."

When I returned to the United States I went to the MIT library to the section where city phone books were stored. Pulling the Chicago directory off the shelf I searched for "Engelbert, Herman" and felt a surge of emotion when I found it. I hurried to my office and dialed long distance to Chicago. A woman answered, speaking perfect English. I told her what had happened to me just a few weeks earlier in Siberia. Was she related to Herman Engelbert?

"He was my husband," she replied. "He died six months ago. I know that he had a brother whom I never met who was lost in World War II, but that is all I know. Everyone assumed that the brother was killed in the war, and now there are no living relatives."

Reflecting back on the discussions with Ershov, the computer scientist, and Englebert, the ex-German POW selling newspapers outside Ershov's office, I realized that I was seeing two different historical epochs co-existing within fifty feet of each other. Ershov had predicted that any person very soon anywhere in the world would be able to communicate instantaneously with any other person anywhere in the world. For over forty years Englebert had been totally cut off from his family, and they from him. The family members did not even know who among them was still alive. But now Englebert could easily have contacted his brother in Chicago, perhaps with the help of a computer scientist from the university.

Imagining this event, I was convinced that the Soviet system of centralized control over information, which gave the government absolute authority over the lives of such people as Englebert, was doomed. The only question was whether Gorbachev could relax the controls without the entire political system coming crashing down. He was betting that he could do so. He would lose that bet.

But the resolution of this issue would require a few more years. In fact, our interview with Ershov was reported back to the authorities in Moscow, and we found that our opportunities for other such interviews were gradually curtailed. When we went back to Moscow and tried to visit computer factories and other centers of automation we were often turned down. We were expelled from one factory, and, at another, our Soviet guide placed her gloved hand over the camera lens so that we could not continue an interview. (We would later show her gloved hand coming down on the lens on the NOVA program that would be broadcast in the United States.)

We also found that our activities each day came under closer and closer scrutiny. We were losing journalistic freedom, and we feared that our program would have to be cancelled.

Martin Smith, the director of our camera team, and I had a long conversation about our problem near the COSMOS Hotel in Moscow, walking outside where our discussion could not be monitored. He asked me if I thought the refusenik scientists would like to be filmed, and, if so, whether I could arrange meetings with them. I replied that I knew many of the refuseniks well, and that I could meet with several of them that evening to ask if they wished to be filmed. I was almost sure that they would agree, since they were eager to attract world attention to their plight. "But," I asked Martin, "even if the refuseniks agree, how will we get our entire camera crew, with all the equipment, out of the hotel and into a refusenik apartment without attracting the attention, and the disapproval, of our Soviet guide? If she notifies the police, we will be stopped."

Martin replied that if he could get the permission of both the refuseniks and the NOVA administrators back in Boston, and if I could arrange transportation with private automobiles, he would do the filming surreptitiously in the evenings, when we were allegedly resting or sleeping. I agreed to try.

That night I visited the Ioffes and the Brailovskys, two prominent refusenik families. Alek Ioffe was a mathematician and Viktor Brailovsky was a computer scientist. Alek had started a hunger strike (which eventually ended successfully), and Viktor had recently returned to Moscow after being arrested and banned from the city for five years. Both were enthusiastic for the plan to include the refuseniks in the NOVA program. In fact, they suggested that we film one of the "Sunday Seminars" in the apartment of a refusenik. These seminars were meetings where scientific papers were read and where the refuseniks gave each other moral support. Since the refuseniks were not allowed to attend seminars in the academic institutions from which they had been fired, the only way they could stay alive scientifically was to arrange their own seminars, held in private apartments on Sunday afternoons. Whenever possible they tried to invite visiting foreign scientists to these events.

We called Paula Apsell at WGBH back in Boston and told her that we were having increasing difficulties, but that we had already obtained much interesting footage. Because we were certain our conversation with her was monitored by the Soviet police, we could not tell her the nature of our difficulties in detail nor of our hopes to film the refuseniks, but Paula understood why we were calling. She said that she would like to come to Moscow to "help out" in the final phase of our filming. We were delighted.

When Paula arrived in Moscow we learned that in the top administration of WGBH in Boston there was controversy over whether we should film the refuseniks and the Sunday Seminar. WGBH was in negotiation with Soviet television authorities about several other possible programs, including a nature film about the polar bears of Wrangel Island, in the far north of the Soviet Arctic; some of the WGBH administrators feared that if the NOVA crew in Moscow defied the Soviet officials who wanted to prohibit us from filming the dissidents all other cooperative activities would be canceled. But Paula's position was firm: she wanted us to go ahead with the filming. After we got back to the United States, she said, the question of what to show could be fought out in the WGBH studios.

With the support of NOVA's top executive, we were more than ready to go ahead. However, we faced major problems. We could film in the evening in dissidents' apartments by simply agreeing to meet there at certain times, coming from different directions. But filming the Sunday Seminar was an entirely different matter. It was held during the day, Sunday afternoon, and all the seminars were under heavy police surveillance. How would we get the camera equipment into the apartment past the burly KGB agents who usually stood at the entrance to the apartment building? For that matter, how could we even get the camera crew out of our hotel without being detected?

We decided to proceed step-by-step, doing the easiest filming first, hoping we would not be detected. For several evenings, therefore, we eluded our Soviet supervisors, telling them we were tired and wanted to go to bed early after a full day's filming of innocent activities scheduled by them. Then, at about nine o'clock in the evening, we would meet in a refusenik apartment, coming from different directions by subway, bus, or taxi. As the one member of the crew who spoke Russian, I was always assigned the most roundabout method of reaching the destination, usually by subway or bus. But before leaving the hotel, I would catch two taxis, give the drivers directions on where they were to go, and then tell the drivers to wait for the other members of the NOVA crew at certain spots distant from the hotel. The hardest part was concealing the bulky camera and sound equipment, but we learned to disassemble the sound equipment into smaller parts, and put the camera in a suitcase. Although we were not invisible, so many people in Moscow were always carrying heavy suitcases and packages on the subways and in the taxis that we did not attract an unusual amount of attention. To the best of our knowledge, we proceeded undetected, and we made valuable films in the homes of several prominent dissidents and refuseniks, including Alexander Ioffe and Victor Brailovsky. Both had been deprived of their jobs for many years, and Brailovsky had been arrested and imprisoned several years earlier. Now both, with their wives Rosa and Irina, were in their apartments, but forbidden to travel. Their plights would eventually attract the attention of tens of thousands of people in the United States and Europe when the films that we made in their apartments were shown.

But the next episode, the filming of the gathering of refuseniks at a Sunday Seminar, was much riskier; in fact, we knew we would be caught, but hopefully after we had the crucial film. We decided that the director, Martin Smith, and the cameraman, Jean de Segonzac, would go with the equipment to the apartment of Iurii Cherniak, where the seminar was to be held, hours early, hopefully before the KGB would have posted their guards. The rest of us, including me, would come later. I would come alone, by subway.

The camera and the sound equipment were bulky, and we needed a car for transportation. We could not use the van assigned to us by the Soviet authorities, since that would be a certain tip-off. To our surprise, one of the refuseniks turned out to be a stock car race driver in his spare time, and he offered to bring his racecar near the hotel in order to pick up Martin Smith, Jean de Segonzac, and the equipment.

I went to an upper floor of the COSMOS Hotel to a position where I could watch the refusenik racecar come to an earlier agreed-upon pick-up spot in what we thought was a secluded location behind the hotel. I saw the red stock car of the refusenik waiting for Martin and Jean. To my horror, I also saw just around the corner a black Volga sedan with four men sitting in it, and I knew that already our plan had been discovered. The KGB was waiting for the pickup. But there was no way, from my position on the eleventh floor, that I could warn my friends.

I saw Martin and Jean approach the racecar, each carrying suitcases in which I knew were the camera and sound equipment. Jean was an experienced cameraman from France, known throughout the video industry for his amazingly steady arm, for his ability to film from a standing position without wavering.

I watched as Martin and Jean got in the red stock car. I desperately wanted to inform them they were already being followed, that our whole scheme to avoid detection had already failed. As they pulled away from the curb and turned the corner I saw the black KGB car pull away from its curb, turn the corner and fall in behind the red car. The refusenik racecar driver immediately saw that he was being followed by the KGB car; he floored the accelerator and at the same moment sharply cramped the steering wheel of his car in a u-turn. The red car roared and squealed so loudly that I could hear it eleven floors above, careened on two wheels, left a long black streak on the pavement from its one rear tire still in contact with terra firma, and shot by the KGB car going in the opposite direction, gaining speed at an incredible pace. The KGB car also wheeled around, more slowly, with four wheels on the pavement, and sped after the refusenik car.

"My God in Heaven!" I thought. "My NOVA crewmates are trying to outrace a KGB car pursuing them in downtown Moscow!" No way, I knew, could this mad escapade possibly turn out well. Surely the KGB car would have radio contact with all the police in Moscow, and dozens of squad cars would soon corner the refusenik and my hapless friends from NOVA. This adventure had all the ingredients of a full international scandal.

Martin Smith later told me about the harrowing race in the red car across Moscow. The race driver literally outraced the KGB and several squad cars, taking his car down little side streets and alleyways that he had carefully plotted in advance, wheeling in inner courtyards, and snaking his way to the Cherniaks' apartment. Martin said it was the most frightening auto trip of his entire life, far more hazardous than when his Latin American driver had tried to elude drug gangsters in Colombia where he made a film on the drug trade. Improbably, incredibly, Martin and Jean made it into the Cherniaks' apartment with the essential equipment before the KGB had time to get there and set up guards at the apartment door. They got in with the equipment and then watched as the KGB cars, about a half dozen of them, pulled up outside the apartment building.

The only reason all this worked, of course, was that we were now in Gorbachev's Soviet Union, a time when the iron grip of the secret police was loosening. The KGB agents were not willing actually to enter the apartment, much less shoot at a fleeing car. When I arrived at the front door to the apartment house several hours later I saw the KGB cars in front and fully expected to be stopped at the entrance to the building. As I came up to the front door I was asked by the KGB agents to open my small brief case, which I promptly did. It contained nothing but a Moscow Russian-language newspaper. To my pleasure and astonishment, the KGB agents let me pass, and I went up to the Cherniaks' apartment where I joined my friends.

Thus, with the KGB clearly visible out the window, we filmed a Sunday Seminar. I still have a copy of the film.

This particular seminar was a meeting of refusenik physicists and mathematicians, including Brailovsky, Ioffe, and about fifteen others. Since these refusenik scientists were prevented from attending any other scientific meetings in the Soviet Union, this Sunday Seminar was the only way they could stay in touch with the scientific world. Foreign scientists were invited to attend and present papers, and also to bring copies of scientific journals, such as *Science*, *Nature*, and *Physical Letters*. The foreign guest the day we filmed the seminar was Thomas Fried from Sweden, who presented a scientific paper. By this time scientists all over the world had united to help the refuseniks in Russia, and at least once a month another from Western Europe or North America would arrive with more periodicals, more reprints, and more moral support.

As we sat in the seminar I occasionally glanced out through the window to the KGB cars below. Why did the KGB let these people into the apartment building? Would they let us leave with our films? It was clear that the police state was unraveling and that no longer was the KGB sure of its powers. Under Gorbachev the Soviet Union had become a permissive police state.

Still, we were afraid that when we left, the police would take the film out of our camera, so we made a copy of it while we were still in the apartment, hid it behind some books in the bookcase, and left. To our pleasant surprise, the police did not stop us as we departed.

As I reflected on these events I realized that we were now in a very different atmosphere than I had experienced before in the Soviet Union. In the old days, not only would we have been prevented from coming to this apartment; we would also have been censured for trying, perhaps arrested, and never again would any of us be given entry visas to the Soviet state. Denial of entry visas would of course affect me more than any other member of the NOVA crew, since only I regularly came to Moscow. But we were not stopped, we left with our film intact, and the next time I applied to come back to the Soviet Union I was given permission. The Soviet Union was changing, and very fast.

When we returned to Boston with our film we were worried that the WGBH senior administration would not allow us to show the footage with the refuseniks and dissidents, despite Paula Apsell's very influential support. However, by the time the editing of the film was finished (a task that required months) the continued political evolution of the Soviet Union had gone so far that the earlier anxieties no longer seemed realistic. Almost all the sensitive footage about dissidents and refuseniks was included in the final version, shown on television a number of times in the late eighties in the United States and Great Britain.

PART IV

INTELLIGENCE, THE COLD WAR,
AND SECURITY CONCERNS

CHAPTER SIXTEEN

THE SCHOLAR WHO DISAPPEARED

When I was selected to go to the USSR the first time I had many questions, as did the dozen or so other Americans selected in the same year. Russia was to us then, long ago, terra incognita. What supplies should we take with us? What restrictions would be placed upon us by the Soviet authorities? How free would we be to meet and talk with Soviet citizens? What precautions did we need to take to avoid becoming entangled or entrapped by the Soviet secret police?

On one evening in the spring of 1960, six months before my first departure for Moscow, Pat and I were invited to the apartment on West End Avenue in New York City of Peter Juviler, a young political scientist, later a long-term faculty member of Barnard College, who had himself recently returned from the Soviet Union. Peter, who was becoming a close friend, told us that he would invite to his apartment that evening several of his American student colleagues who had returned from the Soviet Union after the first year of the exchange program; these people were veterans of student life at Moscow and Leningrad universities, and they could answer our questions.

Among the several recent returnees from the USSR who talked to us that evening, the one who made the deepest impression on me was Thomas Riha, an advanced graduate student in Russian history at Harvard University (he would receive his Ph.D. from Harvard in 1962). Tom was a charming, even somewhat dashing, scholar who had been born in a privileged family in Prague in 1929 and had come to the U.S. in 1947, where he studied at Berkeley, Columbia, and Harvard. Tom was now an American citizen, but he was still proud of his Czech

heritage, and, while speaking fluent English, he preserved and culti-
vated a delightful light Slavic accent which, he was fully aware, made
him seem somewhat exotic.

As a veteran of the Russian exchange program, a speaker of several
European languages in addition to Russian, and a person who spent
his childhood in a French school in Prague, Tom was the sophisticate
who took pleasure in initiating us young American provincials into the
mysteries not only of Moscow life, but also of European life in general.
He was sharply critical of the diplomats from the State Department
who would warn us at "briefings" that no American would ever really
penetrate Soviet society. Most of those diplomats, Tom observed, had
never lived in the Soviet Union, and those few who had were on the
staff of the American Embassy there, where they had lives that were
entirely cloistered from the society around them. Of course Soviet citizens were leery of diplomats, Tom acknowledged, but he reminded us
that we would be students in Russia, alongside other students from all
over the world, including Communists from France, Italy, East Germany and elsewhere, and he assured us that we would be accepted by
our Russian colleagues as fellow students.

Tom told us that the picture that we had of the totalitarian Soviet
Union was only partly true; yes, communist rule was awful — look how
it had absolutely ruined his beloved native Czechoslovakia — but the
way people in Russia lived on the personal level was not that different
from Europeans elsewhere. They sought diversions in food, drink, and
love like everyone else. We would inevitably become a part of those
diversions. The students at the Soviet universities, he assured us, would
draw us into their disorderly lives, sharing their pleasures and their
pains. In fact, one of the main difficulties we would face, he told us,
was not the isolation from Russian life that the communist rules would
force upon us, but the absolute immersion in it that would soon over-
whelm us. So many Russian students would unload their troubles
on us, he said, that we would find ourselves in the most intense atmosphere we have ever encountered. We would be forced to shoulder
the psychological, political, and personal burdens of many fellow students, who would expect us to give them advice on how to handle
situations out of which there frequently were no good paths. So forget,
Tom advised, the fear that you will not be accepted by your Russian
colleagues; worry instead, he said, about how you will handle all the
personal crises and requests for assistance that you will soon meet.

Be prepared, Tom continued, for the fact that you will find little time to study in your dormitory rooms. Russians will be attracted to you as insects to a delectable sweet. If you wish to do research (and we were all obviously supposed to, since that was the ostensible purpose of the exchange program), he added, go to the library or the archives, and stay there all day. They are the only refuges.

Yes, Tom assured us, we should take certain precautions: We should not tell one Soviet citizen about indiscretions, personal or political, committed by another. The most important rule for Soviet social life, he said, was to keep confidences. You will be in social situations, he predicted, where you will know quite a bit about each person present, based on individual conversations we earlier had with them, but we should never short-circuit those friendships by telling one Russian friend a detail about the life of another, even a seemingly innocent detail. Let your Russian friends make all such decisions.

I later found that much that Tom told us was valid, and after returning from my first year in the USSR, I met again with him a number of times and we exchanged remarkably similar stories about relations with Russian students. Tom went on to what seemed to be a promising academic career, teaching Russian civilization at the University of Chicago after 1960. No one would have guessed at that point that Tom would become the most perplexing riddle in the entire Slavic profession.

In 1964, the same year that I began teaching at Indiana University, Tom brought out a three-volume collection on Russian history entitled *Readings in Russian Civilization*. The collection contained basic documents necessary for the understanding of Russian history, from the Middle Ages to the post-Stalin period, a number of them translated into English for the first time. These were very academic materials, such as the correspondence between Andrei Kurbskii and Ivan the Terrible in the sixteenth century. Tom's volumes were a godsend for a beginning teacher of Russian history like me, and I used them in my courses. Tom also went on to publish a number of important articles and a biography of the Russian historian and politician Pavel Miliukov, a man who at the time of the Russian Revolution headed the movement in Russian politics known as liberalism, a strand of political thought that was unsuccessful in Russia then and still is today. With all these publications produced in just a few years, Tom Riha was obviously moving toward a position of leadership in the field.

In the early spring of 1967 I met Tom again at a professional meeting at Georgetown University, and we announced to each other that we had moved to new universities; he was joining the faculty of the University of Colorado and I had shifted to Columbia University. It was the last time I would ever see Tom Riha.

Tom had always been a single man when I knew him earlier, but after arriving in Boulder, Colorado, in the fall of 1967, at the age of thirty-nine, he married a twenty-four-year-old Czech woman named Hana Hrushkovna. Very oddly, another woman interested in Tom, a mysterious older woman named Galya Tannenbaum, followed him to Colorado from Chicago, where he had previously known her. Tom referred to this woman as "the Colonel," and Mrs. Tannenbaum bragged to a number of people that she worked for "military intelligence," just of what country was not clear. The relationship between Galya Tannenbaum and Hana Hrushkovna was obviously troubled, and only four months after his marriage Tom Riha filed for divorce from Hana, although the two continued to live together. On the night of March 9, 1967, the Boulder police were called by a neighbor to Tom's house, where his wife Hana announced that Mrs. Tannenbaum was also in the house, had frightened her and might even have attempted to murder her. Hana never returned to Tom's house, stayed with neighbors for a while, and then left for New York City.

A week later, on the evening of Saturday, March 14, Tom attended a party in a friend's home in Boulder and returned home about 12:20 A.M. He was never seen again, at least not in the United States by anybody who later talked about it. He was scheduled to attend a faculty meeting on Monday, but did not appear; he was scheduled to teach classes on Tuesday, but again the students waited for him without success.

Alarmed by Tom's disappearance a number of us fellow members of the Slavic profession collected money for a reward fund, in the hopes of gaining information about him; no one ever claimed the reward, and the money was eventually used for purchasing books on Russian history in Riha's name for the library of the University of California at Berkeley, where he had once studied.

The police in Boulder and the administration of the University of Colorado seemed amazingly uninterested in investigating the disappearance of a local professor and citizen. The president of the university, Dr. Joseph Smiley, announced that he had been told by "reliable sources" in Washington that Riha was "alive and well," but he would not reveal what those sources were, repeating only that "a confidence is a confidence." The Boulder police also said that "an agency" had told them "not to worry."

However, as the weeks passed, it became ever more clear that no one knew much about Tom Riha and why he had disappeared. The CIA and the FBI began quarreling about the facts of the case and eventually reached a level of animosity so great that J. Edgar Hoover ordered the FBI to cut off all contacts with the CIA, a disruption that lasted from 1967 until 1970, when President Richard Nixon ordered them to start working together again so he could have better information on the anti-Vietnam War movement and domestic dissent.

Galya Tannenbaum was not charged in the Riha case, but she was arrested on charges of killing and swindling several other men. Before she could testify in the investigation of the Riha case that eventually developed she swallowed sodium cyanide pills and died. Just before her death she said to the doctor trying to save her life, "Of everything I've done, I didn't kill Riha."

The Slavic profession was racked by rumors about what happened to Tom, rumors pointing in completely different directions. Some people said that the KGB had murdered him when he refused to cooperate with them; according to some versions of this story, his body had been thrown down a mineshaft in Colorado. Others said that his disappearance was a simple jealousy killing by Galya Tannenbaum, who also intended to rob him, and that Mrs. Tannenbaum had dissolved his body in a vat of acid found in the home of another of her male friends and later victims (the existence of such a vat of acid was actually reported by the Boulder police, but to the best of my knowledge no chemical tests of it were made to see if a body, or bodies, had been dissolved in it). Yet another frequently told story was that Tom had been working for the KGB, or perhaps was a double agent, and had either been killed in a dispute between American and Soviet intelligence agents, or had escaped to Eastern Europe. One prominent professor in the Slavic field reported that a friend of his had seen Riha months later in a hotel in Bratislava, Slovakia. The professor who reported this story was an ex-CIA officer who ruled the U.S.–Soviet exchanges with an iron hand in the early sixties. But this story also, upon close examination, turned out to be one of those "a friend of mine had a friend who said he had seen Riha in Bratislava," and the links could never be identified or strengthened.

To this day no one knows what happened to Tom Riha. Everybody who still cares now assumes he is dead, but no body has ever been found. In December 1971, almost five years after his disappearance, a mutual friend of Tom's and mine—Donald Fanger, a specialist on Russian literature at Harvard—wrote an obituary of Tom for the leading journal in the Slavic field. Don was not certain that Tom was dead but realized that if an obituary was not written at that time, none ever would be.

Even yet when old hands in the profession get together the subject of Tom Riha sometimes comes up. Today the story is just a curious event of almost forty years ago, but in the 1960s one of its chilling effects on people like me who participated in the exchanges with the Soviet Union in those years (I was visiting regularly, often several times a year) was the knowledge that the academic profession of Russian Studies carried with it genuine dangers, especially for those of us who traveled back and forth across the Iron Curtain. As we worked in archives in Moscow and Leningrad, collected notes, and wrote our academic articles and books we often thought of Tom Riha, and sometimes we wondered if his fate might influence our own. I would have particular reason in the future to fear that some of the forces that may have converged on Tom were moving in on me.

CHAPTER SEVENTEEN

BEING FOLLOWED

DURING THE TIMES that I lived and worked in the Soviet Union I was rather frequently followed, often quite obviously. Surveillance was a fact of life for all foreigners in the Soviet Union and for many Soviet citizens as well. Sometimes when I was in the apartment of a dissident in Moscow at certain moments my Russian friends would cover the telephone with a pillow, since the telephone was universally considered to be, and often actually was, used by the KGB to pick up conversations even when it was on the hook and not in use.

Unsettling as being followed and monitored might be, upon reflection there was not much reason to concentrate on the KGB's activities, so long as what one was doing was not espionage. Worrying excessively about the KGB could easily lead to paranoia. During her first year in the Soviet Union, one American student became so concerned about surveillance that eventually her obsession led her to the conviction that a large blue bus with the letter "B" on the front of it (the line that went around Moscow on the circle street Sadovoe Kol'tso, one of the city's main arteries) followed her everywhere she went.

The first occasion when it became glaringly obvious that I was being followed was on a day in the spring of 1961 when Pat and I decided to take a day's excursion to the monastery town of Zagorsk (now called Sergeev Posad), about seventy kilometers from Moscow. Zagorsk was the Soviet-era term for Trinity–St. Sergius Monastery, the holiest Russian seminary and abbey of the tsarist empire, founded in the fourteenth century. In Soviet times it was a standard tourist site, as it is now, and excursion buses regularly ran there from the city. Foreigners in Moscow were encouraged to go to the tourist agency "Intourist" and sign up for one of the buses that left from the downtown hotels for Zagorsk, complete with young women guides speaking the appropriate language. Pat and I, however, wanted to go on our own, without benefit or detriment of tour guides or accompanying crowd. We both spoke Russian, and we enjoyed the independence. We decided that we would travel the way any normal Soviet citizen would, simply by going to the train station, buying tickets, and getting on a train.

Of course, it was impossible at that time, or, rather, impermissible, for foreigners to travel around the Soviet Union at will. All foreigners living in Moscow were restricted to a radius of forty-five kilometers around the city, and some areas even within that radius were closed. In order for foreigners to travel further they were supposed to get special permission, going through the institution with which they were affiliated. This information was of course promptly reported to the KGB, which then would, in its own wisdom, decide whether the foreigner warranted a tail. Not every foreigner complied with this regulation requiring travel permission, but if one violated the rule and was caught, one could be expelled from the country forthwith. Among foreign students studying in Moscow, including the Americans, a number of brave and foolhardy ones regularly ignored the rules. I know one American student who traveled without permission thousands of miles, all the way to Siberia and back, enjoying a jaunt with some Russian friends whom he trusted. His Russian friends were breaking the rules, too, as all Soviet citizens who were away for more than forty-eight hours from the addresses listed in their internal passports were at that time supposed to register with the police. But many Soviet citizens broke this regulation, illustrating once again that Soviet rule was far from totalitarian in practice; in fact, in popular jargon in Russian there was a special phrase to describe this form of illegal travel, *dikim obrazom* or "the wild way." Quite a few of my friends hit the railroads in the wild way and were never caught.

Another American student friend of mine took a boat from Leningrad beyond the limits, was apprehended on the boat, was expelled, and was *persona non grata* in the Soviet Union for many years. Yet another American student acquaintance, living temporarily in Kiev where he was subject to the same restrictions, went a few miles beyond the permitted radius in order to visit the graves of his Ukrainian Jewish grandparents. He was immediately caught, severely chastised, but not expelled. He later speculated that the reason that he was not kicked out of the country for this violation was that the Soviet government would not have cared for the publicity in the foreign press that would have arisen over punishing a young man merely for wanting to see the graves of his grandparents.

For the planned trip to Zagorsk with Pat, I applied for, and obtained, permission to go on the scheduled day. I knew that the KGB would know about our planned trip, but I still doubted that we would be followed, since we were going to one of the most often-visited sites in Russia, and we were unimportant students. To follow us would have been the equivalent of the FBI following a Russian student going to Mount Vernon (actually, in my later more cynical period I would suspect both agencies of such foolishness).

We took the subway to Iaroslavskii Station, getting off at the Komsomol stop, the most ornate of the Stalinesque subway stations in Moscow. The interior of this station, a great hall, is filled with shining chandeliers, mosaics, and grandiose statues of ever-smiling peasant men and women and ever-determined Red Army soldiers. A Moscow story says that when a Russian visitor from a rural area in the provinces came to Moscow for the first time, after being shown this station, he observed "It's a magnificent art museum, but why do trains keep running through it?" The Moscow subway system was built by the Soviet regime in the thirties, a grim time, and was intended to be a promissory note to its citizens for the plentiful and beautiful society that was supposed to be created under communism.

Each of the subway stations was manned by a crew of a dozen of more people (ticket sellers, red-hatted escalator operators in little booths at the bottom of each escalator, cleaning crews, several guards, and a person in charge of the station), and the stations were required to be kept immaculate. As one rode up and down the escalators a white wall was a few inches from one's hand on the moving rubber banister. A pencil or marking pen held motionless there would decorate the entire length of the wall in a few seconds, an almost irresistible temptation for a New York graffiti artist. Yet I never saw such a mark. Soviet citizens were so tidy in some respects, so sloppy in others. I often thought that the U.S. and the USSR should have set up a special sanitary exchange in which the Soviets would teach us how to maintain subways and railroad stations and we would teach them how to maintain toilets. Was there some unknown economic law that decreed that socialist toilets are unspeakable horrors and socialist subways are gleaming cathedrals? For that matter, was there a law of capitalism that decreed that public spaces like railroad and bus stations should be shabby?

After arriving at the railway station we bought two round-trip tickets to Zagorsk, and left in a few minutes, as there were frequent trips. On arrival we were interested in seeing the tomb of Boris Godunov, outside under trees around which wheeled clouds of black rooks, a member of the crow family. Pictures of old Russian churches and monasteries often have these large black birds circling the domes and steeples, and one of the well-known paintings of the famous Russian artist Aleksei Savrasov is called "The Rooks Have Flown In." We felt that in a sense the birds at Zagorsk were doing their duty for the tourists who came looking for Old Russia.

We noticed that although most of the buildings were obviously state-run museums open to the public, one large building was closed. From time to time monks and priests, attired in black, would enter or leave the building. We asked about them and learned that this was one of the two Orthodox seminaries operating in the Soviet Union at that time. The officially atheistic regime had closed all the others. Within sight of the main entrance to the seminary was a book-store, run as a part of the main museum, selling anti-religious books and pamphlets. Here was an example of the intellectual coexistence of different principles — religious and anti-religious — a little bit like the coexistence of rival ideas — collective and individualistic — that one found at the same time on collective farms, where the large communal plots existed alongside the small private ones. The government seemed to realize that it could push the population only so far without excessive costs, either economic or motivational. The intellectual level of the pamphlets in Zagorsk was very low; one of them was a conversation with the Soviet astronaut Iurii Gagarin in which he was asked if during his trip into space he had met any angels or other signs that the heaven described in the Bible was up there. His predictable answer was considered evidence against religion as a whole. Looking at the bookstore and the seminary I surmised that the monks probably thrived on this sort of confrontation.

This monastery town would later become important in my research in the history of mathematics. At the time of the Russian Revolution a priest living here — Pavel Florenskii — was in close contact with two leading mathematicians at Moscow University, N. N. Luzin and D. F. Egorov, whom I mentioned in a previous section of this book. All three men were deeply religious, and together they worked out in secret an approach to mathematics which they considered to be religiously inspired. That approach, which came to be known as the Moscow School of Functions, became famous in the world of mathematicians everywhere. But their fame did not preserve the members of the school from political repression. All three eventually were accused of mixing mathematics and religion (true, but a crime to the regime), and Florenskii and Egorov died in political camps. Thus, in one of the paradoxes of history, the monastery where the Soviet authorities tried to show that religion is conquered by science, as demonstrated by Gagarin's observations, became, for historians of science, a place where an unusual confluence of religion and science occurred.

While we were walking around the fortified walls of the monastery we noticed that a young man was following not too far behind us. At first I did not pay much attention, but it soon became clear that as we paused at different spots, or took little detours, so did he. Pat and I talked about the man, and he seemed to know that we had noticed him, but did not seem to care.

After leaving the monastery we walked through the streets of the town, which were lined with log houses trimmed with the wooden fretwork so common in old Russian villages. The general direction of our stroll was toward the railroad station where we had arrived, but we were not in a particular hurry. In fact, feeling hungry, we decided to get a bite to eat somewhere. Not knowing the town at all, and not seeing any eating establishments around, we suddenly decided that it would be amusing, and perhaps even useful, to ask the man who was following us for information. I turned and walked briskly back to him, noticing his surprise as I approached. He turned a bit to the side, as if to walk in another direction, but I followed him at a pace that soon brought me alongside. "Say," I said, "We are hungry. Could you possibly tell us where we might find a restaurant?" Without much hesitation he replied, "Well, if you walk down this hill about two blocks on the right you will see a low, blue building. Inside there is a restaurant." I thanked him and we walked in the direction he indicated. I noticed as we approached the restaurant that our follower was nowhere in sight.

As we went in the low door of the blue building we were overwhelmingly assailed by a smell that was a mixture of garlic and poorly prepared food. Inside we saw that it was not a restaurant proper, but what the Soviets called a "*stolovaia*" (cafeteria) of the lowest grade. The stench alone quickly killed our appetites. Customers bought their food at grimy steam tables and ate standing at high stools about the size of small barrels. The wooden floor was muddy from the boots of the customers. I walked over and looked at what was being offered on the steam tables: an unappetizing collection of brown gruel, fatty sausage, and sour cream. I turned to Pat who was looking distressed; we said simultaneously that we thought we could wait to eat until we got back to Moscow.

We headed out the door and I noticed that there was a short cut to the railroad station down a back street. We were at the station within seconds, and there we glanced at the posted schedule and saw that a train to Moscow was leaving at the exact time being indicated on the black-and-white clock on the wall. We hurried to the platform where the train awaited, boarded it immediately, and felt the lurch of the train starting before we got to one of the hard benches in the second-class car to which our tickets entitled us. I sat next to the window and looked down the street. I suddenly saw a small figure running toward the station at full speed. As the figure grew larger I recognized our follower, who vaulted the railing near the station, jumped the track, and ran down the platform toward the moving train as fast he could bring himself. He jumped into one of the last cars. He came up and plopped himself into the seat directly across from us, all pretense gone. Barely catching his breath, perspiration running down his red cheeks, he turned to us and exclaimed, "You didn't go to that restaurant, did you?"

Our KGB friend rode with us to Moscow, and occasionally we exchanged conversation with him, although only on very innocuous topics. In Moscow we soon merged with the crowds on the subway headed back to the university, and our follower disappeared.

On the basis of that experience, and a number of similar ones, we concluded that many of the people who followed foreigners—especially young students like us—were not professionals. The image of hardened secret agents in trench coasts keeping watch over foreigners, equipped with radios and probably weapons, was not correct. Perhaps it was a sign of our low status, but the duty of watching over us was often assigned to young Komsomol activists as a part of their training, a little bit like the way a Boy Scout in the United States might be asked to hold the flag at the Memorial Day ceremony. This young Komsomol member had obviously been assigned to keep tabs on us. In my imagination, this assignment was the first he had ever been given, and if he had lost us, as he almost did, he would have started what he hoped was a promising political career with an embarrassing blot on his copybook. No wonder he ran so hard to catch our train.

In later years, whenever I noticed that I was being followed, I often enjoyed asking my pursuers for directions or striking up conversations with them. But I noticed that as I grew older, and became more known as a specialist on Soviet affairs, my followers also grew older and more serious. The camaraderie with my followers that marked our trip to Zagorsk was gradually lost.

In the years that followed I often came to the Soviet Union to do research in the libraries and archives. On one such trip I came to know a man from the foreign department of the Soviet Academy of Sciences (staffed, I knew by KGB officers) named Belousov, a portly fellow appropriately sporting a white moustache ("Belousov" in Russian means "white moustache"). One late afternoon Belousov invited me in to his office, pulled a bottle of vodka from a file cabinet, and proposed that we drink and talk a bit.

I carefully controlled my consumption of vodka, but Belousov imbibed freely. After an hour or so of inconsequential conversation the alcohol began to loosen his tongue, and he talked about his relationship to me. "Our superiors tell us," he confided, "that you may be a spy. After all, you are a specialist on Soviet science, and American intelligence agencies are very interested in that subject. So we have been watching you closely, following you wherever you go. But," he continued, leaning toward me and slurring his words a bit, "if you are a spy, you are the most god-damned boring spy we have ever had to deal with. You are driving our agents crazy. You spend all your time in libraries and archives, and our men sit there watching you and are bored to tears. Why don't you do something interesting to enliven their lives?"

I confessed that the quality of life of KGB agents had not been one of my major concerns. And I was reminded of how, years earlier, I had been criticized by the Komsomol organization of Moscow University for spending all my time studying and ignoring the critical issues of the day. But I now knew that the KGB was definitely paying attention to me, and that the agents following me were no longer Komsomol amateurs.

In the early seventies, like many other people in the United States, I took up the habit of jogging. On my trips to the Soviet Union I continued this practice, one that presented particular challenges to agents following me. Jogging was not nearly as popular in the Soviet Union as it was in the United States, particularly among older people, a status I was acquiring. Soviet men tended to be athletic only while they were young; an ample girth seemed to be almost a sign of respectability and status among older men. I could not imagine the senior academicians with whom I now often associated out on the streets jogging.

When a person was walking around Moscow, almost any half-alert follower could keep up. The greatest challenges were subways and buses, when the follower had to shake a leg to get into the same conveyance and not get stranded by a door suddenly closing or a vehicle quickly departing. But a jogger was different story. First of all, not just any follower could keep up if the jogger was in good shape. An experienced jogger would soon turn an inexperienced follower into a physical wreck, out of breath and desperate. Furthermore, if the follower had to run to keep up, it was more than obvious to the jogger that he was being followed. And joggers could not always be followed by automobiles because they cut across fields, went between buildings, and even preferred soft grass fields to hard pavements.

In 1976 I was staying at the Rossiia Hotel, in sight of St. Basil's Cathedral and Red Square. One day I jogged out the entrance on the Ministry of Defense side and wended my way through the back streets of one of the oldest districts of Moscow. Emerging on "25th of October Street," I headed for a pedestrian passage cutting through buildings to Sverdlov Square, a path that I knew well from past visits. At this point I noticed a man following me, not dressed for jogging and not looking too happy. As I ran through the narrow passageway and popped out on the other side my follower was nowhere to be seen. I did not want to lose him, as this might have been regarded as evidence that I had something to hide. I stopped and jogged in place until my hapless friend found me again. He seemed appreciative. After that, the KGB searched among their ranks and selected as my followers people with more athletic abilities.

This new type of follower became particularly apparent to me in the spring of 1982, when I was staying at the Academy of Sciences Hotel on October Square. On most mornings I would go for jogs, exploring the area. In the process I actually acquired information that was useful in my work, since the area of Lenin Prospect south of October Square was thickly peppered with institutes of the Soviet Academy of Sciences, an organization with which much of my work was concerned. I would run along and pause to read the name plates of the research institutes that lined the streets, such as "General and Inorganic Chemistry," "Physical Problems," "Lebedev Institute of Physics," "Steklov Institute of Mathematics," "Institute of Genetics," and many others, almost all of which were well known to me from my research, but whose location I had not previously noticed.

At first on these jogs I did not see any followers, but after about two or three runs when I emerged from the hotel at my normal pre-breakfast hour, I noticed a jogger nearby in a blue athletic outfit who fell in behind me as I headed down Don Street. He stayed about a block back. Was he actually following me, or was my imagination becoming too active? I switched back and forth between Don and Shabalov streets, demonstrating how diverse my interests were by pausing to inspect both the twentieth-century Kosygin Textile Institute and the eighteenth-century Church of the Deposition of the Robe. My follower made similar switches, keeping a block's distance. I went on down Don Street until I reached the wall of the historic Don Monastery, an ancient walled structure that once was on the southern edge of the city and was a defense point against the Crimean Tatar hordes that rather frequently until the eighteenth century attempted to take Moscow.

On the south side of the Don Monastery is the Moscow Crematorium, surrounded by a cemetery. I turned in the main gates of the cemetery, which were open. My follower came in behind me, and sat down near the entrance where he could watch me. Directly ahead of me lay the gray building of the crematorium. I had recently heard rumors that this is where the bodies of the Soviet soldiers killed in Afghanistan had been brought in the first phase of the struggle there following the Soviet invasion in 1979. According to the rumors the sight of the rows of caskets being brought here had been so depressing to witnesses that later the procedure was changed; the soldiers were either cremated in Afghanistan or actually buried there.

In front of the crematorium, on either side, was the cemetery; from the varying designs of the tombstones it was obvious that this was an old burial place, used both before and after the Revolution of 1917. I have always been interested in cemeteries, and have jogged in them in New Orleans (St. Louis Nos. 1 and 2), London (Highgate), Paris (Pere Lachaise), Cambridge (Mt. Auburn), Cairo (The City of the Dead), St. Petersburg (Aleksandr Nevskii), Buenos Aires (Recoleta), Tokyo, Kyoto, and other places. From the tombstones that surrounded me in these cities I found that I could read much of the histories of the country. I now ran at a very slow pace in the Don cemetery, looking at the stones on each side of me. Directly on my left was the stone of Sergei Muromtsev, the chairman of Russia's first duma, or parliament, in 1905. This parliament gave Russia a far more democratic government than it had ever had before, although it did not begin to solve Russia's social and economic problems. It had been wrested from Tsar Nicholas II only by an almost-successful revolution, but when it and its successor proved too radical for the government's taste, the electoral laws were changed to ensure a more compliant legislative body. On Muromtsev's tomb lay a faded tulip. I noticed that it was not plastic, as many of the flowers on other tombs were, but genuine.

I glanced back at the gate to the cemetery through which my follower had entered. My friend in the blue jogging outfit had struck up a conversation with a man in the little guardhouse near the gate. After a few minutes a militiaman in uniform joined them, and the three sat and talked, no doubt occasionally about me, but they studiously tried to ignore me whenever I looked their way. I continued my tour through the cemetery.

Not far from Muromtsev's stone I saw another marked "Sergei Karavaev, killed by the hand of the class enemy, August 12, 1929." I recalled that Karavaev was an Old Bolshevik who was, according to the Soviet news reports of the time, murdered by the son of his former landlord; I also remembered that the incident was used as a pretext for expelling middle class apartment dwellers from their homes and the takeover of their residences by workers.

Placed in the stone wall around the cemetery were many little memorial tablets with the names and dates of the deceased. Some of these contained urns with ashes behind glass; some did not. I noticed that in one section there were a great many stones with death dates of 1936, 1937, and 1938, and one could see from the birth dates that most of these people died young. It quickly hit me that these were markers for victims of the Great Purges of Stalin's time, and I immediately wondered what was usually done with the bodies of all those people who were shot in the basements of Lubianka and other secret police prisons. I noticed that the markers that seemed to be for victims of the purges did not contain urns for ashes and that in many cases the exact death dates were not given, surely because they were not known. I surmised that the relatives never actually were given the bodies and usually were not told the exact dates of death. (As I learned later from Bukharin's widow she was never given his remains, but she did at least find out when he had been executed.) These memorials were erected by family members, sometimes without knowledge of the basic facts about time and place of death, but who wanted grave markers for their loved ones nonetheless. One tablet simply said "To the memory of Professor Petrov." There was no birth date, no death date, no urn for ashes. The formal title, without a first name, seemed to suggest that persons other than family members had been responsible for placing the tablet. Did Professor Petrov's students put this memorial here? I was certain that they did. Another marker contained the words, "To

Andrei Sokolov. Forgive us, my dear friend, please forgive us." Again, no vital facts. And why the request for forgiveness? Were the relatives and friends feeling guilty because, faced by the fearsome might of Stalin's secret police, they had not protested the detention of their loved one by the authorities? Then a more horrible thought suddenly haunted me; had they actually denounced the deceased to the police? Such denunciations were common in the thirties, and Pavlik Morozov, a little boy, was celebrated by the Soviet authorities for denouncing his father for hoarding grain to the secret police, who arrested him. I also noticed that many of the markers that lacked vital facts bore Jewish names.

Many years later, after the fall of the Soviet Union, we learned what had happened to the bodies of Stalin's purge victims. We still do not know just how many victims there were, but it was certainly in six figures. Some of the bodies were cremated in the crematorium near me, and the ashes were placed in a great pit and then macadamized over. But the crematorium could not begin to handle the flood of victims, and the secret police had to develop a whole network of places to inter the dead—the grounds of Novospasskii and Donskoi monasteries, a dozen or more different cemeteries, the Khodynka Field, already infamous in Russian history as the site of the deaths of over a thousand people in a panicked crowd at the coronation of Nikolai II in 1896, and, finally, on former noble estates and new collective farms, where the victims were sometimes brought live, forced to dig their own graves, and then shot in them.

Looking over the cemetery that day in 1982 I could see signs of the ideological divisions that divided Soviet society and still divide Russian society today. Some markers bore the hammer and the sickle and proudly announced "member of the Communist Party since 1896"; others were surmounted with Orthodox crosses or the Star of David. Still others were stones shaped in the form of the tools of the profession of the deceased, such as a pen or even a microscope. One of the wall markers contained behind glass not a funeral urn, but the cylinder head of an internal combustion engine, complete with spark plug; this obviously was the tomb of an automotive engineer or worker.

I remembered that on an earlier run in the famous Novodevichy cemetery I had seen the grave of a Soviet minister of communications, who was sculpted in stone standing and barking out orders on a telephone. In that same cemetery is the tombstone of Nikita Khrushchev, an interesting modernistic composition by the Soviet (later émigré) sculptor and artist Ernst Neizvestnyi. Neizvestnyi had earlier been re-

viled by Khrushchev at a show of modern works of art; Khrushchev
had remarked that modern paintings looked like they had been made
by the tail of a donkey, and he included Neizvestnyi's sculpture among
the works that deviated unacceptably from the principles of socialist
realism. Incredibly, Khrushchev's family after his death chose
Neizvestnyi to do his tombstone, and Neizvestnyi created a large work
consisting of a pattern of black and white stones, indicating the good
and bad aspects that he saw in the Soviet leader, a person who had
denounced not only him, but also the tyrant Stalin. I counted the
stones and noticed that the black ones were slightly more numerous
than the white ones, a fact well known to the Khrushchev family, but
they still accepted the tombstone.

Along the side of the monastery I saw leaning against the interior
wall very large broken pieces of sculpted stone with religious and Russian nationalist motifs. They extended for hundreds of yards, and obviously had come from an enormous structure. I then realized that these
were pieces of the friezes that had earlier been located between the
main columns of the Cathedral of Christ the Redeemer, the largest
church in pre-Revolutionary Moscow. The church had been erected
in celebration of the victory over Napoleon in the War of 1812. This
cathedral, with its great golden dome, dominated the city and was visible from many parts of downtown Moscow. This prominence was an
affront to Stalin, who ordered the cathedral blown to bits by dynamite.
Photos still survive showing one of Moscow's largest structures collapsing in clouds of dust. After the explosion religious believers somehow
hauled away the largest extant pieces of the sculpture and placed them
inside the Don Monastery, where they remained for decades. As I
looked at them while I jogged along the wall in 1982 I could not dream
that within ten years, after the fall of the Soviet Union, the Cathedral
of Christ the Redeemer would be restored (actually rebuilt, since nothing but these remnants remained). At first it was hoped that the original friezes would be returned to their places on the cathedral walls,
but it was found that they were too damaged. Instead, they were repro-
duced, and the cathedral once again dominates downtown Moscow.
This enormous and expensive effort was carried out at a time when
Russia suffered from great poverty.

It was cold, and I was not running fast enough to keep warm, lost in
my reveries about Russian history. My running outfit was wet from
sweat and was now turning clammy. It was time to go. I ran down the
last row of stones, turned past the crematorium, and headed toward the
main gate. As I passed the guardhouse, my KGB jogger slowly rose

The tombstone of
Nikita Khrushchev,
designed by the sculptor
Ernst Neizvestnyi, in
Novodevichy cemetery,
Moscow. Photo by the
author.

and, once again keeping about a block behind, followed me back to
the hotel.

A few days later I emerged from the hotel for another jog. There, not
far away, was a man different from my previous follower, but dressed in
an identical blue jogging outfit. Must be standard issue of the KGB, I
thought. I also noticed that this man was young and looked very athletic; he seemed to be anticipating what lay ahead.

I headed in a different direction from the previous time, going under
Lenin Prospect in an underground passageway. This spot, near an intersection of two subway lines at the October Square station, was one
of the busiest in the area, and women often chose it as an ideal location to sell flowers to passersby. The private selling of flowers was illegal, like all private trade, but was often tolerated. Once in a while the
city authorities would issue orders to the police to suppress this incipient capitalism, and the police would comply but in such a way that
one could see that their hearts were not in their actions. They would

come stomping their boots on the stairways, blowing their whistles, making a great deal of noise, and proceeding very slowly. The women would hear them coming long before they were visible, would quickly gather up their flowers, and disappear out the other end of the passageway. Once again, the Soviet totalitarianism of the 1980s was a little less frightening than our textbooks told us, and certainly less rigorous than under Stalin.

I emerged on Sadovoe Kol'tso Street, and ran down the hill, past the Institute of Steel and Alloys, toward Gorky Park, the largest park in downtown Moscow. I entered the enormous iron gates of the park and ran along one of the main paths. I looked ahead and saw the huge Ferris wheel from which, in Martin Cruz Smith's murder mystery *Gorky Park*, the police inspector spots the murderer returning to the scene of the crime, a clearing in the woods to the south. Looking in that direction I saw that Smith must not have checked his geography too carefully, as it seemed impossible to see the woods well from the Ferris wheel. But maybe the view from the top of the wheel would be better. The Ferris wheel was now, in the middle of the winter, motionless, and white snow covered the ground except where it had been swept aside by women park attendants in brown shawls and felt boots.

I ran past several concession stands, all closed and shuttered tightly. I cut over toward the wide promenade that bordered the Moscow River. As I emerged on the pathway along the river I glanced back and saw the blue runner not far behind me, his long legs carrying him at an easy pace. He was loafing. I continued along the river, looking directly ahead where I could see, several miles away, the almost-finished garish double skyscraper of the Presidium of the Academy of Sciences. This extravagant monument to Russian science would require a janitorial and service staff of 600, and would, after the fall of Soviet Union, be seen by many Russian citizens as a symbol of the excessive waste and expense of the Soviet regime at a time when basic health care and consumer goods were being neglected: And all in the name of science.

A strong and very cold wind blew off the Moscow River and although I was going at a good pace, I was feeling chilled. I ran with some care, since the snow was interspersed with ice. No one was in sight ahead of me except for two small boys who were trying to take their bicycles through the ice and snow. One of the boys slipped and fell within a few feet of me, and I ran over to help him up. Only his pride suffered. I continued down the promenade, looking across the river at an enormous, columned building that was a military academy. The wind whistled past my ears. I was wearing a complete jogging outfit, with sweat pants and a zippered jacket; on my head was one of those L.L. Bean "Balaklava" woolen hats that can be lowered if the weather was very cold, and provided small holes for the eyes and nose. I decided that I needed such protection, and I reached up and lowered the hat. Now I was completely covered, except for the facial aperture of my hat. I continued to run.

I glanced back at my follower and saw a strange sight. Evidently when I covered my face against the cold he was amused and decided to show me how tough Muscovites are. He removed his sweatshirt, tied it around his waist, and was running with his bare and muscular chest exposed to the icy wind, and he was laughing at me. When he saw me looking at him he proudly pounded his fists on his hairy chest and then gave me a champion's salute.

For the first and only time in my life, I got furious at one of my followers. This was humiliating. What could I do? Obviously I was not going to take off my clothes and freeze to death. But somehow I wanted to show that s.o.b. that he had no monopoly on toughness. I wanted to lose this guy, grind him in my dust. Well, as my father used to say when as a small boy I went with him to stores and asked him to buy things for me, it's one thing to want, and quite another to get. No way was I going to outrun this fellow. I was almost fifty years old, he looked under thirty. He was quite a bit taller and in much better shape. In a sprint he could run circles around me.

I had only one possibility: the long distance. My guess was that this guy was a good athlete, but probably a sprinter, not a jogger. I was not an athlete, but there was a certain slow pace at which I could run a long way. Just exactly how far I did not know, since I had never run a marathon and was not in that class. The longest distance I had ever run previously had been from Jerusalem to Bethlehem and back, a distance of about sixteen miles, when I had been in Israel to read a paper on the celebration of Albert Einstein's 100th birthday. True, that occasion had not ended too well, as I came close to getting sunstroke, and had to rest for a day back in the hotel.

I slowed down and settled in for the long haul. I tried to find a pace at which I hoped I could run forever—well, at least for seven or eight hours. I was so angry at this guy that I was willing to run all day long if necessary, and that, as it turned out, is what was required, on a jaunt that took me from one edge of Moscow to the other, and back.

I ran along the Moscow River until I reached a large and very old white building that looked interesting. I ran up to the entrance and saw that it was the building of a monastery that had been founded by Fedor

Rtishchev in the seventeenth century. I remembered hearing Professor Marc Raeff talk about the monastery in a colloquium at Columbia University twenty-five years earlier. The monastery was the first educational institution in Moscow, and Rtishchev was one of the westernizing boyar predecessors of Peter the Great who tried to bring European ideas to Muscovy. I noticed that the monastery was now a scientific research institute specializing in metrology, and I recalled that the U.S. and the USSR had a scientific exchange in the field of metrology. So, over 300 years after its construction, this building was still serving, among other things, as a place where Western technology was being studied. Above the main door to the institute one could see, very faint, the picture of Archangel Michael. Inside the courtyard were crates containing some kind of scientific equipment.

The conversion of monasteries and churches into scientific research institutes was a very frequent practice of the Soviet regime. The use of religious property for scientific purposes was seen as symbolically important, a victory of scientific rational thought over religious mysticism. The Soviet hydrogen bomb project, headed by Andrei Sakharov, was housed in the monastery of St. Serafim of Sarov, one of the most famous religious sites in pre-Revolutionary Russia. In 1903 Tsar Nikolai II and Tsarina Aleksandra prayed at this monastery for a son and an heir, and the following year their prayers were fulfilled by the birth of Tsarevich Aleksei. Under the Soviet regime it became a secret scientific city called "Arzamas 16." The cells of the monks became scientific laboratories.

I returned to the riverbank, allowing my follower to cut off my detour to the Institute of Metrology. As I headed up the river in the direction, far in the distance, of the spire of Moscow University, I noticed that the path was deteriorating. The ice was so thick and bumpy that I was having trouble keeping my footing. If I stumbled and sprained an ankle I would be in trouble in short order in my sweat-soaked clothing in below zero weather. I wondered if my competitor in the blue suit would come to my assistance.

I decided to turn around and find another path. I wheeled around and retraced my way, passing my follower and giving him a cheery *zdravstvuite* ("how do you do") as I went by. No longer trying to conceal his function, he wheeled and followed. Not far back on the path there was a railroad bridge that crossed the Moscow River. I remembered that alongside the bridge was a path leading up to Lenin Prospect on the other side of the park. I was not terribly eager to go beside the bridge, since the Soviet authorities were unreasonably touchy about railroad bridges, often posting guards along them, but I decided to do so. Foreign tourists were forbidden to take pictures of such bridges. Evidently the security authorities thought the tourists were eager to plan to blow up the bridges and needed the photographs to prepare. As I went up the path by the bridge I noticed that there was no guard, a change from earlier years when I had walked along the same river path. Well, maybe the Soviet Union was softening up after all, I thought. Or maybe the guard had the sense to stay out of the cold.

As I made my way up the hill toward Lenin Prospect I met quite a few people, some with briefcases, coming down. Perhaps they were going to work at the Institute of Metrology. I came out on Lenin Prospect at the large circle in which stood a grandiose stainless steel (or was it titanium?) statue of Iurii Gagarin. To the right was the Institute of Physical Problems where a few days later I would have lunch with Academician Peter Kapitsa and his wife. Up and down the street were scientific research institutes, and atop the shoe store across the square was a gigantic neon sign with the words "Glory to Soviet Science." I looked on the left and saw a large apartment building in Stalinist style, with heavy columns, stone garlands, and pointed entablatures. At the end of World War II this had been the edge of the city, but now it stretched for miles further south. I recalled that Alexander Solzhenitsyn, the Soviet Union's noted writer and dissident, then in forced exile in Vermont, had written in one of his books that when he was a prisoner in a Soviet labor camp after the war he had been brought into Moscow, along with other prisoners, to help in the construction of the building at which I was looking. Solzhenitsyn had been proud that his parquet floors had been constructed with particular care.

I ran down Lenin Prospect toward my hotel. I looked back and saw that my follower was with me. On the right I ran past the Bakh Institute of Biochemistry where several years earlier I interviewed its director, the early researcher of the origin of life, Aleksandr Oparin. On the left, set way back from the street, was the old presidium building of the Academy of Sciences of the USSR, an eighteenth-century mansion built by a wealthy factory owner and later owned by Tsar Nikolai I. Further on the left was the Moscow City Hospital where I had visited my poor friend Vitalii as his kidneys failed.

As I approached my hotel on October Square I was certain that my follower would assume that I would go in, as I had completed a distance that was just about standard for my usual run. Instead, I ran past without hesitation. This little trip is just beginning, I assured myself. I ran under the square and on down past the French Embassy, located in one of the most striking pre-Revolutionary merchants' houses in Moscow, a delightful riot of crenellated brick, colorful wall tiles, and secret gardens. The French ambassador now lived in the old house, and the embassy proper stood next door in a modernistic structure of matching red brick. How much more glorious the whole ensemble is, I thought, than the ratty-looking American Embassy, scheduled soon to be replaced (it was so scheduled for thirty years). Further on the left I inspected the spiffy new hotel for the Central Committee of the Communist Party, surrounded by a massive and secure decorative iron fence, and just being completed.

I reached the Moscow River again near the restaurant-boat *Burevestnik* (Stormy Petrel) where in 1960 I witnessed a party that turned into a brawl in which bottles and mirrors had been smashed, and a Moscow worker was thrown into the river by a fellow reveler. To the worker's misfortune, a small empty rowboat was directly below him and he landed on his head on the bottom of the boat. Some time later he hauled himself over the railing and resumed the battle, blood streaming down his forehead. The melee was eventually quelled by the Moscow police.

I crossed the branch of the river near this spot and ran alongside the famous Government House or "House on the Embankment," featured in the novel of that name by the well-known writer Iurii Trifonov. This apartment house was built in the late 1920s when the Soviet government was experimenting with modern architecture. The enormous structure contained over 500 apartments, all of them fitted out with what was considered to be the most modern conveniences, such as telephones, hot water baths, and garbage pickup. The building was the center of a large complex of services, including a movie theater, department store, auto garage, and a branch of the Kremlin hospital to care for the elite. It became the favored residence of many of the top leaders of the Party and government, who used their influence to acquire apartments there. One of them, Olga Lepinshinskaia, a friend of Lenin's, had been a subject of my research; she developed a false theory of the origin of biological cells that for a time was officially favored because of her political connections.

In the late thirties the secret police often came in the middle of the night in their black vans to this building and hauled away top leaders for imprisonment and frequently, execution. The other residents of the building would hear the steps on the stairs and wonder at whose door they would stop. Attached to the outside of the wall of the building where I could view them as I ran alongside were plaques with the names of some of these unfortunate victims, including that of Marshal Tukhachevskii, the brilliant general whom Stalin eliminated on the eve of World War II, along with many other members of the top leadership of the army.

As I ran off toward the center of Moscow and the Kremlin, I glanced back to see how my KGB nemesis was doing. He had paused as I read the plaques on the wall of the apartment building that marked the work of his predecessors in the KGB and had put his sweatshirt back on. I wondered if he was cold or was concerned about how disrespectful it might seem to run past Lenin's tomb on Red Square bare chested. I rolled up my balaklava hat; I too was getting fashionable for Red Square, and it did not seem cold anymore.

I ran across the street, down a long slope, and reached the other branch of the Moscow River. Here I turned right and ran along the embankment. Looking into the river I saw a bright iridescent oil layer covering the water. I would never be caught in that water, I thought. It looked worse than the Hudson near my apartment in Manhattan. To my surprise I came upon a man who was holding a fishing pole out over the water. "It certainly looks polluted," I said to him. "Do you actually think there are fish in there?" "Absolutely," he replied, "they have become biologically adapted to oil." I was certain that this man accepted the views of the charlatan Soviet geneticist Trofim Lysenko, who believed in the doctrine of the inheritance of acquired characteristics in opposition to international biology.

I continued on down the river past the British Embassy, located in what must be the most glorious location in all Moscow, directly across the river from the golden domes of the Kremlin. The building was the mansion before the Revolution of a very wealthy sugar merchant. The house even has its own river landing, cut into the granite stones of the embankment. The British ambassador told me years earlier that the Soviet government wanted this valuable real estate and each year sent him a letter saying he must get out; each year the ambassador replied that "they were making preparations" and did nothing. Forty years later the British government is still there, but now it is the home of the ambassador; there is a new embassy elsewhere. When I was a student in Moscow I used to visit in the attic of one of the old embassy buildings a British pub, complete with dartboard and bitters. Above the door to the pub was a sign saying "You are entering the only British pub with a view of the Kremlin."

I ran down past the Petroleum Institute and across the bridge leading to Red Square. On my right was the Hotel Rossiia, directly ahead St.

Basil's Cathedral, properly called the Cathedral of the Intercession on the Moat. St. Basil's riotous exterior has always been to foreigners the symbol of Russia. I approached Red Square right under the Kremlin wall, running past the "Tsar's Seat" built on the parapets. As I came to the gate to the Kremlin, suddenly, on a whim, I ran straight for the Spasskiye Gates, at that time closed to all but Party leaders, wondering if I could convince my tail that I had connections he did not know about. As I expected, an armed guard waved me away, toward the center of Red Square. I jogged across the uneven cobble stones of the great expanse of the square, recalling that only a few days earlier a group of six or seven West European students had tried to hold there a disarmament demonstration similar to the ones that were so prevalent in Europe and America. They had raised a sign that said "Peace, Bread, Disarmament." They were promptly hauled away by the police but soon thereafter released with a warning not to return.

I now popped out on Revolution Square. Directly ahead was the National Hotel and to its left, the building that had housed the American Embassy immediately after the United States belatedly recognized the Soviet Union in 1934. The building was now the headquarters of the Soviet tourist agency Intourist, and it had a gigantic neon sign on top of it that said "Kommunizm pobedit'" (Communism Will Be Victorious). A few weeks later I would be jogging in the oldest city in Denmark, Ribe, and there I would see carved in the stone above the entrance of a sixteenth century building the Latin words "Kristus vincit." I was struck by the parallel.

I turned left past the eternal flame in memory of the Soviet soldiers who fell in World War II and headed past the manege, the old stables of the tsar, now used as an exhibition hall. Beyond it was a building with plaques saying that in the 1920s, a time of enthusiasm for the communist movement around the world, several young non-Russian intellectuals rebelling against the political regimes of their native countries lived there while studying Marxism; they included Ho Chi Minh from Vietnam, Bela Kun from Hungary, and Antonio Gramsci from Italy, now famous names in history. A bit farther down the street was a plaque saying that Inessa Armand, an old friend of Lenin's, once had an apartment there. Several Western scholars have speculated that Armand was Lenin's mistress, and one of them, Bertram Wolfe, even suggested that she had a child by Lenin, a supposition not widely accepted. As I ran past her old home I observed that it was only a few hundred yards from the back door of the Kremlin where Lenin lived immediately after the Revolution.

I turned to the right and ran past the entrance to the reception room of the Presidium of the Supreme Soviet, the Soviet Union's legislature, a body with little power. Nonetheless, this entrance was a special spot, and in front of it was a crowd of people, many of them clutching sheets of paper. I realized that this must be one of the days in which Soviet citizens with grievances were permitted to present them to the government. At certain moments a few of these petitioners were allowed to enter, a bit like the way in which kings used to hold hearings for their subjects. Although most petitioners failed, it was not unheard of for some action to be taken. At any rate, people kept trying. From the dress of the people crowded around the entrance I could tell that many had come from far outside Moscow.

I turned up Kalinin Street (now, as before the Revolution, Vozdvizhenka Street; Kalinin was the first chairman of the Supreme Soviet and the man who established the tradition of receiving petitioners), ran past a building that was a very familiar place—the Lenin Library—and continued until I approached Granovskii Street on the right. Granovskii Street had been cordoned off from auto traffic; up and down the street were parked many large limousines, and militiamen were everywhere. Noticing that the sawhorses cordoning off the street were blocking only autos, not pedestrians, I turned up the street to try to find out what was going on. That something significant was happening could not be doubted; I had never seen so many large limousines in my life. With my KGB follower in blue behind me, I ran the length of the street. I wondered if he knew any more about this event than I did. Along the way down the street I saw one Chaika limousine that was larger than any I had ever seen before. Each of its four headlights had a little windshield wiper. But there was no clue to tell me what eminent figure used this impressive automobile, so I returned to Kalinin Street and headed out toward the Old Arbat, an area that before the Revolution was one of the most stylish in Moscow.

Only several days later did I learn what was happening on Granovskii Street. On his return from a trip to Tashkent, where he had given an important speech, the leader of the Soviet Union, Leonid Brezhnev, suffered a heart attack. Of course, not a word about this appeared in the Soviet press. According to official Soviet sources, top leaders never got sick. I learned about the event from Western news dispatches available at the American Embassy. Unofficial rumors rampant in Moscow said that Brezhnev at the Moscow airport had been carried off the plane on a stretcher. One of the main offices of the Kremlin Hospital was located at the corner of Kalinin and Granovskii streets, and I happened to be running near it at the moment when Brezhnev was there under intensive care. (I would later sample the services of the Kremlin Hospital myself.) No doubt the fancy limousine that attracted my attention was his. Later, on Good Friday, rumors spread in Moscow that Brezhnev had died. When he reappeared to celebrate Lenin's birthday, the wags of Moscow maintained that Brezhnev had in fact died on Good Friday but that he arose from the dead on Easter.

I ran down Kalinin Street past the Arbat and the modern buildings that were at that time the showpiece of Moscow. Off to the left were some of the finest old residences of the city. Most of these town mansions were long ago requisitioned from their original noble and wealthy merchant families and turned into public institutions of various sorts. The luxurious mansion of Savva Morozov, an industrialist of the late nineteenth and early twentieth century, became in the Soviet period the "House of Friendship" where Soviet delegations met their touring foreign counterparts. As a student I often went to the basement of this building to eat, since better food, designed for foreign guests, could be found there than elsewhere.

Once my friend Vitalii took me on a walking tour of the Old Arbat and showed me one or two houses that, amazingly, sixty years after the Revolution, were still being lived in by members of the original noble families. The reason that these buildings had been spared was that they were very small and had passed the requirement that no family have more than a certain number (quite restricted) of square meters of living space. One of these homes was the carriage house of the original mansion, to which the family had moved to escape eviction. Their old main house was now a research institute, and they lived in the small, but still elegant, carriage house. Vitalii showed me this house at night, and through the lighted windows and white curtains we could see oil paintings and fine furniture decorating the tiny main room in the carriage house.

I ran on past the "Evening Arbat," a nightclub built for foreign tourists; several years earlier Pat and I spent an evening there with Alan Pifer of the Carnegie Corporation and his wife Erica, Harold Hochshild of Princeton, Iphigenia Ochs Sulzberger of the New York Times family, and Bernard Gwertzman, a reporter for the paper. When I saw the floor show complete with scantily clad performers I could not believe we were in Moscow under Soviet rule, which usually completely forbade such spectacles. Actually we were not in Soviet Moscow, but in a tiny island designed to titillate foreigners and strip them of their

cash. It all worked as it was supposed to, with financier Harold Hochshild paying the enormous bill with good, convertible, hard currency
dollars.

As I passed by the Ministry of Foreign Affairs and headed once again
across the Moscow River, which curled through the city, I approached
the Hotel Ukraina. I wondered how my follower was doing, and I
glanced back. He was still there, but not looking quite as jaunty as
before. On the other side of the river I turned up the embankment and
set my sights for Moscow University, far in the distance. I had gotten
my second or third wind, and I kept up the slow but very steady pace. I
knew that the hill approaching the Moscow Film Studios would be a
trial. Up the hill we went, passing on the left the long line of mansions
that Khrushchev built for the top leaders of the Communist Party. After Khrushchev's demise, most of them found mansions elsewhere, but
Aleksei Kosygin kept his, living there until his death. After Kosygin's
demise, the road past the homes, known earlier as "Sparrow Highway,"
became "Kosygin Highway." I passed all these spots and headed for the
Chinese Embassy, located on "Friendship Street." The embassy was
being built when I had been a student at Moscow University twenty-
two years earlier, and the name of the street was supposed to represent
the state of relations between the USSR and China, which actually
turned sour before the embassy was completed.

My memory of these streets had dimmed a bit, and I got confused.
(Not "lost," just "a bit confused," as Daniel Boone would have said.)
So I wandered around among buildings that were new since the time I
had earlier strolled in this area. In order to find myself again I ran
toward the spire of Moscow University, now close by.

There are seven large skyscrapers in Moscow built in the Stalinist
style, of which the university is the largest. These buildings are unaes-
thetic pastiches of architectural styles, combining Greek columns and
capitals with Soviet heroic statues and pedestals. Towering over the
city, they can be seen from anywhere in it. At one time Stalin planned
to build the highest skyscraper in the world and intended to put it
on the spot where he had blown up the Cathedral of Christ the Redeemer, but, to the satisfaction of religious believers, the soil there
turned out to be soggy and unsuitable for the foundations of a skyscraper. Deprived of the chance to build the world's tallest building,
he built there the world's largest swimming pool and supplied it with
heated water all winter. As a student I used to swim there, surrounded
by billowing clouds of steam escaping into the below-zero Moscow air.

He built his seven skyscrapers elsewhere. They dominate Moscow even today, although none of them is very tall by Manhattan standards. In the recent post-Soviet period, modern competitors appeared.

During the many years I visited the Soviet Union and Russia, I noticed a change of attitude among Russian intellectuals toward these buildings. When I first visited the city, during the height of de-Stalinization, intellectuals often referred to the style of these buildings as "late Stalin imperial" and apologized to foreigners for the affront they made to their sensibilities. In later years, particularly after the fall of the Soviet Union and after many other newer and more attractive buildings had been erected in the city, the antipathy toward the Stalinist skyscrapers seemed to soften. Increasing numbers of people thought that they represented a period of Russian history that was very significant, and it was good to have a visible reminder of that period; it seemed appropriate that the reminder should not be too attractive. And some of the buildings, especially the university, have a certain grandeur, excessive to be sure, but sometimes striking in the foggy distance. As the city grew, the stamp which these old buildings placed upon it was not quite so hegemonic, and people began to point to them with interest the way Midwesterners in the U.S. were beginning to take pride in some of their gaudy nineteenth-century courthouses. In a word, the buildings were becoming camp.

As I passed the university and headed beyond, I looked back at my follower. We had now been running over three hours, and I calculated that we had covered more than fifteen miles. He was lagging behind. I took great joy in that fact, because my legs were beginning to ache. I hoped his legs ached more.

I picked up speed a little as I went toward the university subway stop. When I got to the other side of the subway stop I looked back again. My follower was nowhere to be seen. "Hallelujah!" I thought, "I have run him into the ground." I decided I would sprint down to the Lenin Hills subway stop, and if he still was not in sight, I would hop on the subway and make my way back home in that fashion. So I painfully cranked up the speed and headed down the street. This was the final test.

Arriving at the Lenin Hills stop, I stopped and waited, searching for a glimpse of my blue-suited follower. Nowhere was he to be seen. He must have abandoned the chase at the University subway stop, a mile or two back. I decided to get on the subway.

When I went jogging in Moscow I usually carried with me somewhere some sort of identification (usually my hotel card, which also gave me admission into the lobby in case I was challenged by the doorman, which was rather common in Soviet hotels) and five or ten kopecks for public transportation in case of need. I had done so on this day, but as I felt in my pocket for the money, it was gone. In the lining of the pocket was a small hole, and I realized that sometime during this long jaunt my money had fallen out. I thought of vaulting the subway turnstile in the fashion of a Manhattan teenager, but realized that in the well-attended Moscow subway I would probably be caught. Then I thought of jumping on a bus with an "honor system" pay box and cheating my way home. I had often seen Soviet citizens do the same thing. But I was not sure that I had in fact lost my tail. Maybe the KGB brought in a substitute, someone dressed differently. I did not want to give them the satisfaction of nailing me for cheating the Soviet transportation system. So there was nothing to do but to run home, another three or four miles.

It was a painful final leg. I had to keep running, not walking, because my wet clothing would have frozen if I did not generate enough body heat. The stretch down Lenin Prospect, an area I knew well, seemed three times longer than usual. I arrived back at the hotel still alive, but not a great deal more. I must have run about twenty miles. I felt miserable. Nonetheless, my inward satisfaction was insufferable. I had given my KGB rival a slow but excruciating and humbling treatment, refined by years of jogging around Fresh Pond in Cambridge.

My pride was greatly tempered the next morning when I found that I could barely get out of bed. My entire body was so stiff and sore that I could hardly walk. I made my way down the hallway to the breakfast buffet moving slowly like a wounded crab. The floor lady, who knew me well, expressed great concern and asked if I had fallen and hurt myself. I denied that there was any problem at all and eventually limped off to the library. I did not run again for a week.

CHAPTER EIGHTEEN

SPIES AND SCHOLARS

ANY AMERICAN who made repeated visits to the Soviet Union, as I did, knew that he or she would eventually run into the question of intelligence agents, on both sides. The issue in my case was somewhat simplified by the fact that in my research I never dealt with classified materials and never had classified clearance. It is true that when I was in the Navy, years earlier, I had possessed clearance, but upon entering the academic world I purposely let it lapse. On one or two occasions when, as a specialist on Soviet science, I have been asked to participate in projects that required clearance, I have declined. One of the many reasons that I enjoy being a college professor is that I can talk freely about everything that I study. I would not wish to be forced to have a compartmentalized mind.

Of course, this principle of the uncompartmentalized mind could not be kept pure. Some of my Soviet friends told me things about their personal lives and political opinions that I dared not reveal to other people, especially to other Soviet citizens. And every person, whatever the line of his or her work, knows that personal confidences must be kept. But my academic work has been entirely open, and I have enjoyed talking about it on the slightest provocation.

Studying the Soviet Union presented challenges, however, that scholars working on other topics rarely met. A month or two after my return to the United States from my first visit to the Soviet Union, now forty-four years ago, a man showed up at our apartment on the Upper West Side in New York City, displayed identification, and said that he was from the FBI. He wanted to know if I would talk to him about my recent trip to the USSR. Although I was much more innocent in those days than I am now, my first thought was one of suspicion of a Soviet role in all this. If the KGB wanted to find out more about me, one of the easiest and most informative ways would be for one of their agents to impersonate an FBI agent and come to interview me in the United States. By merely asking me to inform the FBI about the Soviet Union the KGB would learn much about me. Was I already an agent for the CIA? With what political ideas did I sympathize? How willing was I to cooperate with American intelligence agencies?

With these questions in mind, I told the man standing in front of my door that I wished to call the Manhattan office of the FBI and verify that he was who he said he was. The surprised agent assented, gave me his identification card, and waited while I made the call. The secretary who answered at the FBI office could not help me, but within a few minutes a man came on the phone who assured me that my visitor was from the New York office of the FBI.

I was not entirely happy about the situation, but I granted the interview. My main worry was that he would ask questions about my Soviet friends, seeking to find one who might be ripe for approach by American intelligence agencies. In my previous year in the Soviet Union I met many Russians who had confessed their unhappiness with the government under which they lived, but I did not want to be quizzed about these conversations by an FBI agent. I considered these conversations personal confidences.

To my relief, the questions which the FBI man asked me were very simple and very few. None of them gave me any trouble. When I was in the Soviet Union did I witness any military activity? (Only the May Day Parade, where there were rockets and troops on display, seen by the entire world.) Did I know the location of air defenses or other military installations? (No.) Had I heard any stories about the capabilities of the Soviet armed forces or their equipment? My answers to all these questions were inconsequential or simply "no," and upon hearing my replies, the agent left. He had been very courteous.

This visit occurred in 1961. Like most people in the United States in that pre-Vietnam period, I was rather trusting of American authorities. I did not see anything wrong with the visit. So long as his questions were of the nature of those he asked, I did not mind answering them.

As I reflected on the visit, however, one troubling thought did occur to me. I was then twenty-eight years old, looked forward to decades of study and teaching involving the Soviet Union, and planned to visit that country many times in connection with my work. If such an agent came to see me after every visit, the nature of my cooperation would almost surely change. One or two interviews by a local FBI agent seemed to be a citizenly duty. Many, on a regular and predictable basis, seemed more like a professional act. Would I become, in effect, an unpaid agent or informer reporting to American intelligence agencies on the Soviet Union? Did I want to acquire that status? In order to avoid this, the question of frequency of contact seemed to be crucial. I decided to watch the situation carefully.

In 1963 I accepted a teaching position at Indiana University in Bloomington, Indiana. From that time to the present I have been a faculty member at other universities, moving to Columbia University in 1965, to the Massachusetts Institute of Technology in 1978, and part-time to Harvard University in 1984. As I taught students and directed doctoral dissertations the question of contacts with government agencies changed in its nature. A number of my students were interested in government employment, especially after the dwindling of available academic positions in the late sixties. These students frequently applied for government jobs, sometimes with intelligence agencies, and listed references, often me.

The procedure by which government agencies check references is different from that of other employers. Instead of asking for the usual letter of reference, in which the respondent carefully lists the strengths and a few of the weaknesses of the candidate, the government agencies send interviewers around to the offices of the references. Soon they appeared at my door, asking to talk about particular students. Their questions were often uncomfortably pointed: Did I have any reason to doubt the political loyalty of this student? Had the student ever criticized the American government? Did he or she use alcohol or any drugs? Was he or she sexually promiscuous? Was he or she homosexual?

Even in the sixties—a time when most students had at one time or another tried marijuana, many were sexually active in a manner that would have been considered promiscuous by the standards of an earlier generation, and growing numbers were critical of the American government—I usually would have been able to answer all these questions negatively, for I did not have facts at my disposal to the contrary. My discomfort with these questions began to grow at a rather alarming rate, however. It seemed highly likely that one day I would be asked about a student about whom I could not answer these questions so confidently. In the heat of anti-Vietnam War demonstrations, Columbia students were known to jump up on chairs and shout "Down with the pigs!" I also knew some students who were homosexuals. If I revealed this information to one of the government interviewers I knew that government employment for that student would be impossible forever. Government dossiers, so far as I know, were not periodically cleansed on the basis of some sort of statute of limitations.

When I returned from the Soviet Union from a trip in 1966 I was again visited by an FBI agent. For the first time, he asked questions about one of my Soviet acquaintances. The person in question was the "Pineapple Man," Iurii Dimitrev. What did I know about him? According to the agent, Iurii was now in the West. His departure was news to me; I had heard nothing of him since 1961. I replied that I knew Dimitrev as a student at Moscow University, that he desperately wanted to study at an American university, and that I hoped he was getting the chance. Again, I thought that my information was innocent enough, but I feared that the agent would ask me about other of my Soviet friends. I dreaded the moment when the agent would ask me a question that I could not answer both honestly and innocently. The agent did not ask more questions, nor did he tell me any more about Dimitrev. I guessed, without knowing, that he had applied for a job with an American intelligence agency.

In the next few years I was again, from time to time, visited by agency officers who wanted references for particular American students who sought employment. Gradually, I became aware that the situation in the interviews was very unequal. I was certain, without actually knowing it, that they had small tape recorders in their pockets on which the entire interview was recorded. If I hesitated in one of my replies, they might suspect that I was concealing something. I was also confident that upon their return to their offices a transcript of the interviews was typed up. If a question about exactly what I had said should ever develop, they had a record, but I had none. I might maintain that they were mistaken, but I would have no evidence for my assertion, while they would have an official government document.

I considered refusing to meet with the interviewers. But I could hardly restrict my refusals to the FBI and the CIA; the questions asked by interviewers for the State Department, the Institute for Defense Analysis, the congressional committees, and even the Attorney General's office were just as pointed. If I refused to meet with them all, my students would be excluded from a wide range of government employment.

I was planning another trip to the Soviet Union in the spring of 1970. Furthermore, I knew that soon I would be visited again by agents seeking references on students. With much care and thought I worked out a plan for my relations with the agents with which I could ethically live. I was ready for the next visit.

The next episode occurred early in 1970, before my departure for the Soviet Union. I was spending that academic year at the Institute for Advanced Study in Princeton. I later thought it was ironic that the peak event in my relations with American intelligence agencies occurred upstairs from the old office of J. Robert Oppenheimer, the former director of the Institute.

My office was located on the second floor of Fuld Hall, the central building of the Institute, across from the elevator. Out my window I could look across an enormous expanse of carefully tended lawn, between two rows of trees, to the lovely eighteenth-century residence known as "Olden Manor," the home of the director of the Institute at that time, Carl Kaysen, my future colleague at MIT. As I was sitting at my typewriter two men approached my open door and announced that they were from the FBI. Would I mind talking to them?

Never before had I been approached by two agents at the same time. I never found out why there were two of them. Perhaps it had something to do with my forthcoming visit to the USSR. I asked for their identification, and called the local FBI office to confirm that they were who they said they were. I then asked what they wanted. They replied that they wanted to talk to me about one of my students.

I then launched into the speech that I had carefully prepared in my memory, trying to be as courteous and open as I could. I said that I realized that they were doing their duty. It is necessary, I continued, that our government agencies know that they are hiring reliable and capable people. I observed that I wrote dozens of letters of reference every year, and was prepared to do so for any employer in whom a student was interested.

However, I emphasized that I wished to deal with the government agencies on the same basis as I dealt with other prospective employers. That meant there should be a written record. They should write a letter to me requesting information on a certain student, stating what sort of information they desired and requesting a letter in return. I would then write a letter of reference. I would try to fulfill their requests for specific sorts of information, but if I decided that some questions were improper, such as sexual orientation, I would ignore them in my answering letter. I would do the same for any employer, I assured them.

After I had finished my little spiel, one of the agents asked, "You mean that you want us to put you down as a non-cooperator?" I was astounded. I replied that, to the contrary, I was quite ready to cooperate, but that I wanted a record of the cooperation for my own protection and for my students' protection. The agent responded that if I took that position he would have no choice but to put me down as a non-cooperator. I was certain that the term "non-cooperator" was a standard category in the FBI files and a pejorative one. I had a mental picture of the agent returning to his office, pulling out my dossier, checking off the block opposite "non-cooperator," and going about his other business. I specifically requested that I not be listed as a non-cooperator, since such a description would be false, and repeated my requirements for a letter of recommendation. The agents thanked me for my time and left the room.

I never received a letter from them requesting a letter of reference for the student. In fact, since that time, now over thirty years ago, to the best of my knowledge I have never been visited by an American intelligence agent for any purpose, nor have I received any letters from intelligence agencies requesting references. I visited the Soviet Union and Russia dozens of times during these years, but no longer was my trip followed by a caller from the government. I assumed that in the FBI files I was listed as a non-cooperator, and may still be, and that therefore I am no longer given requests or subjected to visits. The FBI was not willing to have written records of their activity.

I must also truthfully say that one or two of my students have, since that time, taken jobs with intelligence agencies, so I was wrong in assuming that the lack of a letter from me would prevent them from getting a job.

Whether there were any concrete results from the fact that the FBI had placed a black mark in my record is still unknown to me. I have never requested to see my FBI file under the Freedom of Information Act. I look upon that file like I do asbestos in a building: it is best left undisturbed. The FBI probably would not pay much attention to the file unless they had reason to do so, and my request to see it would be such a reason. I did notice that in the five years after I had spurned the FBI agents in my office in Princeton my income tax return was audited several times, something that had not happened before and has not happened since. But that experience with the Internal Revenue Service was only worrisome, not horrible, especially since in each case my wife and I either passed inspection or actually received additional refunds.

One of the strangest brushes I had with intelligence agents from

behind the Iron Curtain came in the 1960s. A student from Czechoslovakia, Karl Koecher, announced that he wanted to study the history
and philosophy of science with me. What I did not know when I first
met him was that he was a spy for Czech intelligence agencies working
closely with the KGB in Moscow. The secret plan was for Koecher to
come to the United States to study, to pretend that he wanted to defect
to the United States and thereby gain American citizenship, and subsequently to work his way into American intelligence agencies. His
secret ambition was to be a mole in the CIA. The fact that he eventually succeeded shows that the plan worked incredibly well.

Koecher first came, in 1965, to Indiana University in Bloomington,
Indiana, where I was at that time a young faculty member. To his surprise, on arrival he found that I was in New York as a visiting professor
at Columbia, where I later accepted a permanent position. Koecher
had chosen the wrong university. After I left, no one at Indiana University could advise him on his planned subject of study, the philosophy
of Soviet science. However, Koecher recovered by applying for a transfer to graduate school at Columbia, where I now was, and where I
taught courses on the history and philosophy of Soviet science.

Koecher and his supervisors in Czechoslovakia and the Soviet Union
had prepared the plan carefully. Koecher had a background in physics,
knew four languages, and was a bright scholar in his field. When he
showed up at my office at Columbia, where I met him for the first
time, he demonstrated knowledge of his intended subject of study and
even showed me several of his research papers. After looking at them I
said that as a philosopher of science, not a historian, he should study in
the philosophy department at Columbia, not the history department,
where I was a member of the faculty. This was an important point
since the major professor of a doctoral student has to be in the same
department as the student. In retrospect, I am sure that Koecher's papers were drawn up when he thought he would work with me at Indiana, where I was a member of the history and philosophy of science
department, and where I could have supervised his work. This bureaucratic detail saved me from being the major professor of one of the
most infamous spies in American postwar history. But I did meet regularly with Koecher and was a member of his dissertation committee. There was nothing in his work that would make one suspect he
was a spy.

After receiving his doctorate in 1970, Koecher took a job teaching
philosophy at Wagner College on Staten Island. Shortly thereafter he
came again to my office at Columbia, where he complained that Wag-

ner College was not a distinguished enough institution to warrant his attention, but added that "it would do for now." He then invited me and my wife to dinner at his apartment in mid-town Manhattan, where I noticed what should have been my first warning that Koecher was not a poor beginning professor. He and his wife Hana lived remarkably well, in a fairly expensive condominium that was nicely furnished. Koecher explained his comfortable status to us by pointing out that his wife Hana worked "in the diamond trade" on West 47th Street in Manhattan. His explanation was correct as far as it went; Hana did indeed have a good job with a diamond company and was paid well. What he did not tell us was that this position gave her the opportunity to travel frequently to Europe, where she could pass on to agents there the intelligence information gathered by her husband. Diamonds were also very suitable means of making illegal payments to informants, since they are difficult to trace and easy to hide.

Karl Koecher became a naturalized citizen of the United States in 1970, as his wife Hana did the following year. Now Koecher felt free to seek employment elsewhere; he had become an established academic by teaching and publishing, and he had acquired American citizenship. He applied to the CIA for a position, and, incredibly, was accepted, easily passing the lie detector test that the CIA required of all new employees. After his arrest twelve years later Koecher confessed that he had received training in Czechoslovakia on how to pass lie detector tests.

After being offered a position at the CIA Koecher came to see me for the last time, and we had a conversation that, in retrospect, was ludicrous. Koecher said he was considering taking a position at the CIA and wondered if I would advise him on the wisdom of leaving his academic job for a career in intelligence. I advised him against accepting a position in the CIA, saying that for an American academic such employment could be a fateful step. Even if he later decided to leave the CIA and enter the academic world again he might have trouble finding a good position. I told him that many American academics were critical of the CIA and might suspect that he had not severed all ties with it. I said that he was making an important choice: Would he enter the intelligence world with all its restrictions on free academic inquiry, or would he remain an academic operating outside these restrictions? For myself, I said, I vastly preferred the free academic life.

Koecher must have been inwardly laughing at this moment, since the CIA was the whole reason he had been sent to America. He probably came to me with his deceptive question not because he wanted advice on CIA employment but because he wanted to know more about me. His Moscow supervisors knew that I traveled frequently to the Soviet Union and they wanted to know if I had any intelligence ties. If my answer to Koecher revealed sympathies on my part with the CIA, this was something his friends in Moscow wanted to know. I am sure that he filed an intelligence report on my conversation with him. Evidently he and his colleagues in espionage decided that I was a totally uninteresting academic.

Koecher went on to a sensational, bizarre, and cruel career. At the CIA he learned the name of one of the CIA's major agents in Moscow, a Russian citizen, and revealed that name to the KGB. The Russian, Aleksandr Ogorodnik, committed suicide when Soviet police came to arrest him. Koecher himself was eventually arrested by the FBI, on November 27, 1984, an event that quickly became first page news in the United States. Koecher was not interested in a heroic suicide, but instead tried to escape imprisonment by offering to become a "double agent," to work simultaneously for the FBI and the KGB. When that plan failed, he began from prison to agitate for a "spy exchange" that would let him return to Eastern Europe. He succeeded, and on February 11, 1985, he and his wife were exchanged at the famous Potsdam bridge between West and East Berlin for the well-known Soviet dissident Anatoly Sharansky, who went on to become a prominent political figure in Israel. Koecher obviously had excellent contacts with top government officials in the Soviet Union.

I never again saw Koecher, but in the fall of 2000 I thought about contacting him once again. I envisioned him as a retired spy living comfortably in Prague and willing to talk about the old days. After all, the Cold War had ended almost ten years earlier, and I thought it might be interesting to meet Koecher all these years later and ask him some questions about his decision to study with me, first, at Indiana, and subsequently, at Columbia. Had his superiors in Prague and Moscow really decided that this young professor Loren Graham (at that time I was thirty-two years old and had not yet published a single book) was the right person for him to work with? Why did they single me out?

I went on the Internet to try to find Koecher's current address or location. What I found gave me such a cold chill that I canceled my plans to meet with him again. I saw clearly that the man is a complete scoundrel in ways that have nothing to do with old Cold War passions.

According to Western press reports, in 1999 Koecher was part of a conspiracy to defraud Mohammed Al Fayed, the owner of the London department store Harrods and the father of Princess Diana's lover, Dodi Fayed. Koecher and his associates allegedly offered the senior Fayed, in return for payment of $15 million, CIA documents (later shown to be forged) stating that his son and Princess Diana did not die accidentally in the terrible auto accident in Paris on August 31, 1997, but instead were intentionally killed by agents working at the request of British intelligence and sanctioned by Buckingham Palace.

An important question was where the exchange of the forged documents and financial payment was to take place. Koecher and his associates favored Prague (Koecher's home), but Fayed and his assistants favored a city in Western Europe. A compromise was struck on Vienna. On April 22, 1999, two of the alleged conspirators, an Austrian-born American named Oswald Le Winter, and Karl Koecher, booked rooms in a hotel in the city. However, Fayed and his men informed American authorities of the proposed exchange, and an elaborate sting operation was set up with the aim of arresting the conspirators. Le Winter was indeed arrested, and put in jail in Austria, but the wily Koecher escaped back to the Czech Republic. May he rest with his conscience.

———

It was inevitable that my trips to the Soviet Union would also attract the attention of Soviet intelligence agencies, but, except for the sporadic episodes of being followed, which I have described in an earlier section, I was long unaware of any activity from their side. I was sure that they knew about me and that somewhere in the offices of the KGB resided a file with my name on it, steadily growing as I made repeated trips to that country. I wondered how well they did their job; did they add clippings to the file with the Soviet reviews of my scholarly works that were appearing in journals? In those reviews I was sometimes called a "bourgeois scholar" connected with that "nest of anti-Soviet activity," the Russian Institute at Columbia University, and, later, the Russian Research Center at Harvard University. The fact that I had written a book that described, among other things, a violent purge of the Soviet Academy of Sciences did not endear me to Soviet reviewers. Soviet suspicions of me probably grew when I was featured on the NOVA television program participating in seminars with dissidents and refuseniks who were in trouble with the Soviet government.

In the 1960s, like many other young academics, I became active in the anti-Vietnam war movement. I was never a radical, but I participated in a number of demonstrations, including several "marches on

Washington." My suspicion about the legitimacy of the American effort in Southeast Asia had been awakened by the newspaper accounts of the Gulf of Tonkin incident, which, as a former Navy officer, seemed unconvincing to me. Both my wife Pat and I were caught up in the civil rights and peace efforts of the sixties. In 1964, while Pat was participating in the pro-integration "March on Selma," I took part in a demonstration against the Vietnam War at Indiana University, where I was a beginning teacher. The *Indianapolis Star* printed a letter from an irate citizen demanding to know how much of his state taxes went to pay the salaries of outside agitators like Loren Graham. I would like to have informed him that, rather than being an "outside agitator," I was born and raised in southern Indiana, a short distance from the university in which I was teaching, and that I was a fifth-generation Hoosier, a descendant of middle-west pioneer farmers.

One way or another, the news of some of my political activities got back to Moscow. Perhaps it was a letter of mine in the *New York Times* in 1969 protesting the massacre of Vietnamese villagers at My Lai by American soldiers. At any rate, on a trip to the Soviet Union in 1970 I suddenly became aware that I was being treated a little differently than before. When Pat and I and our daughter Meg made a trip to Leningrad under Soviet Academy of Sciences sponsorship, instead of being assigned the usual third-class type of accommodation to which we were accustomed, we found ourselves in the finest hotel in Leningrad, the Astoria, with a large room, private bath, and a balcony with a view of St. Isaac's cathedral. As I took a photograph of Pat and Meg standing on the balcony I remarked that this luxury could not be an accident and said that I did not much care for the implications of it.

After we returned to Moscow I received a telephone call from a man who said that he had heard about my research on Soviet history in the 1920s and 1930s, and that he would "like to talk to me about it." I was immediately suspicious. My research at that time was not on Soviet history in the twenties and thirties, but, instead, on Soviet philosophy of science in the post–World War II period. Nonetheless, it was true that I had earlier written a book on Soviet science in the twenties and thirties, and therefore, the telephone call was possibly legitimate. The man said he was knowledgeable about Soviet history and would come to my hotel the following day in order to talk to me about topics of mutual interest. He said he would meet me at the hotel entrance at a certain time.

At the appointed time a black Volga automobile pulled up to the hotel entrance with not one man in it, but two. My suspicions were

now growing rapidly; I knew that Volgas were usually owned by government officials, not private individuals. The two men got out of the
car, introduced themselves as "library employees," and said they were
greatly interested in Soviet history. They proposed that we go to a restaurant and talk about history. I got in the car and we sped off on a long
trip to a restaurant outside Moscow, close to a former nobleman's mansion, an estate that was now, it seemed, a park. (I later learned that the
estate had become a "rest home" for the KGB.) Over lunch we talked
about Soviet history, and it soon became clear that I knew immensely
more about it than they did.

Finally, the peak moment of the conversation came. One of the men
reached into his brief case, pulled out a light brown book which he
described as "very important" in Soviet history, but not available to
scholars. The men said they would be happy to give the book to me if I
would agree to continue to have conversations with them on later occasions. I immediately recognized this offer as the first seemingly innocent piece of bait described in spy novels. I knew that I would not take
or even touch the book because my imagination had already provided
the walls of the restaurant with a camera that would record the moment of transfer of the book to me. The photo could be used as "proof"
that Loren Graham and Soviet agents were transferring information to
each other. And the first "gift" would inevitably be followed by others,
of an increasingly incriminating nature, until I was hopelessly involved
with the KGB. As I looked down at the book with concern and even
a flicker of fear, I immediately recognized it, and was overwhelmed
with a sense of amusement. What ham-handed agents! The book was
the official Soviet transcript of the trial of Nikolai Bukharin in March
1938. Totally unavailable to the public in the Soviet Union, and kept
in secret collections of Soviet libraries, the book could be found on the
open shelves of a number of good research libraries in the United
States, including my own at Columbia University. I had even once put
the book on the reserve-reading list for one of my graduate seminars
in which all the students were readers of Russian. The book detailed
preposterous charges against Bukharin, such as his involvement in
the murder of the writer Maxim Gorky and the attempted murder of
Lenin.

I told them that I did not want the book and that I wanted to return
to my hotel. They protested that our conversation was "only beginning." I said I had an appointment back at the hotel with an American
colleague and that I needed to leave immediately. They replied that
they had not finished their food yet (nor had I, but I ate not another

bite) and that I could not get back to the city without their car, which stood outside the restaurant. And they continued to eat and talk, obviously not concerned in the slightest by my "appointment" back at the hotel. Perhaps they had correctly guessed that there was no such appointment. I became alarmed at a rapid rate. I was now being held unwillingly. Would they soon turn from polite invitations to "cooperate" to threatening attempts to blackmail me? I had visited the Soviet Union many times, and they probably had numerous photographs of me in different situations. Somewhere among them had these agents already chosen one as evidence, false to me but persuasive to others, that I had done something condemnatory, or was already in league with the Soviet secret police? I remembered all those vodka bottles in my Metropole hotel room in 1966 and the rather disorderly parties among them, and also thought back to my days as a student at Moscow University, wondering what could be used against me. As they continued to eat and talk, innocently for the moment, I became convinced that I had to get out of this situation as fast as I could. I recalled my old friend and fellow historian Tom Riha who disappeared forever after, some people said, getting involved with and then spurning the Soviet secret police.

I stood up, excusing myself, announced that I needed to go to the mens' room, and walked toward it at the back of the restaurant. I did not know if there was an avenue of escape there or not, but I was going to try. I opened the white door marked with the usual small black figure of a male, and found myself in a narrow corridor leading back to the actual men's room. Glory be, halfway down the corridor was an open window! (It was summertime.) I was on the ground floor, and it was simple to jump out of the window into a small courtyard. I straightened up and ran for the opening to the street, hoping I would see a taxi. I did not, but the street was full of traffic heading toward Moscow, and I held up my hand with several large-denomination ruble notes in it, knowing that many private drivers worked on the side as gypsy taxi drivers. The second or third car stopped, I jumped in, and gave the name of my hotel, the Academy of Sciences Hotel on October Square. We were off immediately, and as we sped by the parking lot in front of the restaurant I looked back at the Volga in which I had come with the two suspicious characters and noted the license plate. I then glanced at my watch and saw that not enough time had yet elapsed for my hosts in the restaurant to become concerned. I took satisfaction in the fact that they were stuck with the bill.

The next day when I met with my old Russian friend Vitalii I told him the story. I remembered his saying earlier that the KGB, despite their supposedly secret activities, often traveled around in cars with license prefixes that were known to many Moscow residents. When I told him the license prefix of the Volga, he laughed, clapped me on the shoulder, and told me what I already knew—that I had just had a brush with Soviet intelligence. Soon thereafter I left the Soviet Union.

I did not inform any American authorities about this episode with Soviet intelligence agents, although I realized that an argument in favor of such an action could be made. American intelligence personnel at the American Embassy in Moscow, for example, would have been very interested in the identities and behavior of Soviet agents trying to enlist American students and professors. However, I was certain that if I informed the American agencies of how I had rebuffed the KGB they would say to me, in effect, "Good work! Now cooperate with us by providing more information." They would have quizzed me very closely, involving me more intimately with them than I wished to be; although I was firmly on the American side in the Cold War contest between the United States and the Soviet Union, I did not trust the intelligence agencies on either side. I wanted to be a simple professor, not a person involved in ambiguous relationships with intelligence agencies, so I stayed clear of all contacts, from whatever country. At the same time I realized that such behavior was also open to criticism. During the Cold War, there was simply no correct path of behavior for people in the field of Russian Studies, only better and worse ones.

The next time I applied to go to the Soviet Union, in 1973, my visa application was turned down. Such a rejection had never happened to me before, and I was curious to learn why. I called the Soviet Embassy in Washington, which handled all visa applications from Americans, and requested an explanation. The man at the other end asked me to wait for what seemed forever and then finally came back to the phone and said "Professor Graham, all I can tell you is that you are not welcome in our country." I knew that my rejection of the advances of the KGB was the reason.

I remained *persona non grata* for the next few years. Several times I applied for admission to the Soviet Union in the mid-1970s and was turned down. In 1976 I was invited by the National Academy of Sciences in Washington, D.C., to participate in a delegation on "science policy" that was a part of official science exchanges between the USSR and the U.S. I was interested in the topic, so I agreed to participate, along with five or six other Americans. Most of them were distinguished natural scientists who were familiar with Soviet research in their areas. The National Academy of Sciences applied for our visas as a group, sending the requests off to the Soviet embassy in Washington. All the participants were granted visas except me. Again, I was rejected as "not welcome in the Soviet Union." To my surprise, delight, and gratitude, the other members of the delegation told the National Academy of Sciences to inform the Soviet Embassy that if Professor Graham was not permitted to go to the Soviet Union on this science exchange, all the rest of them would withdraw. The exchange would be canceled. In face of this threat to science exchanges that the Soviet government valued, the Soviet officials relented, and I was permitted to be a part of the American delegation to Moscow. I had broken the spell cast by my refusal to cooperate with KGB officers, and from that time until the collapse of the Soviet Union fourteen years later all my requests for visas to visit the country were granted.

Now, long after the collapse of the Soviet Union and the end of the Cold War, I sometimes reflect on my relationships with intelligence agents, east and west. The fact that I refused to cooperate both with the KGB and with the FBI/CIA during the long years I visited the Soviet Union still seems right to me, but I realize that there are some very complex issues here which I have not fully explored. An even-handed refusal to work with intelligence agents on both sides seems to imply the attribution by me of a certain equivalence between the Soviet Union and the United States. But I do not, and never did, accept such equivalence between the authoritarian Soviet Union and the democratic United States. For all the flaws of the American system, including the horrors of the McCarthy period at the height of the Cold War, it provided an inestimably more humane treatment of its citizens than did the Soviet Union. It is significant to notice that although I severed relationships with the FBI, and was (I assume) listed by it as a "noncooperator," to the best of my knowledge my academic career did not suffer because of my behavior, despite the somewhat suspicious income tax audits. Indeed, I was able to continue my teaching and research, including trips to the Soviet Union, without hindrance. An academic in the Soviet Union who similarly stayed aloof from the KGB would have suffered much more severe consequences. We now know that every Soviet exchange participant who came to the United States in these years had to pass a security check before departure (an examination of his or her "*kharakteristika*") and was required to file a report with the KGB on return. In addition, a record of non-compliance with security organs could severely affect a Soviet academician's career, perhaps even end it.

My reflections on this history also causes me to admit that if I had been an active academic during the height of Hitler's fascism my attitude might have been different. I can conceive of myself working against fascism in any way that I could, including cooperating with American intelligence agents. Yet the similarities between Hitler's Germany and Stalin's Soviet Union in terms of numbers of victims and treatment of citizens are rather numerous. So why, then, should I not cooperate with the FBI and the CIA when they asked me to do so, seeing such cooperation both as my patriotic duty and an ethical act?

Even today I do not have a fully satisfying answer to this question, but I think it would start with recognition of the fact that I was supposed to be an academic specialist on the Soviet Union, not an intelligence agent. I still believe that I could not have fulfilled both roles simultaneously without compromising both. But I still worry about this conclusion. Would I have felt the same way if I had been an American academic specialist on Hitler's Germany? If all academic specialists had protested and taken action soon after Hitler appeared and made his intentions clear could such horrors as the Holocaust have been prevented? At base there is a conflict here between the goals of the pursuit of knowledge and the goals of the pursuit of politics. We academics like to say that the pursuit of knowledge is more important, but if we reflect sufficiently deeply we will realize that we only have the ability to pursue knowledge if we are in a political setting that permits it. Securing that political base may, in extremis, take priority.

The tension between academic freedom and the need to defend national security in the political setting of the 1960s affected not just me but everyone in my field of study. The enormous expansion of Russian Studies after the Second World War was largely driven by the exigencies of the Cold War. Simply stated, the U.S. government followed the precept of "know thy enemy" by contributing funding and support to programs in and centers for Russian studies that supplemented primary funding from foundations. The first two such centers were at Columbia and Harvard Universities, where I studied and taught.

But this growth initially took place in the McCarthy era when contacts with Russians for whatever reason were, in the eyes of many, grounds for suspicion. Despite the enthusiastic support of the U.S. government, some people on the political right were opposed to the new centers.

Though excellent work was being done in Russian studies in the face of such difficulties, the impact of the Cold War on the field created additional problems, particularly when academic freedom seemed to conflict with the imperatives of the struggle against the Soviet Union. This quickly gave rise to a very difficult situation, one that involved me personally.

In 1957 the governments of the United States and the Soviet Union signed an academic exchange agreement, the Lacy-Zaroubin Agreement, which for the first time in several decades permitted students and young faculty from each of the countries to study in the other. Unfortunately American universities were forced to deal with a Soviet bureaucracy that insisted on a centralized exchange, with tit-for-tat reciprocity in numbers of scholars involved. In order to meet the Soviet requirement, a centralized organization was formed in the United States, a joint university committee which was a non-governmental organization, but which worked closely with the U.S. State Department in administering the exchange. About 15 percent of the money to run the exchanges, in the early years, came from the U.S. government; the rest came from the individual universities and the Ford Foundation.

Given the political climate, the inevitable question became whether American scholars should be chosen entirely on the basis of their scholarly qualifications, or should their political loyalty and private behavior also be considered? Would homosexuals or scholars of "loose morals" be subject to blackmail by the Soviet authorities, and coerced into cooperating with the KGB? Were not the exchanges, therefore, a concern from the standpoint of American national security?

The American university committee decided that a purely academic committee, one that would not be concerned with security matters, should make the selection of candidates for the exchanges. The names of candidates (and spouses, when they planned to accompany a husband or wife) were then sent to the State Department, where a check of all the names on the list was made against the classified files of the FBI and other governmental agencies. If "derogatory" information on any candidate or spouse was found in the security files, that name was then "flagged." Then a senior scholar in the field of Russian Studies with appropriate security clearance, or several such scholars, would be invited to come to Washington to inspect the file. These files contained information on the political, sexual, and other activities of the candidates and their spouses collected by governmental agencies. After viewing this classified material in Washington the invited professors then made a recommendation to the American committee in charge of the exchange either to accept or reject the candidate. This recommendation was usually accepted.

This procedure directly contradicted frequent statements by those academics administering the exchange program that the U.S. government did not influence the selection procedure. It also effectively put professors in the position of being security agents determining whether or not a candidate posed a "risk." Those academics reviewing classified files had to agree not to make public either the information in them or the ways in which it was collected, which effectively made any subsequent protest against the system impossible. And when it inevitably became known that a few members of the academic community had access to such classified personal information great resentment from other members naturally arose. It also should be noted that during the first ten years of the exchange the applicants were never told that they were being submitted to a security check. But gradually, after some people were rejected on political grounds, academics became aware of what was going on. I believed then, and I still believe, that it was a dangerous precedent, one that raised the same issues that arose from the concurrent imposition of loyalty oaths in many American universities.

The first indication I had that candidates were being subjected to this vetting process was the initial rejection of Leonard Kirsch because these files included information on his and his father's association with "radical causes" in the U.S. labor movement. In this case, however, the dispute had a happy ending because Lennie's professors at Harvard strongly defended him and managed to get him accepted for the exchange program despite the security objections to his candidacy.

Other problems arose in the program's first ten years when some of those administering it came to Moscow to check up on candidates, usually about midway in the academic year. They asked questions not only about the conduct and academic progress of students but also inquired into their sexual and political proclivities. In some cases, Americans were ordered on the spot to return immediately to the United States, usually within forty-eight hours. Such orders were sometimes given on the authority of one person alone, the visiting inspector. In one case known to me the reason for such an order was the fact that the inspector had been told (by whom I do not know) that an unmarried American male exchange student was sleeping with an unmarried American female exchange student. Imagine what could have happened to my friend Lennie, who slept with every available Russian girl and then fell in love with one and married her.

When in February 1961 I was quizzed in Moscow by the American inspector—a former CIA officer—about whether I knew any American colleagues who were sleeping around, I made a quick decision to lie, and said that I did not. I justified the lie by telling myself, "Well, I didn't actually see Lennie in bed with a Russian girl."

Fortunately very few American exchange students were barred from the exchange program or stopped from participating in it or expelled from the USSR or Eastern Europe because of security considerations. From the beginning of the exchanges in 1958 until the debates began in late 1967, 13 out of 580 candidates initially chosen were "flagged" because of the security files, and five of these were not permitted to participate. Also, in the same period nine of the exchangees studying in the USSR or Eastern Europe were expelled by the American authorities after having arrived at their places of study (another six were expelled by the Soviet authorities).

During the early sixties I frequently heard complaints about the system, and the demoralizing impression gradually grew in the field of Russian Studies that the university committee administering the exchanges was heavy-handed, inquisitorial, and security-obsessed. The impression was not lessened by the fact that the head of the committee for many years was a professor, Robert Byrnes, the former CIA officer who quizzed me in Moscow, who was known for the rigidity of his moral views and who defended publicly the position that the committee should not nominate anyone who was clearly promiscuous. He favored eliminating candidates who were either homosexual or "overtly heterosexual."

The conflict that broke out in my field of studies should be seen in the context of what was happening in America during the 1960s when society became more permissive, universities abandoned their role of *in loco parentis*, and protests against the Vietnam War led to an erosion of trust in our government. Many Americans were alarmed by these changes and resisted them for moral and political reasons. The field of Russian Studies was not sheltered from the turbulence of this *kulturkampf*.

Things came to a head in 1967 and 1968 when the American governing body for the exchange program realized that not only were the number of applicants declining (some thought it was due to the hardships of studying in the Soviet Union; others believed that being under the surveillance of both the U.S. and the USSR had a chilling effect on potential candidates) but the selection process was also seen as part of the problem by many people in the field. From 1967 until mid-1968 the discussion of the selection process grew increasingly contentious. I took the position, one some branded as radical, that members of the academic community should stop participating in this security vetting process. (Indeed, Russian Studies had made a radical departure from the accepted process, one still followed in every other academic area, of evaluating candidates for fellowships and grants according to strictly scholarly criteria.) This involvement in security considerations, I believed, was a threat to academic freedom.

Not until April 1968, when the decision-making advisory council for the academic exchange met in Seattle, Washington, was an attempt made to deal with the core issue. Changes were made to the old system—important ones and it was agreed that we should not use government security files in the selection process. Moreover no exchange participant should be either recalled from the Soviet Union or dropped from sponsorship for reasons other than "academic performance, mental or physical health, involvement in intelligence, or deception of the exchange authorities." But then the inevitable "catch" came: a special "committee of uncles" (officially called the Board of Review) with the necessary classified clearance would be appointed. It would be headed by a chairman who was a scientist not in the field of Slavic studies and two members from the Slavic field. As the 1968 report stated:

> The chairman reviews the files of nominees to which the government has raised objections, and discusses the principles involved with his fellow committee members without disclosing the identities of the nominees . . . The recommendations of this Review Board would be binding.

Thus, the Slavic field had distanced itself somewhat from security checks, but it still took ultimate responsibility for them. At the meeting I continued to object to this compromise and called for a complete separation of the two functions.

More than thirty years have passed since this dispute raged, emotions have long since cooled, and most of my younger colleagues are totally unaware that the controversy ever occurred. And although I still believe that the position I took was correct, even I feel less strongly about it now than I did at the time.

At the heart of the debate is a very serious question, so difficult that there may not be a completely satisfactory solution to it. My hubris may have been that I thought I could solve it. How does a free and democratic country conduct academic exchanges with an authoritarian one that does not follow the same rules? Without question, the Soviet secret police could have used compromising information on an American exchange student in order to attempt to blackmail and coerce him or her to work for them. But is it the responsibility of

American academics—instead of the U.S. government—to try to guard against this possibility? Only the government has competence in and proper responsibility for dealing with such security concerns. But my opponents maintained that if the government took over the security function entirely, the result would be much worse than if the academics performed it, and that many more scholars would be stopped from traveling abroad, those the government decided to stop on its own.

Is this the argument that forces a compromise? Now that I am older and possibly wiser, I understand better than I did in 1968 how government programs cannot ever be entirely separated from political issues, and I am wavering on whether my proposals were realistic.

While I am no longer absolutely certain what was the right thing to do in 1968, I still draw two lessons from this experience: first, it is crucial that we maintain private institutions and private academic programs, as distinguished from governmental ones, because only private organizations have a chance to resist governmental pressure when the political situation becomes polarized. The criticism of my position that I never managed to overcome was that this exchange was governmentally sponsored and subsidized by the government, and therefore this program had to answer to governmental rules. (There was no question of colleagues in the Soviet Union doing anything other than what the government ordered them to do, much less protesting such orders.) The second lesson I draw is the damaging effects of classified materials when they are introduced into the academic world. Once scholars accept classified information they give up a bit of freedom, for they cannot discuss openly (or properly cite the source of) what they know. And the government has a hammer over the head of the scholar who accepts clearance; that scholar can always be threatened by withdrawal of clearance by the government, if the government disapproves of what he/she is doing. The lifting of clearance is usually interpreted as disgrace and punishment, as it was in the case of J. Robert Oppenheimer.

We are fortunate today to be spared, usually, such difficult issues dealing with academic freedom and national security. The end of the Cold War has brought a healthier atmosphere to our academic institutions. I doubt, however, that these fractious issues are gone forever. Indeed, I suspect that they are present today in Middle Eastern Studies, as the government tries to combat terrorism. Intelligence agencies still understandably wish to take advantage of scholarly knowledge and research but to borrow again from my colleagues in anthropology, how does one draw a line between being an observer and acting as a participant?

PART V

FROM THE USSR TO POST-COMMUNIST RUSSIA

CHAPTER NINETEEN

A MAN OF FERVOR

ALEKSANDR NIKOLAEVICH YAKOVLEV has frequently been described as "the architect of *perestroika* and *glasnost*" (see "Biographical Notes" at the end of this book). During the last few years of the existence of the Soviet Union he was a member of the ruling Politburo and was Gorbachev's most influential advisor. His ideas were fundamental to the dismantling of the Soviet police state.

History will always be kind to Yakovlev for the role he played. But as someone who knew him for forty-seven years, I see many ironies in his life. Neither the Yakovlev I knew before he became Gorbachev's advisor nor the Yakovlev I continued to know after he left that position would have been capable of guiding Gorbachev during *perestroika*. Both the early and the later Yakovlev rejected the goals of *perestroika* and the ideas on which it was founded. Yet Yakovlev was rightly proud of what he did, unintentional though his greatest achievement was. He and Gorbachev brilliantly coincided in their mistaken views for one brief moment in a way that changed history.

A key to Yakovlev's paradoxical greatness can be seen, in my opinion, in an encounter I had with him in Butler Library at Columbia University in the spring of 1959. In the months preceding this meeting Yakovlev and I, as fellow students at Columbia, had become friends, despite our different political views. Contacts between Soviet citizens and American ones were very rare at that time, and when he arrived in New York on a new student exchange program, we sought each other out. Together we scoured upper Broadway for cheap meals and met for long conversations about the state of the world. We were able to talk and disagree without having arguments. We were curious about each other. Eventually I invited him to dinner at our exceedingly modest student apartment at 105th Street and Broadway, where he enjoyed playing with our two-year old daughter Meg. He was also enthusiastic about the tuna fish casserole with potato chips that Pat prepared for him.

By the time I saw Yakovlev emerging excitedly from the stacks of Butler Library in early 1959, I already knew him fairly well. He was doing research on his dissertation on Franklin D. Roosevelt and the New Deal. On seeing me at the entrance to the stacks he exclaimed, "Loren, I've been reading FDR's right-wing critics. They all said that Roosevelt was a traitor to his class, that he was destroying capitalism in America. But it's obvious to me that Roosevelt was not destroying capitalism at all. He was saving capitalism when it was on its knees."

The idea that Roosevelt's election made a crucial difference in American history was contrary to what Yakovlev had been taught back in the Soviet Union: that the Republicans and Democrats were indistinguishable servants of capitalism. But most of all, the example of Roosevelt suggested an intriguing possibility: a reformer was not necessarily a traitor.

In the late eighties Yakovlev and Gorbachev emerged as the reformers of communism, and they were accused by the old-line supporters of the Soviet system of being traitors to the cause, just as Roosevelt had been accused of betraying capitalism. A former head of the KGB, Vladimir Kryuchkov, even explained Yakovlev's behavior during *perestroika* as a result of his being a spy for the United States, a relationship that Kryuchkov said began many years earlier, when Yakovlev was a student at Columbia.

I met Yakovlev a number of times in the years after he was at Columbia, once in New York at the height of *perestroika*. In our conversation at that time I reminded him of our conversation years earlier at Columbia, and asked if he and Gorbachev were trying to save communism the way that Roosevelt saved capitalism, by softening its most harsh features, and I inquired if his knowledge of Roosevelt's policies helped him as Gorbachev's advisor. He smiled, and said, "Yes, you are right." But Roosevelt succeeded in his salvage effort while Yakovlev and Gorbachev failed in theirs. In their attempt to save Soviet communism by humanizing and softening it the whole system spun out of control and collapsed. American capitalism proved capable of reform, and Soviet communism did not, a realization that propelled Yakovlev

further along in the tortured ideological journey on which he contin-
ues to this day.

Yakovlev is a man of fervor, and during his life that fervor has been
expressed in contrasting directions. He was still an ardent defender of
Soviet Communism when we first talked in 1958, as he was for many
years after. Much earlier, as an eighteen-year-old marine, he had been
thrown into some of the most vicious fighting of World War II, on the
front near Leningrad. He told me that when he and his comrades
charged the German lines they shouted at the tops of their voices, "*Za
Stalina!*" ("For Stalin!"). He added, "We were true believers in the
cause."

The marine unit in which Yakovlev served in World War II was a
special one that was supposed to embolden the regular Soviet army
troops with its bravery and ferociousness. Known informally as "The
Black Devils," they usually drank 200 grams of vodka before throwing
themselves against the enemy. German troops later recalled that when
these Soviet marines charged, shouting epithets as they overran the
German lines, they were an overwhelming force of nature stoppable
only by an unending hail of bullets. When these marines ran toward
them the German gunners were forced to calculate whether they
would be able to cut all the Russians down in time, or whether they
should turn and run before they were shot or bayoneted at their posts.
Eventually, in 1943, a German machine-gunner found the courage to
stay at his weapon as Yakovlev and his Russian comrades charged.
Yakovlev was hit repeatedly, and, severely wounded, fell helplessly to
the ground. Five of his Russian comrades tried to pull him back to the
safety of the Russian line; in the process of retrieving him, four of the
five were killed. Yakovlev spent most of a year in a Soviet hospital
recuperating, and he was left with a severe limp the rest of his life.
When he and I later walked together down Broadway I had to slow to
his halting and erratic pace.

For the intensely patriotic Yakovlev the first element of doubt about
the righteousness of the Soviet cause entered his head when he saw
what happened to repatriated Soviet prisoners at the end of World War
II. Stalin feared that Russians who had been in German hands might
have been enlisted as spies, so he ordered that all repatriated prisoners
be sent to labor camps in Siberia. "A true Soviet soldier," Stalin said,
"is never taken prisoner by the enemy." For all his reverence of Stalin,
Yakovlev knew that if four of his marine comrades had not sacrificed
their lives to bring him back to the Russian lines, he would have been

taken prisoner by the Germans and would ultimately have ended up in a Siberian labor camp. At the end of the war Yakovlev watched trains filled with Russians who had just been released from German prisoner-of-war camps being transported under guard to Siberia, and he was deeply ashamed of his country. But his faith was only shaken, not destroyed; he went on to a distinguished career serving his country and the Communist cause. He soon won a position working in the central apparatus of the Party in Moscow.

The next traumatic event for Yakovlev's communist faith occurred in 1956, when he was present, as an invited junior political functionary, at the session of the Central Committee of the Communist Party at which Nikita Khrushchev denounced Stalin's crimes, the famous "Secret Speech." This speech was a sensation in its day, but now it seems guarded and rather tame. Yes, Khrushchev divulged some of the truth about bloody purges and torture, but the crimes he described were primarily those of Stalin against the Party itself, not against the Russian nation as a whole. Khrushchev did not discuss the millions of victims of collectivization and famine, results of Stalin's policies, policies he had helped to implement. Nonetheless, the speech was a revelation to its pre-selected audience of Party faithful.

Yakovlev later described the event:

> We were shocked. There was a deadly silence in the hall, people did not look at each other. I remember that I sat in the balcony, and when we descended from the balcony I heard only one word, uttered by one person after another, "Yes . . . " You heard only this "yes . . . " No other conversations occurred, people left, hanging their heads. They could not find a place in their minds for everything they had heard. It was very hard, very painful—especially for those of us who were not infected with cynicism, who did not know the truth.

But once again Yakovlev recovered his communist composure. When I first met him in New York it was two years after this event, but he displayed no doubts about the Soviet cause; on the contrary, he defended it uncompromisingly in our conversations. In retrospect, if I look for any sign that the Yakovlev of 1958 might have had important political thoughts that he did not express, the only evidence for it was that he obviously enjoyed talking with me even though we disagreed politically most of the time. He quizzed me about the poverty in nearby Harlem, and I took him there, agreeing with him that the mode of life we saw was a disgrace to America. For a convinced Soviet communist like Yakovlev, being plunged into crowded upper Manhattan in 1958, with poverty, racism, and suffering clearly visible around us, was not the most effective way of shedding his ideology. If Yakovlev had his problems occasionally with the realities of Soviet life, I had a few of my own with American life.

But I had by this time read Khrushchev's "Secret Speech," which had been printed in American newspapers but not Soviet ones, and I asked him about it. He did not reveal at that time that he had been present during the speech, and declined to comment on its significance, but he was obviously interested in the fact that I knew about it. Without disclosing his own thoughts, he attempted to elicit mine.

At Columbia I attended one or two courses together with Yakovlev, including Alexander Dallin's class on Soviet foreign policy. On several occasions in Dallin's course I sat between Yakovlev and Oleg Kalugin, another Soviet exchange student attending Columbia. Now I look back on that time and marvel at the fact that I was sitting between two men who would rise to very high positions in the Soviet Union, only later to turn against it in spectacular ways. Kalugin went on to become a top official in the KGB, where he was for a time responsible for supervising spying on foreign visitors to the Soviet Union, including, at certain moments, me. Eventually, after years of dirty work, Kalugin left Russia in disgust, resettled in London after the collapse of the USSR, and wrote his memoirs castigating the Soviet order and his previous profession.

Yakovlev told me in 1958 and 1959 that he was offended by the questions he was asked in Manhattan stores by clerks and shopkeepers who learned that he was a visiting Soviet citizen. He swore that it was not a joke when one shopkeeper took off Yakovlev's hat to see if he had horns. He also said that he was confronted constantly by such questions as, "How much soap should you take with you when you visit the Soviet Union?" "What are the ways in which Communist organizations choose wives for young men?" "Why do communists make wives and children common property?" "Are there bears on the streets of Moscow?" "Why do you want to drop atomic bombs on the United States?"

After leaving New York and returning to the Soviet Union Yakovlev wrote a series of books that excoriated America in the most inflammatory terms; among them were *A Call to Kill; The Ideology of the American Empire; The USA: From a "Great" Country to a Sick One; On the Edge of an Abyss;* and *Pax Americana.* In the last book he described the United States as "an antagonistic class society that cannot live without the exploitation and oppression of the majority of people by an insignificant minority of the rich. The propertied class cannot rule without creating an enormous apparatus for the repression and deception of the masses. Vampires are insatiable for blood, and the exploiters are insatiable for money." He singled out private property and pathological individualism as the roots of American misery. The United States was a land of exploitation, racism, militarism, and cultural degradation, while the Soviet Union was a country of equality, progress, and peace.

Writing in 1967, he maintained that "the power of the workers, the creativity, enthusiasm and energy of the people, have given the Soviet Union a colossal jump forward in economic, technical and social development." These writings make vivid comparison with Yakovlev's books thirty years later when he described the Soviet Union in blacker terms than he did earlier the United States, and when he praised private property and individualism as the roots of human freedom.

Even as late as 1984, when he was already one of Gorbachev's advisors, and one year before Gorbachev came to power, Yakovlev wrote in *On the Edge of an Abyss*, "The U.S. is a nation governed more by deception and demagogy than by conviction, more by force than by law, more by deadening habits and traditions than by respect of and interest in whatever is new, more by hatred, suspicion and intolerance than by the ability to recognize there may be another way of life and thought."

By the time Yakovlev wrote his anti-American books in the sixties, seventies, and eighties, he was a high official, first in the Communist Party, then as Soviet ambassador to Canada for many years. It is likely that he did not write all these books himself; he certainly could call upon research and writing assistants when he wished. But he admitted later that he subscribed to these views at the time. Once, many years later, when he was asked why he had written such dogmatic books, he replied with customary fervor that he still remembered the ignorant and insulting questions about the Soviet Union he had been asked when he was a student in New York, and he also read a steady criticism of the Soviet Union in books and newspapers when he was in Canada. "Had I not been in the USA and Canada, I would never have written such books about America," Yakovlev said, "But being an impulsive man, when I read newspapers and books criticizing my country, well, this hurt me deeply. For example, I know that I am crippled. But when people every day tell me, 'You are crippled, you are crippled,' I get furious. And then I answer back: 'You are crippled! You yourself are the fool!'"

The complexities of Yakovlev's life are further illustrated by the reason he was sent to Canada as Soviet ambassador. His Canadian post was actually a demotion, not a promotion, an exile forced upon him by political controversies in which he was embroiled in the Soviet Union. In the early 1970s Yakovlev had risen to the position of head of the Communist Party's propaganda department, where he was responsible for giving ideological directions to the senior newspaper editors and television producers of the Soviet Union. In this position Yakovlev kept close track of editorial policies being espoused in the leading media. He soon noticed that certain editors and journals were promoting a revival of Russian nationalism, often combined with anti-Semitism. These editors were concocting a bizarre hybrid of Marxism, nationalism and even religion, a mixture that contradicted Yakovlev's conception of Soviet ideology as universalist, internationalist, atheist, and anti-capitalist. Yakovlev wrote a long article in the newspaper *Literaturnaia gazeta* attacking these editors for subverting authentic Marxism. But Yakovlev had badly miscalculated the mood of the leader of the Party and state, Leonid Brezhnev. Brezhnev was a conservative man who wanted political support wherever he could get it and was not concerned with authentic Marxism. He and a few other top leaders had realized that the Soviet public had tired of Marxism, and needed more traditional slogans and symbols, such as patriotism and nationalism, in order to continue to support the Soviet regime. Furthermore, Brezhnev knew that Yakovlev's Marxism left little room for the glorification of individuals, even though Brezhnev was supporting a campaign of self-glorification. To get Yakovlev out of the way, he was sent to Canada, where he found solace by churning out the anti-American tracts already described. In later years Yakovlev stated that he requested the assignment to go to Canada, but only after he realized he was falling out of Brezhnev's favor. It is possible that one of the reasons he wrote such strident anti-American books in Canada was an attempt to regain official approval in Moscow.

While Yakovlev was in Canada from 1973 until 1983, he had an opportunity to travel throughout the country, visiting towns, farms, and cities. He was particularly impressed by the productivity of Canadian farms, located in a harsh northern climate very similar to the Soviet Union's. He puzzled over the question, "Why could not Soviet farms duplicate this agricultural success?"

Although Canada was a capitalist country just like the United States, to the best of my knowledge Yakovlev never wrote criticisms of Canada like those he wrote about the United States. Part of the reason, of course, was that as ambassador to Canada he wished to avoid unnecessary offense to the country hosting him. But Yakovlev also noticed that Canada had softened capitalism more than the United States. It had, for example, a universal governmental health plan, something the United States lacked, and it provided a more extensive system of social welfare. It was, Yakovlev thought, as if Roosevelt's New Deal had been given a much greater scope for development in Canada.

Yakovlev had met Mikhail Gorbachev before he went to Canada, but he did not yet know him well. In 1983, however, Gorbachev, a rising star in Soviet Communist circles, and currently in charge of agriculture, came to Canada on a ten-day tour. The two men immediately hit it off, and Yakovlev shepherded Gorbachev around Canadian farms, dairy plants, and meatpacking plants, which he already knew well. It was obvious to both of them that the productivity of Canadian agriculture far exceeded that of the Soviet Union. And it was also clear to them that people in Canada, even those who were not affluent, had a standard of living far superior to that of Soviet citizens. Yakovlev told Gorbachev that things simply could not go on in the Soviet Union as they were. Some kind of dramatic and drastic reform was needed. Gorbachev agreed and said that Yakovlev should return to Moscow. Soon thereafter Yakovlev became director of the prestigious Institute of World Economy and International Relations. He was now in Gorbachev's inner circle and soon was to become the second-most important man in the Soviet Union.

When Gorbachev came to power in March 1985, and turned to Yakovlev for advice, he recommended fundamental political reform. Gorbachev was not yet ready for such dramatic steps, and put Yakovlev back in his old job of head of the propaganda department of the Central Committee of the Party. Turning Yakovlev's recommendations for political reforms aside, Gorbachev adopted a milder economic program, called "acceleration" (*uskorenie*), thinking that greater discipline and tighter management could bring economic improvements. But within a year it became obvious to Gorbachev that the limited economic reforms were going nowhere, and he began to think in more radical terms. The words that Gorbachev now began to use more and more frequently were *perestroika* (restructuring) and *glasnost*, "giving voice," or "openness." The policy of publicizing facts under glasnost

gained tremendous momentum after the spring of 1986, when it became clear that the Chernobyl power plant disaster had been made
worse by the traditional Soviet policy of secrecy. Gorbachev turned to
Yakovlev, in charge of public media, to rectify the situation. Yakovlev
promised to appoint new editors to leading Soviet newspapers who
would tell the truth, who would inform the Soviet public what was
really going on in the country. The first of these appointments was
Vitaly Korotich, who was made editor of the weekly *Ogonyok*, and
quickly transformed it into the liveliest, most controversial publication
in the Soviet Union. Yakovlev also brought in new editors to many
other Soviet publications, and soon the Soviet public was treated to
shocking stories of past Stalinist abuses and current bureaucratic scandals. For the first time in two generations it became possible to discuss
openly the flaws of Soviet society. As freedom of the press began to
spread in the Soviet Union the names of Gorbachev and Yakovlev became known throughout the world.

Gorbachev pushed a more radical program of political reform, and
Yakovlev provided the architectural plans for the new changes. His
political star steadily rose. In 1987 he reached the pinnacle of Soviet
power when he became a member of the Politburo of the Party, the
tiny group of men who still tried to keep control under increasingly
difficult conditions as dissenting political groups found their voices.
Only four years later Yakovlev would be expelled from the Communist
Party for his success in destroying the old Communist monopoly on
information and power.

Yakovlev received many invitations in these years to come to the
United States in order to explain the new reforms to American audi-
ences. He gave lectures at Columbia, Harvard (where I was his host),
and at many other American universities. American businesses also
celebrated Yakovlev, and on one of his trips to the United States the
Archer-Daniels-Midland Company provided him with its corporate jet
to travel around the country. On a trip from Boston to Chicago Yakovlev invited me to ride with him on the company jet, and as we sat there
together in corporate splendor I could not but recall Yakovlev's books
in which he had castigated American capitalists as "vampires" sucking
the blood of the American people. And, as a matter of fact, the Archer-
Daniels-Midland Company was soon to be involved in a scandal about
its price-fixing practices; one of its executives was even recorded saying
that "the customer is our enemy, our competitors are our friend."

Yakovlev told me that he wanted to buy a chain saw to use for building his dacha outside Moscow, so I helped him purchase one at Sears Roebuck. I later carried the chain saw for him to the airport and noticed that people made way for us with unusual alacrity.

I visited the Soviet Union often during these years while doing research on several books and also while chairing a series of conferences entitled "Science and Technology with a Human Face"; at these conferences Russian and American academics discussed ways in which unbridled Soviet technological enthusiasm, which resulted in terrible pollution and environmental destruction, could be brought under control.

On several occasions I attempted to get Yakovlev to participate in these conferences, but his concerns were more directly political than academic, and he did not accept. Nonetheless, we met several times. He was now in such a high political position that I could not call him directly on the telephone, but I found another way to communicate with him. The headquarters of the Central Committee of the Communist Party were located on Staraia Ploshchad (Old Square) but the main entrance was impenetrable to a foreigner and heavily guarded. By poking around the building, however, I found around the corner a tiny entrance marked "sovershenno sekretno" (completely secret). Opening the door and walking inside I found a second wall with a tiny window behind which stood a Red Army soldier with rifle and fixed bayonet. I learned that if I went up to that window and thrust through its tiny aperture an envelope with the words written in Russian on it "Aleksandr Nikolaevich Yakovlev, Member of Politburo" the letter would be accepted. In the letter I would tell Yakovlev that I was in town and ask him to call me, which he usually did. It was so simple that I wondered why Western newspaper reporters had not discovered it as a way to communicate with the top leaders of the Soviet government.

In January 1991 Pat came with me to the Soviet Union, and we both decided to try to meet with Yakovlev. I left a letter for him at the "secret window" and soon our telephone in the hotel rang. Yakovlev's assistant told us to come at a certain hour to the main Kremlin gate, the Spasskaia tower, where we would be met. Pat and I went to the tower where the assistant was waiting and took us inside the Kremlin past the old Voznesenskii Monastery to a building in which the offices of the Soviet leaders were located. I noticed that the offices on the northeast side of the corridor had windows looking out over Red Square, but most of the important offices were on the other side, with windows looking in to the interior of the Kremlin. The assistant showed us briefly the office of the founder of the Soviet state, Vladimir Lenin, preserved as a museum, and then led us a few more feet past Gorbachev's office to that of Yakovlev. In the spacious anteroom Yakovlev's assistants were watching television, and to our amusement we noticed that the program was a "Woody Woodpecker" cartoon suitably dubbed in Russian.

After being escorted into the main office, we met with Yakovlev, who immediately told Pat how well he remembered the tuna fish casserole that she had served him years ago in our New York apartment. He also inquired about our daughter, two years old when he first met her, and now a thirty-four-year-old social worker in Chicago. The conversation was almost entirely social, although he did express interest in my academic work in Moscow. He was not interested in describing his own political difficulties. He did suggest a photograph of the three of us in his Kremlin office, with a large picture of his boss Gorbachev visible on the wall.

Within a few months Gorbachev fell from power and Yakovlev was out of a job. In 1992, with the Soviet Union dismantled, he became the chair of President Yeltsin's Commission on Rehabilitation of Political Prisoners. He also founded and chaired a new political party, that of the Social Democrats, and eventually split with his old boss Gorbachev.

As chair of the Commission, Yakovlev was in charge of investigating the crimes of the Soviet regime. In order to do so he began digging into the archives and bloody records of the Soviet secret police, now open to him. It was Yakovlev who announced in November 2000 that the Swedish diplomat Raoul Wallenberg, who rescued so many Jews from Nazi persecution, had probably been executed in the basement of Lubianka prison in Moscow. The experience of going through the secret police records had an absolutely transforming effect on Yakovlev and his writing. In the year 2000 he published a book that is striking in its bitterness and despair. Entitled *The Sowing of Crosses*, it contains the following explanation of its title:

> Russia to its horizons is sown with the crosses and nameless graves
> of its citizens, killed in wars, dead from hunger, shot at the whim
> of the Leninist-Stalinist fascist regime. Millions lie under crosses
> but even more millions are nameless, buried without markers.
> They lie in ditches, in gutters, in swamps, in mountain crevices,
> and many skeletons are simply scattered in the forests of the Russian land. . . . My many years of work in the archives now reveal
> that the number of people killed for political reasons and those

Patricia and Loren Graham with Aleksandr Yakovlev in his Kremlin office when Yakovlev was Gorbachev's chief advisor, January 1991.

who died in the prisons and camps during all the years of Soviet power is 20 to 25 million people.

As a young man Yakovlev had revered Stalin and the Soviet order. Then, under the pressure of the revelation of Stalin's crimes, he changed his views, but for a long time he still considered Lenin to be a great revolutionary, a person who was true to the principles of social-ism that Stalin betrayed. But in the archives of the secret police Yakov-lev learned that Lenin himself had personally ordered the execution of a great many imprisoned Russian citizens. The records and papers of frightful events that Yakovlev studied in the archives totally destroyed his last hopes for something salvageable in Soviet socialism. In fact, these revelations nearly vanquished all hopes he had for his native land, under any form of government.

He now spoke of his boyhood hero Vladimir Lenin, founder of the Soviet state, in the following terms: "He constantly ordered executions, hangings, arrests. He was responsible for the deaths of millions of Rus-sians. By all the norms of international law he deserved a death sentence for crimes against humanity." On the cover of his new book Yakovlev quoted Lenin as saying "The more representatives of the reactionary clergy we can shoot the better."

Yakovlev was so disillusioned, so embittered, by what he discovered that he began speaking of Russia as a ruined nation, hopelessly condemned by decades of destruction. He wrote:

> Lenin, Stalin, Hitler make up the trio of the creators of neo-Cainism—the crime of brother against brother, of Cain against Abel. They are the chief criminals of the century. This century was fatal to Russia. Its thousand-year-old model of development has been betrayed and replaced. Russia used to be a peasant country—it became a society of mean scoundrels. It used to be a country of orthodox religion—it became an atheistic society. It used to strive forward—it now pulls back. To the core it has been ruined by the poison of scoundrels. It is rightly scorned by normal people. What is left to respect in Russia? Laziness, drunkenness, envy of the prosperity of one's neighbor, incompetence? . . . The Russian people are capable of anything, but especially of drunkenness and the intoxicating feast of laziness. It has been impoverished, but it does not wish to work hard. Money lies on the ground, it is being trampled, but to bend over and pick it up is impossible because of laziness. That person who does not wish to be idle, that person has nowhere to live in Russia.

I read this book as I was traveling by plane to Moscow in December 2000 to participate in a selection committee of an American philanthropy, the John D. and Catherine T. MacArthur Foundation, to award fellowships to citizens of the former Soviet Union in areas of work such as human rights, environmental studies, legal reform, and peace and security. I had spent the previous weeks reading the applications of many young Russians who still had hope for their country, who wanted to help create a truly democratic, free, and just society. Furthermore, in trips around the country I had visited universities and research institutes in Vladivostok, Kazan, Novisibirsk, Tomsk, Perm, Samara, Nizhny Novgorod, Taganrog, Krasnodar, Rostov, St. Petersburg, and Moscow. Yakovlev was absolutely right in his description of the mind-boggling horrors of the Soviet period, but I could see that he was wrong in thinking that these awful decades had destroyed everything good in the Russian people. Even after the catastrophe of Soviet rule, there are numerous talented, honest, and promising people in the former Soviet Union, many of them educated by that regime. I understand why Yakovlev was so disillusioned, and I further understand why he was so shaken, but the goodness of human beings is more robust than he thought. Russia is in crisis, but it is not lost. Looking at these applications, and later meeting many of these highly talented young people, I could see that Russia still has hope. One must build on that hope.

But although I am now critical of the position that Yakovlev had taken, just as I was critical of those he adopted years ago, his historical significance is very clear to me. He helped change history. The ironies here abound. At every moment in his life Yakovlev was a fervent man who gave in to extremes: he was extreme in his adulation of Stalin, he was extreme when he thought the Soviet regime could be saved by a few reforms, and he was extreme when he considered Russia to be a lost country deserving of scorn by all normal people. But those who have not lived through horrific events should not rush to judge him —or denigrate the significance of his accomplishments. Aleksandr Yakovlev died on October 18, 2005.

CHAPTER TWENTY

THE SOVIET UNION AND I COLLAPSE TOGETHER

IN EARLY DECEMBER 1991, I went to Moscow in order to work in the archives, now open to foreigners to a degree I had never before seen. The Soviet Union was in complete disorder and, although I had no presentment when I arrived, would disappear, along with the Gorbachev government, while I was there. My subject of study was the purges of Russian engineers at the end of the 1920s, a topic on which I had been collecting information for several decades. I was particularly interested in the life and experiences of Peter Palchinsky, an engineer executed by Stalin in 1929 after he had been accused of organizing an anti-revolutionary conspiratorial group, the "Industrial Party." What I already knew about Palchinsky led me to believe that the real reason Stalin had silenced this brilliant engineer was that he was a sincere socialist who wanted to industrialize Russia in a way that would truly benefit the workers. Stalin regarded Palchinsky as an obstacle in his drive to concentrate all power in his own hands while increasing the military might of the Soviet Union, whatever the effects on the workers. On this Moscow trip I would gain access to archival records about this episode of Soviet history that would result in a book, entitled *The Ghost of the Executed Engineer*.

Although I was paying my own way for the research trip, I had received an invitation from the Soviet Academy of Sciences to stay in a guesthouse of the Academy, Neskuchnoe (which translates: "not a boring place"), which was located on the edge of the city. The guest-house was on the estate of a prominent local nobleman before the Revolution and had extensive parklands situated around it. Scientists had taken over the estate and converted it into a sanatorium and resort for the several hundred full members of the Academy of Sciences of the USSR, who were, in a sense, the new nobility. The Academy hotel was located on the perimeter of these restful grounds, which were covered with a blanket of snow. The hotel was clean and modern, but modest in the services that it offered. On several evenings I was the only person in the dining room, and the menu usually offered only one main course. But the food was good and even tasty, and green salads, heretofore unknown in Soviet hotels, were available.

It was difficult to force myself to work in the archives when so much was happening on the city streets. Political groups of all sorts were organizing meetings, the street kiosks offered a broad range of literature that earlier had been banned—ranging from monarchist and neo-fascist leaflets on the right end of the political spectrum to anarchist and neo-Marxist writings on the left. And pornography, also heretofore unknown except covertly, was appearing everywhere. After decades of Soviet puritanism in official publications the thirst for anything related to sex was intense, and such materials were being churned out by newly flourishing private and illegal presses.

On one street a woman had set up a card table and was selling photographs, arranged in two piles. A line of women had formed in front of one pile, and a line of men in front of the other. The women were patiently waiting their turn to buy photographs of nude men, arranged in photogenic poses, and the men were lined up before nude women, similarly displayed. The business was brisk. By contemporary standards, the photos were not pornographic, just nude pictures.

Before I had left the United States, I had experienced what I thought was a very minor health problem—intermittent flashes of pain on my face, often traversing down my nose onto my cheek. I had checked with my MIT doctor in Cambridge, who diagnosed the problem as "trigeminal neuralgia," an inflammation of a facial nerve sometimes called "tic douloureux." He gave me some pills to control the pain, which he acknowledged could be severe, but he assured me that the disease was not serious, it would probably eventually clear up on its own, and that with the help of the pills I should be able to continue my activities in a normal way.

During the first ten days or so that I worked in the archives I noticed that the flashes of pain were coming more and more often, but the pills were still effective, and I was eager to get as much work done as possible in these precious days between semesters when I did not have to be in Cambridge. If I took a pill whenever I felt a flash of pain in the morning I would be free of further trouble that day.

And the fruits of the archival labors were very exciting. When Palchinsky had been arrested in 1929 the secret police who took him away collected all his papers and letters and deposited them in the secret police archives. These materials were now available for the first time in over sixty years, and I was retrieving them as quickly as I could, limited in my speed by the archival rules that allowed me to look at only ten folders a day. Here were Palchinsky's prophetic warnings about the disastrous way in which the Soviet Union was industrializing, exploiting and alienating the workers the Revolution was supposed to benefit, and, through haste and carelessness, creating environmental disasters and inefficient industrial plants.

Not only did the archival materials contain all Palchinsky's official reports and critiques, they also held his personal letters to his wife and friends. These sources demonstrated that while Palchinsky was opposed to Stalin, he was a convinced socialist and believed rather naïvely that the Russian Revolution would usher in a new era in history. That new era would bring with it not only novel social and economic relations, but distinctly different sexual and personal behavior as well. Peter and Nina Palchinsky were in rebellion against "bourgeois mores" and freely confessed to each other in their letters when they had love affairs with other people. Nina observed to her husband that far more significant than sexual loyalty between a man and a woman was "mutual commitment to the benefit of society as a whole, honesty with each other, and a communion of souls." Reading through these materials was certainly more interesting than studying the official protocols that the Soviet government earlier had made available to me.

In the middle of the second week of my archival research I was awakened early in the morning by excruciating pain in my face that, however many pills I took, would not go away. I should have called for help at that moment, but I feared to do so because I knew that Soviet hospitals were in chaos, like all Soviet institutions as the country was beginning to break up, and I had read many appalling stories about what happened to people who ended up in them. Furthermore, earlier the pain had always eventually gone away, and I was sure that it would again. I still believed that I was suffering from a minor ailment.

As a result I delayed asking for help for several hours until the pain had reached such intensity that I could only lie on my hotel bed in a comatose state. I would drift in and out of consciousness, and all sense of time disappeared. I later learned that I spent over two days in this state. When I needed to go to the bathroom I found that I could only crawl, not walk. On the first occasion there I managed to pull myself up by the sink and look in the mirror to see, to my horror, that my entire face was twisted into a grimace. I tried to slake my thirst with a drink of water, only to find that my jaw was paralyzed shut and that I could not open my mouth. I remembered that my wife Pat had put some paper straws in my luggage (how could she have anticipated this event?) and I crawled to my suitcase and retrieved one. Returning to the bathroom, I turned on the water for the tub, jammed the straw between my lips and up to my teeth, and, by sucking hard, managed to drink water through my clenched teeth, my upper torso draped over the porcelain side of the bathtub. Several times during the next days I obtained water in this fashion.

Lying on my bed I continued to drift in and out of consciousness. At the moments when the flashes of pain were greatest the torment was far beyond the limits of anything that I had previously experienced in my life, and just withstanding the agony without going into convulsions took a major effort. I tried playing mental games in which, when the pain was at its apogee, I would try to imagine even worse pain so that what I was actually experiencing would seem tolerable. It seemed to work for a while, then the pain overwhelmed my psychological defenses, and I would pass out again. Upon returning to consciousness, the waves of pain built up again. I alternately was soaked in sweat and freezing from cold.

Gradually I became aware of what should have occurred to me much earlier: if I did not get help, I was likely to die in that hotel room. I decided to wait for a moment when the pain was not at its worst and then try to make my way to someone who could aid me. My first thought was to try to call someone on the telephone, but I feared that with my jaw paralyzed shut and my throat wracked with nervous twitches I would not be able to speak. At what I thought was the best moment I crawled out of the bed and made my way to the telephone. With my knees on the floor and my arms stretched across the desk I dialed the number of Anton Struchkov, a young Russian historian of science who knew me well and with whom I had met just a few days earlier. At that time I had told him that I was not feeling well.

I recognized Anton's voice when he answered the phone, and I desperately tried to speak to him. My jaw was still frozen shut and my throat would not respond but by making a concentrated effort I was able to grunt into the phone a deep and guttural "aargh" that meant nothing and would have frightened away almost anyone who heard it.

From Anton in response came at first only silence. He did not hang up, as I thought he would, but said nothing. After a moment I repeated the grunt, and again heard nothing from Anton. Then, after what seemed to me to be an interminable time, he said, in Russian, "Loren, is that you?" I repeated the grunt once more. Again Anton hesitated a while, and then said, "Loren, if that is you, could you make that noise twice?" I gathered up my strength, held the phone to my mouth, and emitted two "aarghs", one after the other. Then Anton quickly asked "Loren, if you are in your hotel and you want me to come to help you, could you do it once more?" I once again emitted the noise, heard Anton say "I am on my way," dropped the phone into its cradle, and collapsed onto the bed. Then fearing that I would pass out and not be able to let Anton into the room when he arrived, I crawled to my outside door and unlocked it. Then I crept back to the bed and collapsed from pain and exhaustion.

Anton lived on the far side of Moscow from where I was located, and he had no car of his own. Taking a bottle of vodka from his closet, where it was kept with several others as a negotiable currency for moments of need, Anton went to a neighbor who had a car and offered him the vodka if he would make his car available for a rescue mission. The neighbor agreed and together the two men started off for my hotel. The car was an orange vehicle, an inexpensive Zaporozhets that emitted smoke and coughed through three cylinders.

Meanwhile in my room I had once again lost consciousness. Some time later—it must have been close to an hour later—I partially came to my senses and heard my telephone ringing. Before I could push myself off the bed onto the floor I heard steps outside my door, and Anton and his friend burst into the room. I could see his horror when he looked at me, and I realized that my face was still contorted, as it had been when I earlier peeked in the mirror. I pointed at the telephone, still ringing, and Anton went over and picked it up. The person on the other end of the line was Nikolai Nikolaevich Vorontsov, the minister of environment of the Soviet Union (see "Biographical Notes" at the end of this book). Anton was a historian of environmental science, and certainly knew who Vorontsov was, but had never met him, and was clearly astonished to be talking suddenly to a member of President Gorbachev's cabinet. As he tried to adjust to that situation, his eyes roamed over the dark hotel room, taking in my demented state and the disheveled surroundings with discarded clothing and open bottles of medicine and pills scattered about.

Vorontsov, an old friend of mine, told Anton he had talked to me a week or so ago, and that he had invited me to visit him and his wife at their governmental dacha outside Moscow. I had declined, saying that I was not feeling well, but had promised to call him within a few days. Not having heard from me, Vorontsov was concerned and wanted to know how I was. Anton, who still was trying to assess the strange situation, replied that I seemed to be partially paralyzed and could not talk. Vorontsov commanded, "Get that man to the Kremlin Hospital. I will call the Kremlin ambulance and order it to pick him up. You stay with him until he is safely in the care of the hospital and then call me and let me know the situation." Anton assured Vorontsov that he would wait for the ambulance.

The Kremlin ambulance—a Mercedes-Benz van-sized vehicle with a crew of two physicians and two nurses—arrived at the hotel about fifteen minutes later. Its ostentatious appearance at the hotel entrance, red light flashing and siren wailing, and "Kremlin Hospital" emblazoned on its side, caused the entire hotel staff to collect and follow the medical delegation to my room, where Anton and his friend were waiting with me. Anton explained to the two young physicians that my jaw was paralyzed shut, that I alternated between consciousness and unconsciousness, and that I could not talk. The Kremlin doctors briefly examined me, then reached into a black bag, dipped a swab into a bottle of liquid that I later decided because of its dramatic effect must have been codeine or morphine, and rubbed the inside of my mouth and jaw. The result was incredible; not only did the curtain of pain that was overwhelming me disappear, but my jaw relaxed and I suddenly felt good, maybe even wonderful. Soon I was joking with the doctors, enjoying the situation, and wondering what the Kremlin Hospital would be like.

The nurses put me on a stretcher and the whole crew went out to the ambulance, loaded me in, and started off at a fast pace. In Moscow at that time the central lanes of the main roads were still reserved for police cars and ambulances, but also for the official vehicles of Kremlin leaders. We went down the central lane at a speed of what must have been in excess of 100 miles an hour. Anton and his friend, who had been commanded by Vorontsov to stay with me until I was safely in the Kremlin Hospital, steered their little Zaporozhets automobile into the same central lane, the friend put the accelerator on the floor, and all three cylinders of their car strained to chase after the fast disappearing Kremlin ambulance. I shouted to the ambulance driver that the Zaporozhets contained my friends and hoped that he would not lose it.

The Kremlin Hospital was a part of a great network of institutions specially created for the care of the Soviet Union's top leadership. The network included special grocery stores, meat markets, cleaning and shoe repair facilities, rest sanatoria, clothing stores, and a variety of other facilities. Health care for the elite fell under a special division of the Ministry of Health called "the Fourth Chief Directorate." At first the clinic for the leadership was in the Kremlin itself, but even after it grew too large for the crowded Kremlin it continued to be called "the Kremlin Hospital." In the late twenties a large headquarters for the hospital was built not far from the Kremlin at the corner of Kalinin and Granovskii streets, and later smaller clinics were located in the apartment buildings where many of the top government bureaucrats lived, such as "Government House" on the Moscow River (on Vsekhsviatskaia Street, later named Serafimovich Street). In 1978 the Kremlin Hospital opened a large complex known as "The Moscow Clinical Center" at 6 Michurinskii Prospect, near Moscow University, and—most importantly—close to the mansions of the top Kremlin leaders on Kosygin Street, along the Moscow River. This new facility was so close to the homes of the upper crust of the Party and government they could be taken from their home beds to their hospital ones within five minutes.

The hospital is a collection of buildings, rather like a small university campus, surrounded by a high brick wall. Inside are modern surgical and therapeutic wards. It was to this hospital, the best and most modern in the Soviet Union, that I was being taken. At the entrance to the hospital is a giant metal gate next to a guardhouse with uniformed Kremlin police. The ambulance pulled up in front of the gate, which immediately began to open. Anton and his friend came dashing up behind in their little orange car, and as the ambulance entered, they drove right behind it. At this moment one of the guards emerged, walked in front of the Zaporozhets, and commanded that it stop. He explained to Anton and his friend that private cars were not permitted on the grounds of the Kremlin Hospital. Anton noticed that the Kremlin ambulance had also stopped, so he jumped out of the Zaporozhets and ran up to ask the ambulance driver to intercede with the guard and let him drive in. The driver replied, "They will never let your car in, but just hop in the ambulance and you can come in with us." Anton did, and there were now seven of us in the ambulance—two doctors, two nurses, a driver, Anton, and me.

I was wheeled to my room on a gurney, with the whole crew in tow, Anton gaping at the oriental rugs, chandeliers, and parquet floors. No one seemed to question Anton's authority to be with me. Waiting for me in the room were two more doctors and several nurses. Although I was still lying down, I said that I felt so good that I thought I could walk, and I got up and did. The doctors insisted that I get into bed, the nurses stripped me naked, put a rather elegant Kremlin nightgown on me, and firmly placed me in the bed. The doctor in charge collected information from me, the ambulance doctors, and Anton about my condition, gave me a couple of large pills that he said would put me to sleep, swabbed my mouth again with the wonderful elixir, and ordered everybody out of the room except one of the nurses.

I awoke several hours later when a nurse came in the room. In my now relatively stable condition I immediately noticed that she was one of the most beautiful women I had ever seen in my life. Obviously, when the top Communist leadership supplied and staffed its hospital, they demanded the best of everything. She said that she had come to "check my vital signs." She was a wonderful stimulus to vitality. Asking for my arm, she took my pulse and then my blood pressure, and expressed surprise that the latter was so high. I observed that I suffered from "labile blood pressure" that varied enormously, and that under different conditions my pressure might be much lower. Whether she understood that her presence might be provoking my blood pressure was not clear, but she told me "Dr. Gorbunov is soon coming to see you, and he will take your pressure again." She then announced that she was going to take a blood sample. I had read that Russian hospitals often used the same needles repeatedly, and that diseases were often spread by them, so I said that I did not want to have a blood sample taken. A bit offended, she inquired, "Why not?" Before I could reply, she continued, "I know why. You are afraid we are going to give you AIDS (in Russian, *spid*), aren't you?" I admitted that the thought had crossed my mind. She then proudly and firmly announced, "*This* is the Kremlin Hospital. We use only the best French disposable needles," and she opened a plastic case in which a number of such needles were displayed, each in its own plastic envelope. In the face of such evidence, I relented; she took a blood sample and left.

Soon Dr. Gorbunov came in my room. A somewhat pudgy man with an air of authority, he announced that he had studied my record and was going to give me "therapy," but first wanted to take my blood pressure. It turned out to be almost normal, slightly high. Dr. Gorbunov smiled, asked me to turn over, opened the back of my nightgown and began a long process of applying acupuncture needles. "My God," I thought, "What if they don't use disposable acupuncture needles?" It was too late to object, and Dr. Gorbunov did not look like the kind of man who would have paid any attention if I did. So I decided to try to start a conversation by remarking that his name, "Gorbunov," was the same as Lenin's personal secretary and assistant in the Kremlin in the early 1920s. Was he related? "Yes, of course," Dr. Gorbunov replied. "All the members of my family are highly educated and have occupied important positions. The man you refer to, Nikolai Gorbunov, was educated as a chemical engineer and was a personal advisor to Vladimir Ilich Lenin." I did not tell Dr. Gorbunov that I knew that his relative Nikolai Gorbunov had been shot in 1938 during the Great Purges. Dr. Gorbunov was at that moment puncturing my back with needles, and I did not wish to disturb either his aim or his composure. For the same reason I did not tell him that I knew that in 1953 Stalin threatened to purge all the Kremlin Hospital doctors for allegedly conspiring against him.

Dr. Gorbunov continued his enlightening lecture. "I am a Kremlin physician who has treated the most important people in our country," he bragged. "You will receive here the best medical treatment in the world. You know, we Kremlin doctors are much more versatile and thorough than your Western doctors. Your doctors know how to do only two things, give pills and cut. Your doctors are very good at drugs and surgery, but they do not treat the whole patient, as we do. For example, I am now giving you acupuncture and soon I will give you a back rub with a special lotion. You have a nervous problem that I know how to treat."

He twiddled with the needles for about twenty minutes. The treatment was not painful and was obviously applied in a systematic fashion that I did not understand. Then Dr. Gorbunov removed the needles, and began a back rub. Suddenly I was assailed by a strange and pungent odor that came from the lotion he was applying. When I inquired what it was, Dr. Gorbunov replied that he was applying "bee sting venom" to my back to quiet my nerves. He rubbed it in with expert motions and seemed very accustomed to the treatment. He worked away for another fifteen minutes or so and then said that he was leaving, but that if I had any future problems I should inform the nurse who would call him.

After he left, and I was alone, I inspected myself, stretching my legs and arms, and trying to feel my back, which had been so dramatically treated. Everything seemed fine. In fact I felt great, and was ravenously hungry, not having eaten anything in several days. I decided to get up and inspect the premises. My room was enormous and had a desk, telephone, and fresh flowers on a table. The bath was similarly commodious, and contained both a bidet and a Jacuzzi. I emerged from my room and started walking down the hallway in what was obviously the main section of the Kremlin Hospital. As I passed each room I looked in; every one was empty. At a time when normal hospitals in Moscow were jammed with patients, often a dozen or more in a single room, the Kremlin Hospital was practically deserted. It was also excellently equipped and clean, contrary to most other Russian hospitals. I had visited a number of Russian friends in the regular hospitals, including my unfortunate friend Vitalii, and I knew just how bad they could be. At the far end of the hallway I was walking down there was a desk where a nurse was seated with her back to me, so I silently turned around and returned to my room, not wanting to alarm her with my peregrinations.

Soon a different woman came in the room with a menu. She said that at the Kremlin Hospital patients could order their own meals. I found that the menu was more extensive than any Russian hotel I had seen and to my surprise included French wines. I ordered Kiev chicken, green salad, and white wine. I was enjoying myself immensely. The pain was entirely gone.

I stayed in the hospital for three more days, enjoying having the best personal service I had ever experienced. The pain never returned, and the mouth swabs were discontinued. I began to think that maybe Dr. Gorbunov was on to something with his acupuncture and bee sting venom. On the fourth day I told the nurse that I had recovered and that I wanted to leave. The nurse replied that I would have to talk about this with "the chief administrator," whom she would send to see me. A few minutes later the chief administrator arrived, a very polite and seemingly competent woman. "Why do you want to leave?" she asked, "Are you not happy with your treatment?" I replied that I was delighted with my treatment, but that the reason that I was in Moscow was that I needed to work in the archives, and I must get back to my work. "Well, fine," said the administrator, "Why don't you just leave each morning for the archives and then come back here in the evening, where we can keep an eye on you?" I was simultaneously amazed by her generosity and suspicious of her motive.

"Who is paying for this treatment?" I asked. "You are," she replied, and then explained the whole situation: "You are the first private patient in the history of the Kremlin Hospital. You know, everything is changing in the Soviet Union now, and there is much criticism of the exclusive privileges, like special grocery stores and hospitals, that the top leadership traditionally has received. We here in the Kremlin Hospital have decided that we can no longer exclusively serve the political leadership; we must open our doors to the public. But we are afraid that if we just admitted anybody we would be deluged by the crowds trying to get good medical service. So we have decided to start very gradually by admitting only a few foreigners who can pay hard currency. You are our first such patient and we are doing everything we can to make you feel perfectly at home. So why don't you stay with us a while longer?"

I replied that I appreciated her hospitality and thoughtfulness, but needed to know just how large the bill was that I was running up. Maybe I did not have enough money. "Oh, I am sure we can handle that," she cheerfully replied, "We have applied to American Express to accept their cards. Do you have such a card?" I admitted that I did, but added that this was not exactly a solution to the problem, since eventually the bill would have to be paid. I had visions of a bill of thousands of dollars. Could she add the bill so far? She pulled out an abacus and mused as she flipped the little wooden wheels, "Now there also was a special ambulance trip for you, and you have been eating our best food and wine, and then there is the therapy and the medicine." My worries increased. Working away at the abacus, she announced, "Your bill so far is $275.50." Four days in the Kremlin Hospital for less than one day in a good hotel! And meals were included! Suddenly I dreamed of living permanently in the Kremlin Hospital. "Of course you understand," she added, "that as our first private patient we have not had time to work out an appropriate rate schedule. We need to consult with hospitals in the West to find out how much they charge."

I then realized that they did not have the slightest idea how much a hospital should charge for its services. During the entire previous history of the Kremlin hospital everything had been paid for by the government, and no individual financial accounts for patients were kept. Even in the commercial sector of the Soviet economy, all prices had been set by the government, not determined by the market, and therefore no one really knew what something was worth. I had heard a story that Stalin in the 1930s was inspecting a list of prices for groceries, and noticed that the state price for a kilogram of flour was greater than for a kilogram of sugar. He simply reversed the prices, saying, "everyone knows that sugar costs more than flour."

Mulling all this over, I decided that however attractive the thought of staying in the Kremlin hospital might be, I had better get out while the getting was good. Once they found out what a private room in an exclusive hospital in the West cost, I was in for trouble. I pulled out my American Express card and said that I appreciated very much her hospitality, but that my family back in the United States would be alarmed if they learned that I was living in a hospital, and that I needed to leave. She reluctantly agreed, but soon demonstrated that she did not know what to do with the American Express card. She stared at it and turned it over several times, but was obviously at a loss. In my belt hanging in the closet I had several hundred dollars in a "secret" pocket, so ultimately I paid her cash.

I then returned to the Academy of Sciences hotel, and soon was back in the archives. In a few days, however, I felt the first flash of pain in my cheek, and now knowing what was coming, I left immediately for the airport and the trip back home.

In Boston, neurological tests recommended by my new physician— Dr. Martin Wohl of Harvard—soon established that I had a brain tumor, an acoustic neuroma, which was slowly squeezing the top of my spinal cord and would soon kill me if it were not removed. In just a few weeks I had at Massachusetts General Hospital a successful seventeen-hour operation led by Dr. Robert Ojemann, a surgeon specialist on just this sort of tumor.

A few months after the operation, when I had almost returned to normal, I met Mikhail Gorbachev in Chicago at a meeting arranged by the MacArthur Foundation, and I then had lunch with him at the Sheraton Hotel near Michigan Avenue. By this time Gorbachev had been thrown out of office by Boris Yeltsin, and was in the United States to enjoy American adulation for dismantling (unintentionally) the Soviet Union. During the lunch, someone took the accompanying photo of Gorbachev and me chatting.

We both look like large birds with distinct head plumages, Gorbachev the sand hill crane with his famous red birthmark on his forehead, while I am a turkey with a neck wattle of a surgical scar running down my skull. When the photo was taken I was telling him about how the Soviet Union and I had collapsed together, and about my adventures in the Kremlin Hospital. Gorbachev observed that I seemed to be doing better than the Soviet Union. He knew Dr. Gorbunov and was pleased to hear that I had benefited from his services. I did not tell him that the Kremlin Hospital had not diagnosed my brain tumor. Who knows what Dr. Gorbunov would have done to me if he had known? Faced with a brain tumor, I preferred Dr. Ojemann, who knew only how to "cut well," to Dr. Gorbunov's treatment of "the whole patient." Still, to this day, I have only the fondest memories of the

Mikhail Gorbachev and the author, Chicago, 1992.

Kremlin Hospital. For anything but cutting, I would be happy to try it again.

I later learned that the experiment with "outside patients" at the Kremlin Hospital was subsequently abandoned. How many private patients it served before once again closing its doors to all but the elite I do not know. Today it serves exclusively the top leadership of the Russian government. No doubt Vladimir Putin knows Dr. Gorbunov and enjoys the beautiful nurses.

I visited the Kremlin Hospital once again, in March 2000, but not because of my health, but because of the death of a friend.

CHAPTER TWENTY-ONE

AN AMBIGUOUS FUNERAL

WHEN MY CLOSE FRIEND Nikolai Nikolaevich Vorontsov died in Moscow on March 2, 2000, I wanted with all my heart to attend his funeral. Not only were he and his family dear friends, but also, as Soviet minister of the environment in 1991 he possibly saved my life by getting me into the Kremlin Hospital.

In the last years of the Soviet Union Nikolai Nikolaevich in his governmental post had desperately tried to correct some of the rampant environmental abuses. He soon found that whenever his effort to curb pollution meant opposing the "power ministries"—the ministries of defense, police, and heavy industry—he was treated contemptuously and simply overridden. But he also noticed that in the administrative chaos that spread in the Soviet Union as it began to collapse there were opportunities earlier not present to increase silently the acreage of the nature preserves in the distant Arctic and Siberian regions of the country. Everyone in power was so concerned with the political maneuvering in Moscow, and particularly the struggle between Gorbachev and Yeltsin, that they did not notice what was happening along the shores of the Arctic Ocean, the Pacific Ocean, or in remote areas of Siberia. Nikolai quietly increased the size of the preserves by hundreds of thousands of acres, and most of these areas remain under protection—to be sure, inadequately enforced—today.

But the true political strength of the man emerged in August 1991 when military and security officials took over the government and tried to restore authoritarian rule in Russia. Vorontsov rallied troops in their barracks to support democracy, and he took a place beside Boris Yeltsin

Nikolai Vorontsov, Minister for the Environment of the USSR, and the author. Photo taken in Vorontsov's apartment by his daughter Masha.

on the tank in front of the "White House," the seat of the Russian government. The putsch failed, and the reform movement continued.

When Nikolai died I was home in the United States, with no plans for a trip soon to Russia, and his funeral was to be held a few days later. I had no visa for entry into Russia, and getting one—I knew by long experience—was usually a process taking several weeks, sometimes a month or more. Furthermore, I learned of his death on a Saturday afternoon, and the Russian Embassy in Washington was closed for the weekend. If I waited until Monday afternoon to leave the United States, after in the morning miraculously persuading the notoriously bureaucratic consular officers in the Russian Embassy in Washington to give me a visa, I would still miss the funeral in Moscow on Tuesday. The dilemma was a seemingly intractable one for me. I could not just get on a plane in Boston or New York for Moscow in the hopes of convincing the officials at Sheremetevo Airport to let me in on a special basis because the airlines will not permit one to board a plane for Russia unless one shows an entry visa along with the ticket.

I decided to gamble, to take an exceedingly long shot by flying on Sunday to Paris, appear at the Russian Embassy there Monday morning, and then try to talk the Russian consular officers into giving me an entry visa in time for me to take a plane out of Paris at 4:00 P.M. on the same day and arrive in Moscow the evening before the funeral. If I failed, I decided that I would go for a long walk on the streets of Paris, think fondly of my friends in Moscow, living and dead, console myself with a meal and some wine in a French bistro, and then fly back to the United States.

I arrived at Charles de Gaulle Airport at 7:30 A.M. on Monday morning after a sleepless night, took the train to Paris, and at the Chatelet station caught a taxi to the Russian Embassy, which is located on Boulevard Lannes, near the Bois de Boulogne. My historian's sensitivity immediately reminded me of the appropriateness of the location, since the Bois de Boulogne was where the Russian army camped when it occupied Paris after defeating Napoleon. My historical reveries were interrupted when I caught sight of the Russian Embassy. It is an enormous modernistic building, occupying an entire city block, and giving the impression that it houses an impenetrable bureaucracy. My feeling that my mission was hopeless deepened when I entered the basement of the building, where the visa section is located, and found that a crowd there was milling around eight or ten windows behind which sat impassive Russian officers responsible for handling visa requests. The shortest line had ten or twelve people in it. No way, I thought, am I going to receive a visa—with the requisite stamps and photos—in the four or five hours that I had available before I had to leave to catch my flight to Moscow.

I impatiently waited in line for about forty-five minutes until I found myself at a window facing a woman who looked like someone hired by the loan department of a bank for the specific purpose of forcefully saying "no." Taking a big breath and managing a smile, I said in Russian that I was Loren Graham, a professor from the United States, and that I had come to make a special plea that she grant me a visa immediately so that I might fly to Moscow to attend a funeral. To my amazement, the woman replied, "We are expecting you, Professor Graham; we will have a visa ready for you in a few minutes." It turned out that Vorontsov's family in Moscow, hearing of my plan, had contacted a friend in the Ministry of Foreign Affairs in Moscow, who had in turn sent a fax to the Russian Embassy in Paris asking the officers there to grant me a visa immediately "on urgent grounds." For once in my life the Russian bureaucracy turned out to be incredibly efficient. (I could not help but recall the difference between this new Russian bureaucracy and the old Soviet one, which had caused the death of my friend

Vitalii by delaying the issuing of his exit visa. At the same time, I realized that the contrast was not entirely justified both because the Soviet Union was no more, but also because I now had more influential connections in the bureaucracy.) In about half an hour, and a hundred dollars poorer, I left the embassy with my visa in hand. I was able to get to the airport so soon that I caught an earlier flight to Moscow, happily missing my nice meal in a French bistro.

Russia in the post-Soviet period is crime-ridden, and I knew that the most dangerous moment for an arriving foreigner was the trip from the airport to the city. If one just went out on the curb and caught the first cab it might turn out that the driver who appeared was not a cabby at all, but a robber eager to relieve incoming foreigners of their cash. Since travelers' checks are still not widely accepted in Russia, most arriving foreigners have large amounts of cash on them, something the Russian mafia knows well. I had heard stories about such incidents, one of them resulting in a fractured skull for the foreigner. Therefore, I was determined to make special transportation arrangements, catching one of the buses sent to the airport by hotels. Still, I had to wait for that bus, and I therefore went to the designated spot on the curb outside the airport terminal.

As I stood there I glanced downward, and saw very near my feet a package about the size of half a brick. It was wrapped in clear plastic, with several rubber bands around it. Through the plastic I could see what appeared to be a large roll of one hundred dollar bills; at least the top bill on the roll quite visibly carried the $100 label, and one could surmise that the package contained a great deal of money. As I stood there contemplating this surprising development a little voice in my brain warned me "Loren, do not touch that package." I actually moved a few feet away from the apparent bonanza. At that moment a man moved in beside me, reached down, picked up the package, and put it in his coat pocket. I could not resist saying to him, "You are a very fortunate man." He smiled at me and said nothing. Then, as we both stood there, a third man rushed up, tears streaming down his face. He exclaimed to us both, "I just lost my life's savings, $5000. It was a package I must have dropped here a few minutes ago, right where you are standing." Turning to me, he asked, "Do you have my money?" I answered, "No, I do not have your money." The tearful man then turned to the person whom I knew had the package, and asked of him "Do you have my money?" The man replied, "I know nothing about it. I do not have your money."

The distressed man then began running back and forth along the curb, looking for his package, while still sobbing. When he was out of earshot I turned to the man who took the money and said, "Give that man back his money. I know that you have it." He replied, "I'll split it with you." I said, "No, I do not want any of it. Go over and give the money back." My partner stared at me silently for quite a while, apparently wondering if I would actually turn him in, and then ran after the crying man and gave him the package. Then both of them quickly disappeared, going in opposite directions. I noticed a remarkable lack of appreciation expressed by the man who got his package back.

Later I described this incident to several of my Moscow friends. They all agreed that I had narrowly escaped a rather well known scam. The two Russian men, I was told, were working together. The package had no money in it, just a piece of paper on top that looked like a hundred dollar bill. If I had picked up the package, or if I agreed to split the money with the man who offered to do so, yet a third man in a policeman's uniform would have appeared and "arrested" us both for possession of stolen goods.

At that point one of two things would have happened; either I agreed to pay a large bribe to escape arrest, or I would be hauled off, ostensibly for arrest, but actually to be hit over the head and relieved of all my money. After hearing from my friends about the ruse, I could not help but ask myself, "Why did these men go to all the trouble to invent such a clever scheme? Why not follow me until I was alone, perhaps in the restroom of the airport or hotel, and simply bop me over the head and take my money? Were they humble robbers, or perhaps unemployed scientists still being creative?"

Dazed by the kaleidoscope of events in the previous twenty-four hours, I made my way to an airport hotel and collapsed in my bed. The next morning my old friend Anton Struchkov picked me up and took me to the funeral. The poignancy of his coming to get me was striking; it had been Anton Struchkov who, at Nikolai Vorontsov's suggestion, had taken me to the Kremlin Hospital when, nine years earlier, I had collapsed physically in Moscow at roughly the same time the regime collapsed politically. Furthermore, not only had Vorontsov died in the same hospital, but the funeral was to be held there, in a facility constructed in Soviet times for the final rites of the elite of the Communist Party and the Soviet state. This funeral hall, or "traurnyi zal," of the Kremlin Hospital, is located on the grounds of the hospital itself, at 25 Marshal Timoshenko Boulevard. To reach it Anton and I drove by the hospital gates through which years earlier Anton had accompanied me in an ambulance.

Once inside the funeral hall of the Kremlin Hospital I found myself in a very strange and striking location. Soviet ideologists, leaders of an atheistic state, had always attempted to replace the religious symbols that traditionally surrounded such momentous events as birth, marriage, and death, not to speak of all the religious holidays of the Orthodox calendar. They created parallel, entirely secular, ceremonies to supplant the older religious observances.

In the 1920s, a small sect of Communists, known as "God-Builders," had held great outdoor ceremonies in the Soviet Union celebrating with a semi-religious fervor communism as the replacement of Christianity, and replete with secular substitutes for each element of the Orthodox liturgy. During the French Revolution, Robespierre had done something similar, holding a "Festival of the Supreme Being" in front of the Parisian masses while dressed in a magnificent sky-blue coat. The funeral hall of the Kremlin Hospital reflected a latter-day continuation of this effort.

How does one bury someone important without falling back on religious themes and motifs? The architecture of the Kremlin funeral parlor was in the heavy Soviet grand style, utilizing the most expensive building stone, and the marble walls, of alternating grey and cream blocks, were festooned with heavy brass garlands which supported drooping black drapes extending around the large room. At one end there was an enormous glass window, and here the flirtation with religious symbolism came closest, but the glass was not of the type that recalled that of the stained glass windows of Christian cathedrals, but, instead, of secular blue and white panes that allowed the weak wintry light to penetrate the chamber. On the opposite wall were the pipes of an organ, silent and possibly never designed actually to play, since nowhere visible was the organist's seat. In the background could be heard the recorded piano version of Chopin's funeral dirge.

But the date was March 7, 2000, and the Soviet Union was long gone. Furthermore, the man being buried had proudly refused to join the Communist Party and had bravely fought against the restitution of Soviet rule when such a possibility became all too real. Vorontsov was, in fact, the only member of the Council of Ministers (the equivalent of the President's Cabinet in the American government) in the entire history of the Soviet Union who was not a Party member.

Vorontsov was well known as a Westernizing pro-democratic intellectual who, paradoxically, had also been a very high official in the last Soviet government, and therefore was entitled to final rites in what was still an obviously Soviet setting. The family had been presented with the difficult assignment of accepting the honor of having a funeral in the place reserved for top Soviet leaders even though they were determined to show that they were opponents of the very Soviet system that had constructed the place and even of the architects who had designed it according to communist ideological principles.

The obvious answer was to "Christianize" the ceremony, to introduce clearly religious elements defying the Soviet surroundings. But there was a problem here, too. I knew that Nikolai Nikolaevich had never been a conventionally religious man. He was an ardent evolutionary biologist who saw a conflict between science and religion and who came down on the side of science. So the family introduced just enough religious elements to show that they were anti-Soviet while retaining many secular features. In the main hall, near the open casket, were two tiny brass crosses, but no other religious symbols. However, outside the main hall, in the cloak-room, an Orthodox priest was present, and he had hung religious icons and other symbols of his faith on its walls. Religion was held at a distance, but it was there.

The ceremony was divided into two halves, a secular service and a religious one. At the secular service several people, including me, eulogized Vorontsov. The director of the secular service was Sergei Kapitsa, the well-known scientist and television personality whom I had first met many years before. Sergei introduced each of the eulogizers. The previous speakers had gone far beyond their alloted time, so when my turn came I abbreviated my prepared remarks, speaking first in English, in the name of the Davis Center of Russian Studies at Harvard and of other American academics who sent their condolences, and then in Russian, speaking for myself. Among the other speakers were Yegor Gaidar and Boris Nemtsov, leading politicians at the time and democratic colleagues of Nikolai Nikolaevich.

Following the secular service came the religious one. The Orthodox priest moved out of the cloakroom and came into the main hall. The Orthodox funeral service is very long and moving, accompanied by chants and music. One of the singers was so pale and frail that she had to leave during a song. The priest moved around the casket, casting the brass censer with its smoking incense in looping arcs over the deceased. At certain moments in the service the mourners standing around the casket (there were several hundred of us) were supposed to make the sign of the cross. Here again, the Christianization of the congregation was distinctly partial. I noticed that only a small minority of the people present, maybe a fifth, actually followed the priest's cues and made the sign of the cross. Several people stood with such rigid postures that their avoidance of the gesture seemed to be more a proud refusal than an act of abstinence.

Standing there during the ceremony I had ample time to look over the people who had to come to honor this marvelous man, and I found that I knew quite a few of them. Many of them were biologists and activists in the environmental protection movement, as Nikolai Nikolaevich had been; others were participants in the democratic political movement that had transformed the Soviet Union in its last years; a few were government leaders, colleagues of Nikolai Nikolaevich when he was a minister in the government and a member of the first four dumas (national legislatures) of the incipient Russian democracy.

Almost all of the mourners were members of the Russian intelligentsia, a small minority that had traditionally defined itself in terms of what it was opposed to. These people, especially the evolutionary biologists, had roots in the rise of science in Russia at the end of the nineteenth century and early twentieth century. Many of their intellectual forbearers had regarded evolution as inherently opposed to tsarist autocracy and religious orthodoxy. The best-known partisan of biological evolution in Russia, Kliment Timiriazev, openly sided with the Bolsheviks at the time of the 1917 Revolution, a rare event among scientists at the time.

In the early Soviet period, many of the biologists had been alienated by the wasteful industrialization program that destroyed their beloved natural areas and polluted the environment. When they found that they could not resist the industrial onslaught, they retreated to nature preserves (*zapovedniki*) where they created little organizations that were totally free of Communist influence and which democratically elected their officers at a time when that happened nowhere else in the Soviet Union.

The two historians who chronicled this nature protection movement —one an American, the other a Russian—were both present at the funeral, my countryman at least in spirit. Douglas Weiner, author of the aptly named book *A Little Corner of Freedom*, sent a statement of condolence that I read out to those gathered at the funeral. The Russian, Felix Shtilmark, was standing a few feet away from me, in a rumpled suit, looking like he would much have preferred to be snowbound in a little log hut in the remote taiga of Siberia, an area whose natural beauty he loved.

Also present were many older biologists who in the forties and fifties had opposed Lysenkoism; they had stood against it and its creator at a time when such opposition was very dangerous. A number of them had served time in the labor camps. Elsewhere in the room was a younger generation, people who in the late Soviet period had vocally opposed Communism, many of them either participants in or sympathizers with the dissident movement.

Now the Soviet Union was gone, and I sensed that all these people, rooted in different generations but bound together by their mutual resistance to tyrannical authority, were having great difficulty deciding what authority they should now be opposed to. They were bereft of the oppositional ideology that had sustained them all their lives. Traditionally opposed to religion, they had to fall back on it to show that in this Soviet shrine they were not Soviet. Opposed to communism in the name of democracy and the Russian people, they were finding that in free elections the Russian people did not support democrats like them, but inclined toward authoritarian leaders like the Communist Gennady Zyuganov, the ultra-nationalist Vladimir Zhirinovskii, or the "strong hand" Putin who, several weeks later, was elected president.

The intellectuals in this room had thought that democracy would provide them with their hour, the moment when their opinions would count. Instead the nation, acting democratically, had gone in a different direction. These members of the intelligentsia had become superfluous people after decades of believing that they represented all that was good in Russia. I sensed an enormous ideological vacuum in that funeral hall.

After the funeral, the mourners went to the cemetery for the graveside ceremony. In the supposedly egalitarian society that Communism created, the place a person was buried was one of the significant indices of status, of class in the "classless society." The creme de la creme were interred in the Kremlin Wall, or in graves immediately in front of it. That is where Lenin, Stalin, some of the members of the Politburo, and a few foreigners, including the American radical John Reed, ended up. But quite a few leaders lacked the political support required for interment in the Kremlin, and they, including the former head of the Party and government Nikita Khrushchev, ended up in Novodevichy Monastery, the second-ranking place of burial. But now Novodevichy was full, so members of the governing elite were increasingly sent to the third-ranking cemetery, Troekurovskoe Cemetery, not far from the Kremlin Hospital. That is where Nikolai Nikolaevich was to be buried.

The graveside ceremony, also prolonged and attended by the priest, was held in the middle of a late winter blizzard, with swirling clouds of large snowflakes covering us as we stood surrounding the casket, still open. The snowflakes fell on Nikolai's face, covering his eyes and eyebrows so rapidly that every few minutes one of the mourners would wipe the dead man's face with a handkerchief. It was desperately cold and windy, and we shivered as we stood there. There were many more speeches, and each speaker always stood bareheaded as she or he spoke, exposed to the wind and the falling snow.

As I stood before the grave and listened to the speeches I looked around me. The gravestones on each side of Nikolai's grave indicated not only who was buried there, but also stated the deceased's highest rank: there was an admiral in the navy here, over there a general, here a "narodnyi artist" (people's artist, an official rank given to performing artists), there a minister in the government, there a full (and therefore immortal) member of the Academy of Sciences. Often the likeness of the deceased was engraved on the stone.

As appropriate for a governmental cemetery, most of the tombstones were government-issue: standard rectangular blocks, some larger than others, but without much variety. But I noticed that a few of the most recent tombstones, those erected since about 1994, were shaped in the form of the double-barred Orthodox cross. Thus religion, earlier banned from official occasions, was creeping into the governmental cemetery for the top leaders. I counted the new orthodox crosses visible from the gravesite and saw maybe ten or twelve. I noticed that there were no Stars of David in sight, nor did I see any as I walked along the snow-covered path leading out of the cemetery. I did, however, see one quite unusual tombstone: the man had been buried in 1972, almost twenty years before the fall of the Soviet Union, and his marker was a standard Soviet government product, an anonymous block of stone. But someone, no doubt a member of his family, had very recently brought a stone Orthodox cross and attached it, with metal bands, to the secular tombstone of their loved one.

At the conclusion of the graveside ceremony the cemetery workers, clad in soiled crude clothing and boots, closed the casket lid and nailed it shut. Then they lowered it with two large fraying ropes into the grave, acting so hastily that the casket descended at a precipitous angle, no doubt causing chaos within. There was no place here for the automated unrolling gears with suspension straps that one sees at gravesites in the United States.

Once the casket was in the bottom of the grave, the workers, eight or nine of them, began furiously shoveling dirt on the casket. The mourners stepped forward and threw handfuls of dirt on the casket, as was the Orthodox custom. I followed suit and found that the task was not so easy, for the earth was frozen in unbreakable lumps. When the grave was almost two-thirds full of dirt, one of the workers appeared with a wooden Orthodox cross, and hastily thrust it into the hole while other workers shoveled dirt around it.

As I turned and left the grave I said to myself that Nikolai probably would not have agreed with much that happened at his burial, including the implanting of a cross over his body. But just what kind of symbol would have appropriately marked this man's grave, a man who spent most of his life combating orthodoxy? Now new orthodoxies were crowding in, ones with which he and his life were out of step. To his dismay, he would not have known whether to support or oppose them.

CHAPTER TWENTY-TWO

GEORGE SOROS TRIES TO SAVE RUSSIAN SCIENCE AND CULTURE

FOR THE LAST FIFTEEN YEARS, starting even before the collapse of the Soviet Union, I have been engaged in an effort, working with American foundations, to save and reform science and higher education in Russia. The foundations have included George Soros' International Science Foundation, the John D. and Catherine T. MacArthur Foundation, the Sloan Foundation, the Civilian Research and Development Foundation, and the Carnegie Corporation. These programs, for which I have been an advisor or member of selection committees, have disbursed several hundred million dollars to scientists and scientific organizations in the former Soviet Union. This activity brought me in contact with a strikingly generous but puzzlingly idiosyncratic philanthropist and businessman, George Soros, with whom I traveled in Russia several times. My work with these programs also alerted me to a series of questions that I had not earlier considered, such as the difficulty of many Russians in understanding philanthropy, and the mixture of motives of philanthropists themselves.

For all its many defects, the Soviet Union was remarkably successful in education and science. Evidence in support of this observation can be found in the fact that many, if not most, American universities today employ scientists educated in the Soviet Union, including tenured professors at Harvard, Princeton, California, MIT, Minnesota, and many other leading universities.

As a historian of Russian science I knew both the weaknesses and strengths of the Soviet record in science. On the one hand, the Soviet government politically persecuted many of its scientists and forcibly harnessed them to the military-industrial complex; on the other hand, it magnificently educated some of them, and the Soviet Union became a world leader in areas such as theoretical physics and mathematics.

When the Soviet Union collapsed in 1991 the support for science and higher education virtually ceased at the same time. Under the Soviet centralized economy the government had controlled prices, including the lucrative concealed "turn-over tax" on consumers, and was able to direct the large central budget coming from these controls in whatever directions it wished. The military and scientific establishments were the primary beneficiaries. When the Soviet Union disappeared, controlled prices and hidden taxes vanished at the same time, and the earlier beneficiaries were suddenly without money. The new more representative legislative bodies of Russia were, understandably, not as interested in science as had been the autocratic Soviet government, devoted to military and technological prowess. To a certain extent this adjustment was healthy, since the Soviet Union had a distortedly large scientific establishment and produced more scientists and engineers than any other country in the world at a time when its economy was a fraction of the size of several other countries, such as the United States or Japan. A shift in priorities was natural, but became extreme. I soon heard distressing stories of unemployed or unpaid scientists at the leading research and educational institutions of the former Soviet Union. The families of many Russian scientists faced poverty, even starvation. American scientists and foundations began to organize to see if something could be done to help, and I was quickly drawn in.

The John D. and Catherine T. MacArthur Foundation was one of the first foundations to respond, spurred on by its native Russian-speaking vice-president Victor Rabinowitch with the full support of its president Adele Simmons. I became an advisor on its programs in the former Soviet Union, and, over a decade later, under a different president at MacArthur, Jonathan Fanton, I still am. I have also been a member of the "Governing Council" of a program of the Civilian Research and Development Foundation helping strengthen Russian research universities. This foundation was long headed by another Russian-speaking American, Gerson Sher. However, in the natural sciences the efforts of established private foundations like MacArthur were soon surpassed by those of one individual: George Soros. Here was a man who out of his own pocket financed efforts that, at least temporarily, dwarfed the programs in science and education in Russia of the largest American private foundations, and, in several years, compared with those of entire governments.

Soros is an extremely complicated individual who once confessed that he had been afflicted with messianic fantasies from childhood, which he felt he had to control, lest he end up in the loony bin. Controlling but not suppressing these fantasies had helped him to become the most successful hedge fund manager in history. Anyone who put one thousand dollars in his Quantum Fund in 1969 would have over two million dollars today; Soros himself, starting with relatively modest resources, became a multi-billionaire. In September 1992 he "broke the British pound" in a speculative venture in which he made over a billion dollars in a few days.

Several months after this spectacular success Soros announced that he was going to establish the International Science Foundation (ISF) with the specific goal of supporting science in the former Soviet Union. To supervise the new foundation he formed an "executive board" on which I served during its entire brief history, four years. Most of the members of the board were distinguished natural scientists, including seven Nobel laureates. Soros himself usually participated in the frequent meetings of the board, and he also personally supervised the operations of his foundations in Russia, of which there were soon several. In these meetings, and during our travels together in Russia, I had an opportunity to witness at first hand his mode of operation and behavior.

It soon became clear that we were an "executive board" only in name; real power rested entirely with Soros. On the other hand, he did not ignore us; he listened carefully to our opinions, and we could see him visibly processing the information that we gave him. But we were definitely advisors, not members of a normal board of trustees with authority to make important decisions on our own. After listening to all our opinions Soros would reflect a bit, maybe even admit a few uncertainties, and then he would decide the question. Once his decision was announced, there was no further debate.

Watching him in action I realized that this was a man whose administrative mode had been entirely formed by his long experience as an investor. In that position it was not important to be "right" or "wrong" in the terms familiar to me as a member of the academic world. It mattered little to Soros that he was frequently wrong; he operated on the assumption that all his decisions, like everyone else's, would be flawed, and many mistaken. In fact, he possessed a philosophy based on the incompleteness and fallibility of human knowledge. That, to him, was the key to understanding both financial markets and human history. All that mattered to Soros was that, on a statistical and financial basis, he take more winning positions than losing ones. He obviously had been fantastically successful in doing so in the financial world. He was in the habit of getting up each morning and then, on the basis both of intuition and the latest information available to him, deciding to "buy" this or "sell" that. At our board meetings he made similar quick decisions, not worrying about the rough-cut or approximate character of his recommended policies. It was an education to watch him in action.

Despite his belief that all knowledge, including his own, was incomplete or flawed, Soros could be impossibly arrogant and rude. I once saw him dismiss a member of his staff by simply turning on him and saying "You have become a source of negative energy. You are fired." Several times during the years I worked for him I considered resigning from the board, irritated by his imperious method. But each time I decided not to do so, since I so strongly agreed with his goals. I deeply admired him because he spent his money on such good causes, not on the yachts and expensive playthings in which many other rich people indulged. Today, when his interests have moved rather far from Russian science, I still admire him for this reason. And, after all, the money that he spends is his own, and he should have authority over it as long as he obeys the laws on taxes and financial dealings.

Soros once told me that people who suspected that he mixed his philanthropic and business interests were wrong; instead, he said that when he was acting as a businessman, he acted within the law, but that he showed no mercy. If he could make a profit, he did so. However, when he acted as a philanthropist, he told me, charity and mercy were important goals for him. He said he did not mix the activities of business and charity, but kept them separate. I believed him, and was certain that he would not invest in any businesses in Russia connected with his philanthropic activities. I later found out that I was wrong.

In December 1992, at the first meeting of his executive council, Soros was obviously distressed by reports that the families of many Russian scientists might not make it through the coming winter; they simply had no money for food or clothing. He decided that he wanted to get emergency grants into their hands almost immediately. Even $500, he said, would make the difference for the average Russian scientist. At that time, at the existing exchange rate between the dollar and the ruble, $500 was almost a year's salary for most Russian scientists (perhaps an irrelevant fact, since most of them were not receiving even these miserable salaries). He turned to me with the following challenge: "Loren, you are an expert on Russian science, can you give me a list of the names and addresses of the 20,000 best scientists in the former Soviet Union?"

My mind whirled. I knew what his goal was, and I strongly supported it. I also knew that under the circumstances I had to say "yes"; if I did not, my services would probably be terminated. But how would I do it? I knew how to get a list of the leading research institutes and universities in the former Soviet Union, but how would I decide in a very short time which 20,000 scientists (out of the over a million with the appropriate degrees) should get the emergency grants? How would we measure financial need? How would we evaluate scientific quality? Not knowing the answers to these fundamental questions I nonetheless replied "Yes, I can, but it will take me several months."

Soros cut me short with a curt, "That's far too long." He observed that "he who gives quickly gives twice." He challenged me with a suggested answer to his original question: He asked me if there was not something called the Science Citation Index. Could I not go into the computers of this service and search for all scientists in the former Soviet Union who had published at least five articles in the last three years? If it turned out that there were more than 20,000 such scientists, I should make another computer search requiring each scientist to have published six articles in the last three years. I should keep doing this, changing the publication requirements, he suggested, until I got a list of approximately 20,000 scientists. Then I should send each of them $500.

This approach was typical of Soros—brilliant, but rough, inequitable, and formidably difficult. What journals would be considered legitimate? And how could we send $500 from America to 20,000 scientists in Russia at a time when there were in Russia no banking system, no personal checking accounts, no credit cards, and Russian prohibitions against importing foreign currency? I also knew that in Russia many senior directors of research institutes, privileged people who were in the least need of financial aid, forced all junior researchers to attach the director's name to the list of authors of all important published articles. I knew of one such director who published, as a co-author, an article every week on average, obviously an impossibility if he were doing the work himself. We would end up rewarding quite a few old fogies in the Russian science establishment who were no longer doing innovative research. I pointed out to Soros some of the drawbacks of his approach, but it soon became clear that he had made up his mind. He wanted a method that would produce results fast, and he was willing to live with the drawbacks.

Actually, Soros' approach was probably the best of all imperfect means of getting $500 into the pockets of excellent Russian scientists within the shortest possible time. We advisors worked out the details, deciding which journals to consider on the basis of an "impact factor" that measured their citation standings in the field, and in a few weeks came up with a list of 20,000 scientists.

Delivering the money into the hands of the scientists in the former Soviet Union was another matter. Russian custom and tax laws prohibited the importation of large amounts of foreign cash, or imposed exorbitant custom duties. Furthermore, in the absence of a Russian banking system, accounts could not be transferred over national borders by electronic means. Trying to overcome these obstacles, American scientists carried large amounts of cash to the former Soviet Union, usually in $20 or $100 bills, ignoring the requirement to declare on customs declarations the amount of cash they were bringing with them. In this first phase of the American help to Russian scientists, before Soros worked out special legal channels, all sorts of methods were used to transfer money, most of them illegal. The chairman of the mathematics department at MIT, Robert McPherson, smuggled in $20,000 by concealing it in his clothing. On several occasions I also illegally took money to Russia destined for scientists, although usually only several thousand dollars at a time. Many American mathematicians and physicists did the same thing, sometimes carrying large amounts of cash in brown paper bags. Any one of us could have been arrested and imprisoned for violations of Russian customs laws, but luckily no one was. Then on January 10, 1993, George Soros met with Boris Yeltsin in the Kremlin and worked out a way to exempt the funds of the ISF from customs duties. Still, cash had to be taken to Russia by hand in the first weeks of the program, and one Russian member of the Executive Council, V. P. Skulachev, carried an enormous amount of money from New York to Moscow in his briefcase. Even though, according to the agreement just made by Soros with Yeltsin, the transfer was now legal, the risk of theft was breathtaking. Eventually Soros obtained permission to establish his own bank in Russia, which could receive wire transfers.

The Emergency Grants Program was tremendously successful. Although it lasted only a short time the payments made under that program are still remembered by many Russian scientists as what made the difference for survival in one of the most difficult years of transition from the Soviet Union to the new post-Soviet Russia. It was followed by an even more important program of long-term grants, with full peer review that served as a model for other foundations and the Russians themselves, and other forms of support. In all, Soros expended approximately $130 million in the period 1992–1996 on science in the former Soviet Union.

Starting in the early nineties and continuing to the present time I have made more frequent trips to Russia than ever before, sometimes four or five times a year, and usually for the purpose of helping Russian science. One trip I remember particularly well came in 1995 at a time a meeting was scheduled in Moscow of the Executive Council of the International Science Foundation. When I purchased my ticket I got in step with the heady atmosphere of the times and bought a business class ticket. Always before, in my many trips to Russia, I had traveled tourist class, but now my way was being paid by one of the richest men in the world, and that thought may have gone to my head. Furthermore, I was growing older, and I noticed increased stiffness in my legs on long airplane flights. So I enjoyed the additional space (and the drinks and refreshments) of business class.

About two-thirds of the way across the Atlantic I decided to take a stroll to limber up my legs. The plane was a Boeing 747 that had two aisles, so I could do a circle tour of the entire aircraft as I exercised my legs. In the middle of my amble, to my horror I spied George Soros sitting in tourist class. I had talked with him only a few days earlier in New York. I knew that he was going to the same meeting of the ISF Executive Council in Moscow I was, and that he was paying the transportation costs for all of us. I frantically tried to get out of his line of sight, and hastily returned to my business class seat, which now seemed decidedly illicit. I do not know if Soros saw me or not.

Soros had a distaste for expensive display. In Moscow he found the hotel which his staff had chosen for him to be impossibly expensive and immediately transferred to another hotel. He certainly lived well, had apartments in London, Paris, and New York, an estate in Southampton on Long Island, and dressed in fine tailored suits, but nonetheless had firm ideas about what was necessary and what was unnecessary expense.

In Moscow in these first years after the fall of the Soviet Union I witnessed poverty, distress, and crime in Russia at every hand. Near the subway stations stood long lines of people, usually women, holding up items for sale, pathetically simple things like socks and toothbrushes, or a bottle of vodka. Deprived of their salaries, they were exhausting their closets and wardrobes in order to obtain, by selling their personal possessions, enough money to survive for another week. Inside the subway stations, beggars, again often women, were holding out their palms to everyone who passed, often beating their heads against the pavement as I came near, crying out "God have mercy!" When I went to a post office to mail a package of books home I noticed an old woman hurrying along with me, dressed in threadbare clothing. She was going to pick up her monthly pension, which was disbursed in cash at the post office. When we arrived together we both saw a sign posted on the post office door saying, "We have no cash. Pensions are not being paid." The old woman burst out in tears and collapsed at the door. I thrust a ten-dollar bill into her hands and quickly fled from the scene. Why, I asked myself, am I trying to help scientists, who had at least some advantages, when people exist in such worse circumstances? (George Soros would eventually react the same way, and shift his millions away from science, to health, basic human services, and the support of a civil society.) What Russia most needed at the moment, it was clear to me, were old-fashioned Salvation Army food kitchens and clothing disbursal units. Eventually the Salvation Army moved to Moscow, even though subjected to considerable criticism by Russian nationalists and religious spokespeople who feared they were religious proselytizers.

It is only natural that Russian citizens protested their new poverty and blamed Boris Yeltsin and his "economic shock" policy for their misfortune. In these years, the early nineties, it was not at all rare to see on the streets of Moscow demonstrations against the government. I took a photo of a man standing in the center of Moscow with a sign saying "Yeltsin is an enemy of the people!" "Prosecute Yeltsin and his whole crew!" The phrase "enemy of the people" is of course a Stalinist one, and the red flags carried by the man and the people behind him show that this was a pro-Communist demonstration.

Perhaps the most wrenching scenes in these early post-Soviet years were at the church doors. Orthodox churches, freed from Soviet controls, were reopening everywhere. I had read in novels and history texts about Western Europe that in the centuries of the middle ages the cathedral door was the place where beggars and lepers traditionally congregated, appealing to the faithful as they went to worship, but I was not prepared for what I saw when I went to Russian churches; I went there not to worship, but to observe (what a coldly neutral anthropological term!) the turmoil of post-Soviet Russian society. Outside the door was a small crowd of beggars, assuming heart-wringing

A protestor carrying signs saying "Yeltsin is an enemy of the people!" and "Prosecute Yeltsin and his whole crew!" Moscow, 1993. Photo by the author.

poses that were designed to loosen the pockets of the worshippers. Men sat in the snow extending amputated limbs, often diseased and ulcerated, with the bandages removed so the onlookers would see the horror of their condition. Women held up their babies, crying out that they could not feed them. And all this at a time when the Orthodox Church was gilding with gold the cupolas of these long-neglected places of worship!

But not only the Orthodox Church should have felt ashamed. I was living at this time, while working on Soros-sponsored projects, in the Radisson Slavianskaia Hotel, a partially American-controlled luxury hotel on the Moscow River. Inside its marble-covered lobby one could buy an American hamburger at its Amadeus Cafe for $20, or spend $100 for a meal in its gourmet restaurant. As I returned to the hotel from one of my trips around Moscow in which I witnessed misery I recalled one of the passages in Tolstoy's writings in which he described how he, as a pampered young nobleman, returned to his mansion for a fine meal after witnessing the suffering poor of tsarist Moscow. I shared some of Tolstoy's feelings of guilt.

While many Americans patronized the Radisson Slavianskaia, it was also a favorite stopping place for the "New Russians," the new elite profiting from the economic possibilities of post-Soviet Russia, as well as the criminal Mafia that imposed "protection charges," often 20 percent of profits, on the newly emerging businesses. The members of this Mafia carefully imitated what they thought were the life styles of the Mafia in the West. When they had earlier been citizens of the USSR they had been told by the Soviet propaganda organs that "capitalism is criminal"; now that they were capitalists, they thought it natural to be criminal.

One time standing at the main entrance to the Radisson Slavianskaia I saw a long Mercedes limousine pull up, with drawn white curtains in the windows. The front two sets of doors flew open, and the bodyguards of the Mafia chieftain inside jumped out, guns drawn. Then the big man himself emerged, dressed in a black silk suit and accompanied by a sexy blonde, while talking ostentatiously on his cellular phone. From inside the limousine, from the CD player, I could hear the theme song of the movie "The Godfather." It was pure theater, and everyone knew it and played roles in it.

The man in charge of the Radisson Slavianskaia, and partial owner, was Paul Tatum, an American from Oklahoma. He also had bodyguards, but he cautiously met each week at a "Happy Hour" with the residents of his hotel. During the half dozen or so times I stayed at the Radisson Slavianskaia while working for American foundations I occasionally attended these events and came to know Tatum. He told me that he was under great pressure from the Mafia to pay exorbitant protection charges, but that he refused to do so. He therefore knew that his life was in danger. He occupied two suites, Rooms 850 and 852, on upper floors of the hotel, and was advised to stay inside whenever possible. On November 3, 1996, he ignored this advice and walked out the front door of his hotel to the nearby Kievskii Vokzal subway station, where, as he descended the steps, he was shot eleven times by two Mafia gunmen with Kalashnikov assault rifles. He died almost instantly. The gunmen fled in a white Zhiguli sedan, one of the most common cars in Moscow. No arrests were ever made, and the Mafia spread the story that Tatum had actually been assassinated by CIA agents.

I did not believe that I had anything to fear from the Mafia, but there was one moment when I wondered if I was mistaken. This incident caused me to think that my association with the famous financier George Soros, hated by some anti-Semitic nationalists in Russia, might have serious consequences. I went on a walk from the Radisson Slav-ianskaia in downtown Moscow. I wanted to get some exercise, and I also needed to buy a few gifts for members of my family and friends. I knew that near the Rossiia Hotel, right off Red Square, was a small restored church that was used by an arts and crafts society as a place to sell handcrafted items from the rural villages of Russia. Here one could buy wonderful whittled wooden birds with exquisitely detailed wings, textiles, oil paintings, and water–colors. In order to reach this small church I walked across the river on Smolensk Boulevard and then down the historic, and now touristy, "Old Arbat" street toward the Kremlin. When I reached Red Square after a long walk I crossed it and then turned left on Varvarka Street. I had intended here to stop in the church with the handicraft shop, but I was by this time so cold I de-cided to go past the church into the lobby of the giant Rossiia Hotel and get warm.

As I started up the curving street toward the hotel entrance I saw on the sidewalk a few feet in front of me a moving red dot, about the size of a quarter. As I watched the dot it came toward me, mounted my shoe, and then started up my leg, an illuminated spot that easily moved on any surface it came to. It moved up to my chest and stopped. Sud-denly I realized what it was and immediately jumped behind the car parked at the curb next to me. I threw myself down on the ground beside the car and saw that the dot did not follow me. The car was between me and the emission source of the red dot. My heart pound-ing, I raised myself up to the level of the window of the car and looked through that window toward the Rossiia Hotel. There, on the fourth floor, in a hotel window I saw a dark figure and another red dot, source of the similar dot searching for me.

As a person who summered in the North Woods of Lake Superior I knew that some of the latest models of hunting rifles come equipped with laser sights that allow the hunter to place a laser dot on the heart of a deer or bear before firing, in that way ensuring an accurate aim. I was somebody's target. I noticed that the figure had disappeared from the window, and I decided that I should leave immediately in case he was coming after me. I ran into the hotel, whose internal layout I knew well from former periods of residence in it, turned right down a long corridor, and then emerged from another hotel entrance that I knew had a taxi stand opposite it. I jumped in a taxi and went back to the Radisson Slavianskaia, even though it did not seem to be the safest refuge one could imagine.

In my room I called a Russian friend and told him what had happened. He listened carefully and gave a rational explanation of the event that did much to calm me. He said that on Varvarka Street, where I had just been, was located a sports shop specializing in hunting equipment, and that the person who pointed his laser sight at me was no doubt not trying to kill me; instead, he probably had come to Moscow from a provincial city in order to buy one of the new laser hunting guns for sale in this shop, and, once back in his hotel room, could not resist the temptation to see how the sight worked, no doubt with an unloaded gun. I was the hapless person who walked toward his hotel at that moment and presented a practice target.

I was not entirely convinced, but several days later I visited the hunting shop, in sight of the Rossiia Hotel, and found that laser-sighted hunting rifles were indeed for sale there. I decided not to become paranoid about the incident. I have been in Moscow many times since this traumatic experience and have seen no more red dots.

Meanwhile, George Soros was being attacked in the newspapers for his philanthropic activities. In February 1994 the right-wing journal *Molodaia gvardiia* published an article entitled "The Secret Diplomacy of George Soros" in which the author, S. Moskvitianin, accused Soros of trying to set up a secret world government, working together with David Rockefeller, Henry Kissinger, and Mikhail Gorbachev. Moskvitianin concluded, "Only the patriotic forces and a national government can put an end to this ruinous duplicity, stop the secret diplomacy, and free the country from the bondage yoke of the transworld government."

Then on January 10, 1995, the major newspaper *Nezavisimaia gazeta* published an article that was purportedly an internal document of the Russian Federal Counterintelligence Service (FSK) accusing American foundations, universities, and volunteer organizations of carrying out espionage and subversion. George Soros and the International Science Foundation were given special attention, but the Ford Foundation and Harvard, Yale, Columbia, Duke and Stanford universities were also accused of espionage. Rather than helping Russian science, the ISF, according to this article, was promoting brain drain and "dooming Russian science and the Russian economy to lag behind, to be controlled by America."

Particularly regrettable was the interview that the famous Russian dissident Alexander Solzhenitsyn gave on Russian television on March 13, 1995, in which he said that Russia needed to boost its "ideological defense against scientific and culture grants from the Soros Foundation."

George Soros was hurt by these unfair charges. The Russian scientific community rose in his defense, sending in protests to the newspapers that published the scurrilous articles. When I was with Soros in St. Petersburg the local society of scientists honored him with a banquet at which great appreciation for his activity was expressed. Eventually the national legislature, the Duma, honored Soros with a special citation. But the attacks never ceased. Indeed, in March 2001, long after Soros ceased his support for Russian science, the Russian newspaper *Moskovskii Komsomolets* published a particularly paranoiac article:

> Known for his charity, George Soros once spent almost $100 million to link Russian research centers to the Internet. There was more to it than charity as such. Russian researchers gained electronic access to the world—and the American financier recouped his money many times over. . . . As a rule, all these foundations (Soros, Carnegie, Fulbright, MacArthur, Ebert, International Scientific-Technical Center, USAID, Eurasia Foundation, and many others) use a similar pattern. They organize a competition, promising grants to impoverished Russian scientists. Acting as a sieve, they sort out heaps of applications with descriptions of projects, and pick out the most promising ones. . . . It turns out that Russia is losing billions of dollars a year through such leaks. . . . And where are the court trials? What have our secret services been doing? . . . The secret services are supposed to protect our national assets, including intellectual property.

This article ominously suggested that American foundation officials trying to help Russians in their moment of need might be accused of breaking the law and put on trial.

I knew from my own experience with American foundations that these charges were completely false. Nonetheless, I was disappointed when George Soros, whom I admired so much for his generosity toward Russian science, enormously complicated the situation by reversing his earlier position that he would not mix his philanthropic and investment activities. In 1996 he invested heavily in a Russian communications company even though in his earlier philanthropic activity he had helped build communications networks for Russian scientists. Seeing possible trouble on the horizon, I was relieved that after 1996 I no longer had a connection with Soros' philanthropy in Russia. But I am proud to have worked for George Soros when he so generously aided Russian scientists. I am also proud to have continued activity with other American foundations, such as the John D. and Catherine T. Mac-

Arthur Foundation, who have done such wonderful work in areas of environmental protection, human rights, law and society, peace and security, and higher education.

The justification that George Soros gave for his shift in policy toward mixing philanthropy and business offers a revealing insight into his complex, contradictory, and fascinating personality. Just after his shift of policy a reporter challenged him: "You said earlier that you did not plan to invest in Eastern Europe, not only because you have enough money already, but also because it could lead to conflicts between your business goals and your philanthropic ones. Why have you changed your mind?" Soros replied, "Because the situation changed . . . My rule not to invest in countries where I had foundations was a simple rule to deal with a complex situation. It was convenient, because it avoided any possibility of conflict of interest. Today the rule is no longer tenable. The eastern European financial markets are developing, and it is my business to operate in financial markets."

Not satisfied with this answer, the reporter pushed Soros harder: "But by refraining from making investments, you could have reduced the grounds on which you can be attacked."

The answer that Soros gave to this question is, I think, one of the most revealing statements he has ever made. He replied:

> Yes, I could have. But I deliberately chose to expose myself. To be a selfless benefactor was just a little too good to be true. It fed my self-image as a godlike creature, above the fray, doing good and fighting evil. I have talked about my messianic fantasies; I am not ashamed of them; the world would be a grim place without such fantasies. But they are fantasies. And to be godlike is to be removed from humanity. . . . I could see, particularly in Russia, that people simply could not understand what I was all about. Previously I never needed to explain my motivation to people who shared my objectives, but in today's Russia, people are so caught up in the fight for survival that the pursuit of an abstract good like open society seems hardly credible. I made the decision to start investing last year at the height of the robber capitalist episode. It seemed to me that to appear as a robber capitalist who is concerned with cultural and political values was more credible than to be a disembodied intellect arguing for the merits of an open society. I could serve as a role model for the budding robber capitalists of Russia. And by entering the fray as an investor, I descended from Mount Olympus and became a flesh and blood human being.

The easiest interpretation of this statement, and one that surely contains much truth, is that it is an eloquent piece of self-justification. Soros saw an opportunity to make money and wanted to take advantage of it (the fact that he miscalculated, and had heavy financial losses in Russia does not change that conclusion). However, in my opinion, this interpretation is only partially correct. Looking at all of Soros' activities, including his heavy expenditures on philanthropy in Russia up to 2003 (when he announced he was pulling out), it is clear to me that he is truly dedicated to the ideal of an open, democratic society, has done far more to help create such a society in Russia than any other individual, and would love to see Russia move in that direction. Such a transformation would benefit both Russia and Soros, including his financial ambitions. In the United States Soros has recently emerged as a critic of the excesses of the capitalist system that made him a rich man, has given money heavily to such unorthodox causes as possible partial legalization of drugs and the study of how Americans avoid the topic of death. Mixed in with Soros' financial impulses are the motivations of a philosopher, an altruist, and a reformer. Soros has so much money that everything he does, good and bad, is magnified enormously, and all his traits—his benevolence, his avarice, and his enormous ego—are all fascinatingly on display.

CHAPTER TWENTY-THREE

DEATH OF AN OLD AMERICAN COMMUNIST

ON DECEMBER 2, 2000, the day before I left for a trip to Russia, I attended a memorial service in Cambridge, Massachusetts, for a well-known American Marxist, Dirk Struik, who had recently died at the age of 106. Struik, a professor of mathematics emeritus at MIT, was a legend in Cambridge, a man who in his long life had many close personal friends but also quite a few political enemies. A fervent sympathizer with Communism until his death, he was asked by a reporter several years ago whether the horrors committed in the name of Communism and the demise of the Soviet Union caused him to question his beliefs. He replied, "No, of course not, because Marxism is an outlook on life. It's the same with Christians; you can be a good Christian despite the fact that Christians have committed horrible crimes in the name of Christianity."

On another occasion, after he had passed his hundredth birthday, someone asked Struik to what he attributed his longevity; he replied, "to the three M's—mathematics, marriage, and Marxism." He was bonded to mathematics from his student days in the Netherlands just after the turn of the century; he was married to the same woman, also a mathematician, for over seventy years; and he was loyal to Marxist socialism for over ninety years. He saw the three M's as all of a piece. Indeed, he said many times that Marxism helped him understand both mathematics and society better, a happy marriage was the key to his personal contentment, and that mathematics provided him with such pleasant intellectual thoughts that he was able to continue to publish long after all his contemporaries had died of old age. At a ceremony several years earlier marking his 100th birthday he gave a paper on the history of mathematics, an event that I attended. At the age of 104 he remarked to a friend that he was "past his prime" (103 is a prime number in mathematics) but expected to return when he was 107 (another prime number).

After joining the MIT mathematics faculty in 1926 Struik was active in both mathematics and politics. He was an apologist for the Soviet Union and once considered moving there. During World War II he was a member of the same communist group at MIT and Harvard as Wendell Furry. He made no secret of his Marxist beliefs. Just as was the case with Furry, Struik became a *cause célèbre* in the McCarthy era. In 1951 he was indicted in Massachusetts on charges of advocating the overthrow of the United States and Massachusetts governments, charges that caused Bertrand Russell to observe, "That Struik must be a very powerful man." At the time of the indictment MIT suspended Struik from teaching duties, but with full pay and benefits until the case could be dealt with in the courts. After five years the indictment was dropped and Struik returned to the MIT faculty, continuing his work there until his retirement in 1960. Despite his restitution to teaching duties, the five-year period in which MIT refused to allow this mild-mannered mathematician to serve on its faculty has always been regarded by defenders of academic freedom in the United States as a serious blot on the reputation of MIT.

The memorial service for Struik at MIT was an event that attracted all the old radicals in Cambridge. And not just from Cambridge; several radical mathematicians who had fled abroad during either the McCarthy or Vietnam periods returned from Canada, Mexico, and other countries just to attend this service and honor Struik. Several current deans and department heads at MIT, no doubt wishing to do penance for MIT's previous administrative harshness to Struik, also attended. A half-dozen or so of my colleagues in history of science, both from MIT and Harvard, were there. In all, several hundred people were present. The memorial service was held in the Sala de Puerto Rico room of the student union building at MIT, a place chosen to symbolize Struik's sympathies with the third world. Dozens of eulogies were given, including one from the Communist Party of the United States of America, delivered by a national committee member sent by the Party for the occasion from its headquarters in New York City. Many of the speakers praised socialism, speaking in a language that was more reminiscent of the 1930s than the new millennium of the twenty-first century. Struik's lawyer during the political and legal struggles of the 1950s was there, pointedly observing "people say socialism is dead, once again."

When a few days later I was in Moscow, ten years after the fall of Soviet communism, I told several of my friends, also people in the academic world, of the ceremony for Struik that I had just attended back at MIT, and of the eulogies, including the one by the U.S. Communist Party, that had been delivered. I was struck with the strength of their reactions. "Loren," they asked, "how could you attend the funeral of an American Communist? No one knows better than you the damage that communism has done to this world in the twentieth century. Would you attend the funeral of a Nazi who had been dismissed from teaching duties at MIT in World War II? You know very well that there have been more victims of communism in this past century than even of Nazism. And as a historian of Russia and Russian science, you can have no illusions about communism. Why would you do such a thing?"

I tried to explain that although I did not share Struik's political views, he was a friend and colleague (not only at MIT, but also at Harvard, where for many years he was an associate of the same department in which I taught, the history of science department). I also pointed out that Struik, as a historian of mathematics, had written books, no doubt influenced by his Marxism, in which he maintained that the evolution of mathematics and science could be related to social and political developments, a viewpoint which I also supported throughout my academic career. Struik and I had often discussed the history of science and mathematics together, and I was grateful to him for these discussions. For a person interested in history, Struik was fascinating to talk to, because his memories spanned the entire twentieth century. The Russo-Japanese War of 1904–1905 and the Russian-Chechen War of the late 1990s were equally personal events for him. Furthermore, I observed that even though I did not agree with Struik politically, I believed that MIT had acted incorrectly, violating the principles of academic freedom, in forbidding him to teach for five years. I added that while I was a friend of Struik's, whose admiration for the Soviet Union I did not share, I was also a friend of many critics of the Soviet Union, such as Aleksandr Yakovlev, whose hatred of the Soviet order was now so powerful that he considered everything good in Russian society to have been destroyed under Soviet rule, another extreme view with which I cannot agree.

My Russian friends quizzed me closely about the "punishment" that MIT had given Struik for his political transgressions. When I told them that although he had been forbidden to teach for five years, he had continued throughout this period to receive full pay and benefits, my Russian colleagues broke out in laughter. They compared this "punishment" to the prison sentences and executions of political suspects in the Soviet Union; one of them even observed that he would like to have the same punishment as Struik, since it amounted to a five-year fellowship without obligations that would give him the opportunity to "get some research and writing done."

I was sobered by the criticisms of my Russian colleagues. They were all intellectuals who had earlier seemed to be thoroughly Westernized, strong defenders of democracy and academic freedom. However, they could not understand the American experience, and they thought that I could not understand the Russian experience, even though I had by this time visited Russia sixty or more times and had lived there, in total, for quite a few years.

As a last resort, I defended my behavior to my Russian friends contextually (as Struik, a strong believer in the influence of society on human behavior, might have done). I said that for an academic institution to dismiss a faculty member from teaching as a result of his political views, while at the same time paying his salary, might not seem like heavy punishment in Russia, but in the United States it was a clear violation of academic freedom. I pointed out that for years Struik was considered by many people to be a "traitor" and was so named by several testifiers before Congress, including the FBI informant Herbert Philbrick. I also observed that even though in Cambridge I had recently attended a memorial service for an American Marxist persecuted by American academic and legal institutions, in earlier years I had honored refuseniks and dissidents who had been persecuted in the name of Marxism by Soviet academic and legal institutions. I maintained that in each society it was appropriate to defend those who were wronged, even if the political beliefs of the accused pointed in opposite directions.

Although my Russian friends benevolently ceased criticizing me, both they and I knew that I had not "solved" the problems we were discussing. I am almost sure that they were correct in assuming I would not attend the funeral in the United States of a Nazi, even if he or she, like Struik, had committed no crimes and had been dismissed from teaching only because of his or her political views. So much for the purity of my commitment to academic freedom. Once again I saw that in the century in which I had spent most of my life, a period of fascism, communism, and the Cold War, it was often difficult to determine what "correct" behavior would be in many circumstances. But while determining what was correct was often difficult in my life, I clung, and I still cling, to the belief that better and worse forms of behavior can be distinguished in all societies, including Russia and America. It comes down, ultimately, to having a conscience—and listening to it. As Edmund Burke said two centuries ago: all that is required for the triumph of evil is that good men do nothing.

AFTERTHOUGHTS

In 2005 Russia displayed striking characteristics of both the post-Communist era and also sobering remnants of its Soviet and even tsarist past. I visited in 2002, 2003, 2004, and 2005 Moscow, St. Petersburg, Velikii Novgorod, Rostov, Taganrog, Perm', Krasnodar, Samara, Vladivostok and Nizhny Novgorod. I was in Moscow in October 2002, at the time of the storming there by Russian special forces troops of a musical theater in which Chechens were holding about 800 people hostage; in this operation about 170 people died, most of them innocent civilians killed by the gas used by the troops. Just a few days before I visited in the south the homeland of the Kuban Cossacks, whose ancestors had been instrumental in conquering Chechnya for the tsar in the middle of the nineteenth century. Everywhere I saw signs of Russia's turbulent, politically repressive, and often violent past.

On October 26, 2003, when the police arrested Russia's richest man, Mikhail Khodorkovsky, I had just returned to Moscow from the Volga River city of Samara. This event alarmed Western businesspeople far more than it did average Russians. Most Russians resented the way in which a few men like Khodorkovsky had gotten incredibly rich in a few years by seizing Russia's natural resources. They failed to see that Putin's requirement that rich people stay out of politics could only be fulfilled by the use of force. Putin's insistence on a monopoly of political power denied the pluralism found in all true democracies.

On the surface, Russia in 2004 and 2005 appeared a very different place from what I had known in the Soviet years. Visually, Moscow especially, but also the larger provincial cities, had changed tremendously. Commercialization was rampant, with the outskirts of the cities transforming into ugly mercantile strips reminiscent of American cities. In Soviet times there were few billboards, mainly those proclaiming "Glory to the Communist Party" or "The Soviet Union is the Bulwark of World Peace." When I first went to the Soviet Union, long ago, Western goods were simply unavailable in Moscow. Private trade was prohibited. Clothing styles were so limited in the old days that I could tell, for example, when a special shipment of white gloves from Czechoslovakia (a brother socialist country and therefore given export privileges to the Soviet Union) for women had arrived in the city; on the buses and subway cars I saw the gloves on the women, and we all realized that a rare novelty was suddenly available.

Now, in 2004 and 2005, billboards were everywhere, advertising all the consumer delights known elsewhere in the world, and large European clothing, furniture, grocery, and plumbing stores were situated in what were becoming suburban malls. What had been precious novelties earlier had now become commonplace. Up and down all the main streets were stores selling Italian clothing, Danish and German kitchen equipment, American computers and software. In 2004 I saw in Moscow Mercedes-Benz and BMW limousines parked bumper-to-bumper outside Gucci, Prada, Armani and Yves Saint-Laurent stores. The Italian fashion house Brioni announced that its outlets in Russia were doing such a prosperous business that they were helping the company survive a recession in Western Europe.

To be sure, many Muscovites could not afford these items. Great disparities existed between the citizens who were prospering from booming commercial activities and those in professions such as education, science, and high culture who continued to try to exist on miserable state salaries, or the retired who were dependent on pensions as low as sixty dollars a month. Capitalism had come to Russia, widening economic and social differences. The subways continued to be populated by beggars, many of them old women, but occasionally one saw younger people, especially poverty-stricken artists and musicians. In the underground passage connecting Red Square with the National Hotel I saw what appeared to be the entire violin section of a symphony orchestra, standing with their violin cases open for contributions, and playing such magnificent music that it stopped me in mid-stride. I stood there for ten minutes, along with other people, and most of us dropped a little money in the worn violin cases.

Despite these reminders of the costs being paid by the economic changes, the spread of consumerism and relative prosperity was obvious. According to a newspaper article published in Moscow in 2005 about 60 percent of the residents of the city had at that time cellular phones, both a convenience and a status symbol. Moscow was also a city where sales of expensive automobiles such as Mercedes and BMW were exaggeratedly high, since they are symbols of power and prosperity, and are often purchased at the expense of the rest of the household budget. On the outskirts of the city the Swedish home furnishings giant IKEA placed a large store, surrounded with parking lots for Russians with their new cars. Russian patriots and nationalists protested, to no avail, that the IKEA store overshadowed and diminished the monument to World War II located next to it, which marked, by symbolic tank-traps, the furthest extension of Hitler's forces toward Moscow. The fascist troops got so close to the city that Red Army soldiers could take the subway or city bus to the end of the line and then walk to the front. Old Muscovites who remembered the war and traveled by public transportation lines to place bouquets of flowers on the memorial had to brave the much larger crowds of younger people arriving in their automobiles who converged on IKEA to buy the latest sofas and tables for their renovated apartments. An indication that the new prosperity extended far beyond a narrow elite was that IKEA's management announced, soon after opening its first store, that the business was so good that they intended to open many other outlets in Russia.

In early 2003 the largest shopping mall in Eastern Europe, called the "Megamall," opened in southern Moscow at the intersection of the Ring Road and Kaluzhskoye Highway. Occupying an area of 130 acres, it already contained by June 2003, 248 retail outlets. Trees imported from Florida and artificial palm trees lined the storefronts. The complex contained eight fast-food outlets, seven sit-down restaurants, and nineteen cafes, as well as an eleven-screen movie theater called "Rising Star." Designed for the newly affluent car owners of Moscow, the mall had parking for 10,000 cars. Only 15 to 20 percent of the shoppers were expected to arrive by public transportation.

As I observed these dramatic changes in the appearance of Russian cities it occurred to me that the time was soon coming when the casual tourist arriving in Russia will conclude that the country is really no different from any other. Everywhere globalization is bringing the same chain stores and products. What that tourist may not realize is that only a few years ago Russia was a very different place. Its appearance and economic culture contrasted sharply with the rest of the world. There was no private property, no commercial advertising, no credit cards, no checkbooks, no residential suburbs, very few private automobiles, no fast-food outlets. Yet it was a superpower in geopolitical terms. And despite the political oppression in the Soviet Union many people lived fairly normal lives, marrying, raising children, and pursuing careers. From a purely anthropological standpoint it was fascinating twenty years ago to see that a modern society could operate in a way so different from the rest of the world. Now that difference was gone. Human happiness has increased, freedom has grown, but anthropological heterogeneity has diminished. A way of living has disappeared forever.

When I have told other people what I just said above, that "a way of living has disappeared forever," some have asked, "Does this mean that you feel nostalgic for the Soviet Union?" No, I cannot experience a longing for a political system that killed several of my friends and millions of the friends of other people. But do I feel that I gained from my times in the Soviet Union? Absolutely. I have experienced emotions and human situations in the Soviet Union that have added entire dimensions to my life. I have seen terror, love, inspiration, cruelty, and beauty in intensities I have not witnessed elsewhere. I must admit that on occasion I have found the United States and Western Europe somewhat bland in comparison. Some people may call that reaction "nostalgia"; I call it "appreciation": a deeper empathy for the world in which I have lived.

The impact of the West on Russia is now massive, at least in visible commercial behavior. But I knew, from my many recent visits to Russian universities and research institutes that the influence of the West also extended to academic practices. During the time of the Soviet Union all research was funded by the government, and that money was distributed in block grants to institutions, not to individual scientists or scholars. Since the money was given to the directors of institutes and the rectors of universities, top administrators had enormous power in the old system, the power of the purse. With the fall of the Soviet Union the amount of money available for such block grants diminished by over ten times, and new ways of funding research had to be found. The Western model of competitive proposals written by individual scholars and submitted to funding agencies—both governmental agencies and private foundations—was now exercising great influence. The Russians created, after the fall of the Soviet Union, a government foundation modeled on the National Science Foundation in the United States. This new approach to funding science, still only very partially adopted by 2005, was transferring power to individual scholars and diminishing the power of the leading administrators.

Naturally, the administrators did not like this system very much. It also should be said that many research scientists did not like the new system either, since it required them to spend a great deal of time writing proposals—something they were not accustomed to—and it also separated the strong from the weak among Russian scholars. Like the new economic system, the new academic system placed a "wager on the strong" that made the average participant in the systems nervous. A Darwinian selection was going on among Russian scholars, with those who were successful in gaining grants surviving, and those who were not gradually disappearing. But for all the ambiguity of attitudes, the new academic system was spreading so rapidly that more and more Russian scientists and administrators were accepting it as the new reality.

Thus by 2005 in both commercial activity and scholarly research the influence of the West on Russia was manifest. However, it would be easy to exaggerate that influence. Underneath the easily observed surface phenomena many old attitudes and practices still prevailed. Opinion polls of Russians showed, for example, that when one compared Russian attitudes toward capitalism and democracy with their actual behavior, contradictions emerged. The polls showed that most Russians strongly favored democracy as an idea, but very few acted in a way that might strengthen it. There were still no true political parties in Russia in 2005—with the possible exception of the Communist Party—in the sense that they exist in the West as representatives of the interests of certain socio-economic groups. Instead, the parties were often transient phenomena cobbled together by individual political leaders to help them get elected. And Russians, with few exceptions, were inactive politically. They rarely started grass-roots political organizations. Most of them continued, as in Soviet times, to consider politics an activity for "them," the political leaders, not something in which they themselves should engage in a democratic manner, exercising rights of free speech.

A similar, but reverse, contradiction appeared when one looked at the activities and beliefs of Russians with respect to capitalism. In opinion polls Russians continued to display suspicion toward capitalism, often considering it a somewhat disreputable, even sordid, activity, as they had been taught in Soviet times. But their behavior was completely out of synchrony with their expressed opinions. In 2005 Russian citizens were actively pursuing their rights as consumers under capitalism: searching everywhere for the lowest prices and the best quality goods, flooding Western stores like IKEA to furnish their apartments. They may be attitudinally suspicious of capitalism, but behaviorally they often make Western consumers look inattentive to the opportunities for personal gain that capitalism presents.

Thus, in their attitudes and behavior Russian citizens still demonstrate incomplete transitional characteristics as they confront what is still a tentative democracy and a growingly robust capitalism. Since the economic urges seem to be stronger than the political ones, the greatest danger to Russia is not a return to economic communism — that is virtually impossible — but arrested development at political authoritarianism combined with a semi-capitalist economic system. Perhaps it could be called "state capitalism," a system in which private enterprises function only under the close controls of the government.

Just as Russians now face great challenges, so also does the West in its attitude toward Russia. A hundred years from now historians will consider one of the great questions of our present generation to have been: "Did Russia gradually become a part of the West, joining intellectually and politically a burgeoning and expanding European and North Atlantic community, or did that expansion of Western attitudes and practices halt at the Russian border?" This is not, in the final analysis, a geopolitical question of alliances and diplomacy; it is a question of ideology and the harmony of ideological beliefs with personal behavior. On this question, the jury is still out, but it is a question on which wise policies and practices by the West can have major influence.

BIOGRAPHICAL NOTES

━━━

ANDROPOV, IURII VLADIMIROVICH (1914–1984) Iurii Andropov was the head of the secret police, the KGB, of the Soviet Union from 1967 to 1982, and in that position persecuted many dissidents and refuseniks. He was also Soviet ambassador to Hungary in 1956 when the Soviet army brutally suppressed the Hungarian Revolution of that year. Despite this record, around Andropov there still swirl controversies today. Some people maintain that he was a reformer who, if he had not died only sixteen months after taking office as head of the Soviet Union, might have been able to reform that country without causing its dissolution, as happened during Mikhail Gorbachev's tenure as leader a few years later. There are few concrete pieces of evidence that support that view.

Andropov was born near Stavropol in the southern Soviet Union in 1914; his father was a railway official. He received a narrow education in the Rybinsk Water Transport Technical College before he became fully occupied in politics. He gradually rose through the Party in the years before World War II. During the war itself we are told that he participated in guerrilla activities. After Stalin's death Andropov was a rival to Georgy Malenkov, who managed to get him "exiled" as ambassador to Hungary. After helping to squelch the Hungarian Revolution of 1956 Andropov returned to Moscow, and in 1967 was appointed to lead the KGB, a position he held for many years. On Leonid Brezhnev's death in 1982 Andropov was made head of both the Communist Party and the Soviet Union. During his few months in office he conducted an anti-alcohol campaign and tried to enforce work discipline by having the police round up "loiterers" on the streets. His time in office was so short that it is difficult to predict what effects, if any, his policies would have. He certainly would not have favored the more radical reforms of Gorbachev, and in that sense he might have delayed the collapse of the Soviet Union. He died of kidney failure on February 9, 1984.

BERIA, LAVRENTII PAVLOVICH (1899–1953) Lavrentii Beria was one of the cruelest of the leaders of the Soviet secret police. Born near Sukhumi, Georgia, he was a Mingrelian, a people related to the Georgians. He was educated as an engineer in a school in Sukhumi, but soon became involved in radical politics. After the Russian Revolution in 1917 he quickly rose in the ranks of the Bolshevik political police, first called the Cheka. Beria was an early ally of Stalin, who was also from Georgia, and he played an important role in suppressing nationalist uprisings in the Caucasus. He was made a Party secretary in Georgia in 1931 and became a member of the Central Committee of the Communist Party of the Soviet Union in 1934. In 1938 Stalin appointed Beria as head of the secret police (NKVD), where he succeeded Yezhov, who was executed in 1940. The Great Purge came into full swing before Beria took over, and he actually moderated its tempo at first, but later participated fully in Stalin's cruelties. In fact, Beria is described by historians as being a sadist and a sexual predator.

Beria was put in charge of the Soviet atomic bomb project after World War II. The physicist Peter Kapitsa refused to join the project because he found Beria to be disrespectful toward scientists and intellectuals. Andrei Sakharov worked in Beria's atomic empire, but later turned against the entire Soviet system. After Stalin's death Beria tried to win support for himself by denouncing some of Stalin's paranoia, such as the "Doctors' Plot," and he urged more relaxed policies in economics and politics. Nonetheless, given his record, he was accurately seen by his associates as a person who might turn on them at any moment, and in 1953 Khrushchev outmaneuvered him and arranged for his arrest. He was executed on December 23, 1953.

BUKHARIN, NIKOLAI IVANOVICH (1888–1938) Nikolai Bukharin was the youngest of the leaders of the Bolshevik Party who accomplished the Revolution of 1917. He remains today somewhat enigmatic, since he made a dramatic transition from the left to the right wing of the Party, and tried to soften the brutalism of Stalin's collectivization policy. He also was more open to non-Marxist ideas in economics and culture than most of his political associates. He was one of the victims of Stalin in the Great Purges.

Bukharin was born in Moscow, where his parents were school teachers. In 1905, when he was only seventeen, he was already participating in radical politics and supported the abortive revolution of that year. From 1905 to 1911 he rose in the ranks of the radical Marxists, and in 1907 convened a meeting that founded the Komsomol, or youth division, of the Bolshevik Party. He was arrested in 1911 and exiled, but made his way to Western Europe, where he continued his education, particularly in economics. He edited Party newspapers and produced a number of publications, one of which was used by Lenin in the writing of *Imperialism — The Highest Stage of Capitalism*. On his return to Moscow he became a leading Bolshevik, and after the Revolution of 1917 the editor of the Party newspaper *Pravda*. At first Bukharin was a "Left Communist," and strongly criticized the Treaty of Brest-Litovsk which brought Soviet Russia a punitive peace, favoring instead a continuation of the war, and a push for World Revolution. Later, he moderated his policies and became a strong defender of the New Economic Policy of the twenties, which promoted a mixed economy with the government in charge of heavy industry. Increasingly, Bukharin became associated with the right-wing of the Communist Party, and he opposed the cruelty of Stalin's collectivization program at the end of the twenties. In response, Stalin attacked Bukharin and caused his demotion. But Bukharin remained a figure in Soviet politics for many years, and became editor of the government paper *Izvestiia* in 1934. Stalin then moved against all potential opponents and had Bukharin, among others, arrested. Bukharin was tried in 1938 and shot on March 13 of that year.

GAGARIN, IURII ALEKSEEVICH (1934–1968) Iurii Gagarin was the first human being to orbit the earth (1961) in an artificial satellite. He was born on March 9, 1934 in a rural area west of Moscow. His father was a carpenter on the collective farm where Iurii grew up. After high school Gagarin attended a technical school on the edge of Moscow. He left this school in 1951 and enrolled in an industrial college, where he became interested in aviation. After graduating in 1955 he joined the Soviet Air Force. Because of his superior abilities as a pilot he was selected to be a test-pilot flying experimental aircraft. When it became clear that the Soviet Union had an ambitious space program (the USSR launched the first artificial satellite, "Sputnik," in 1957), Gagarin volunteered to be a cosmonaut and became a leading member of the first cosmonauts-in-training, a group of six pilots. Gagarin displayed an amazing ability to withstand physical and psychological stress, including thirteen g's in a centrifuge and isolation in a soundless, lightless room for twenty-four hours. His trainers described him as "very difficult, if not impossible, to upset." He was launched into orbit on April 11, 1961, and soon thereafter attended a mammoth celebration of his feat on Red Square, an event that Loren and Pat Graham attended. His flight was headline news throughout the world. He was killed in an accident seven years later, on March 7, 1968, while testing a MIG-15.

KAPITSA, PETER LEONIDOVICH (1894–1984) Peter (Pyotr) Kapitsa was born in 1894 in Kronstadt, a navy base on an island in the Baltic Sea near St. Petersburg. His father was a military engineer, and his mother was active in education and folklore research. Kapitsa completed his scientific education at the Petrograd Polytechnical Institute, where he worked with another future Nobel laureate, N. N. Semenov, on atoms in magnetic fields. In 1921 Kapitsa went to the Cavendish Laboratory in Cambridge, England, at the invitation of its director, Ernest Rutherford. He remained in England for thirteen years, doing important research on magnetic fields and low temperature phenomena. In 1927 he married Anna Alekseevna Krylova, daughter of one of Russia's best-known mathematicians, A. N. Krylov. In England Kapitsa became the Director of the Mond Laboratory (1930–1934) and a member of the Royal Society.

In 1934, while visiting family in Russia, he was informed by Soviet authorities that he would not be permitted to return to England. With the help of the Soviet government, Kapitsa managed to transfer much of the Mond Laboratory from Cambridge to Moscow, where it became a part of the Institute of Physical Problems of the Soviet Academy of Sciences, which he directed for many years. Working together with the gifted theoretical physicist Lev Landau, Kapitsa combined exquisite experimentation with refined theoretical analysis. He received the Nobel Prize in 1976 for work done in the thirties on the superconductivity of liquid helium at temperatures near absolute zero. After World War II Kapitsa was put under house arrest by Stalin for his refusal to work under Beria on the atomic bomb project. After Stalin's death Kapitsa again emerged as an important figure on the Soviet scientific scene. Only after the fall of the Soviet Union did we learn that Kapitsa in numerous personal letters to Stalin and other Soviet leaders defended Russian scientists who were imprisoned or threatened with arrest, including Landau, Vladimir Fock, and N. N. Luzin, all great figures in Soviet science.

KAPITSA, SERGEI PETROVICH (1928–) Sergei Kapitsa, the son of Peter Kapitsa, described above, was born in Cambridge, England, in 1928. He came to the Soviet Union after his father was forced to stay there in 1934. During World War II he spent two years studying in the Volga River city of Kazan, about 600 miles southeast of Moscow. Returning to Moscow after the Germans retreated, he was for many years professor of physics and chairman of the physics department at the Moscow Institute of Physics and Technology. Because of his fluent English, acquired as a boy in England, Sergei is one of the best-known scientists in Russia to foreign scientists, with whom he has many close relations. He is also well-known in Russia, not only because of his family, but even more because for many years

he has been the host of one of the most popular science television shows in the
Soviet Union and post-Soviet Russia. He served as vice-president of the Academy
of Natural Sciences and president of the Eurasian Physical Society. In recent years
he has written much on globalization and environmental issues.

LYSENKO, TROFIM DENISOVICH (1898–1976) Trofim Lysenko was perhaps the most infamous scientist of the twentieth century. He espoused a theory of heredity that
was counter to accepted science, and he refused to accept the reality of either
genes or DNA. Lysenko was born in Ukraine near the city of Poltava, where he
grew up in a peasant family. He received a rudimentary education in science at
the Horticultural Institute in Poltava and then at a plant-breeding station in
Azerbaidzhan. He first worked on the effect of temperature variation on the life
cycle of plants. He soon claimed that he could change a winter variety of wheat
to a spring variety by "vernalization," the subjection of the wheat to specific temperature changes. In later years he tried a great variety of nostrums for the cultivation of plants and animals: submersion of seeds in cold water, nest and cluster
planting, natural fertilizers, controlled feeding of dairy cows, etc. Many of his
claims were tested in Western laboratories, and none has stood the test of time.
Nonetheless, Lysenko would have been only a crank, not a threat to both biology
and his colleagues, if he had not begun using the power of the Soviet state and
the secret police to destroy his opponents. He was able to do this because he had
the political support of Soviet leaders, at first, Stalin, and later, Khrushchev, neither of whom knew much about biology. In 1948 he won a complete victory, and
for many years biology as it was known abroad could not be practiced in the Soviet Union, or, if so, only in secret. He was discredited in 1965—after the fall of
Khrushchev from power—as a result of an investigation of his claims carried out
by the Soviet Academy of Sciences. It took many years for biology in Russia to
recover.

SAKHAROV, ANDREI DMITRIEVICH (1921–1989) Andrei Sakharov was probably the most
famous Russian scientist of the twentieth century. His scientific reputation was
established by his playing a key role in the development of the Soviet hydrogen
bomb. His fame as a defender of human rights and democracy came later, when
he moved into opposition to the Soviet regime.

Sakharov was born on May 21, 1921, in Moscow, where his father was a teacher
of physics and author of textbooks and works of popular science. Sakharov grew
up in a cultured family of the Russian intelligentsia. In 1938 he entered Moscow
State University as a beginning student, but three years later was evacuated because of the German invasion and graduated university in Ashkhabad, in faraway
Turkmenistan. He returned to Moscow in 1945 to study at the Physics Institute
of the Academy of Sciences, where he received his *kandidat* degree (usually considered equivalent to a Ph.D.) in 1947.

At first his research was on cosmic rays, but soon he became involved in the
Soviet atomic bomb project directed by Igor Kurchatov. After the explosion of the
first Soviet atomic bomb in 1949, Sakharov was a leader in developing the hydrogen bomb. While the design of the Soviet atomic bomb was highly similar to the
U.S. atomic bomb, and based on much espionage, the Soviet hydrogen bomb was
original in its design. Together with Igor Tamm, Sakharov also proposed an idea
for a controlled fusion reactor, the tokamak, that is still the basis of research in the
area. Gradually Sakharov became more and more aware of the danger posed to
humankind by nuclear testing, and his first steps toward dissent with the Soviet
government stemmed from this awareness. In 1968 he wrote an essay, *Reflections*

on Progress, Peaceful Coexistence, and Intellectual Freedom, published outside the Soviet Union, that resulted in his being banned from all military-related research. The essay actually called for a convergence of the Soviet and Western systems, and not for the overthrow of the Soviet Union, but was still totally unacceptable to Soviet leaders.

Later he moved to the defense of dissidents and prisoners of conscience, especially after his marriage to the human rights activist Yelena Bonner in 1972. In 1975 he was awarded the Nobel Prize for Peace, but was not allowed to leave the Soviet Union to collect it. Sakharov gradually moved into complete opposition to the Soviet form of government and economy, and in the years after the collapse of the Soviet Union, as a member of the new parliament, he was a major force for democratic reform. He died of a heart attack on December 14, 1989.

VORONTSOV, NIKOLAI NIKOLAEVICH (1934–2000) Nikolai Vorontsov was an outstanding zoologist and evolutionary biologist who ended up as a government official— in fact, he was the only member of the Council of Ministers of the USSR (roughly equivalent to the president's cabinet in the United States) during the history of that state who was not a member of the Communist Party. He was a brave defender of reform and democracy.

Vorontsov was born on January 1, 1934, and attended Moscow University in the department of vertebrate biology, from which he graduated in 1955. These were years in which the science of genetics was suppressed in the USSR by Lysenko (discussed in this book); Vorontsov, his colleagues, and his wife Elena Lyapunova, also a biologist, spent much time struggling against Lysenko's mistaken theories of biology. From 1955 to 1963 Vorontsov was located at the Zoological Institute of the Russian Academy of Sciences in Moscow.

In 1964 he moved far away to Siberia, where he was in the Institute of Cytology and Genetics of the Siberian Department of the Academy of Sciences in Novosibirsk. The remote location of this institute meant that in secrecy some of the geneticists there were able to keep the ideas of modern genetics alive. From 1971–1977 he was director of the Institute of Biology and Pedology of the Academy of Sciences, located even farther away from Moscow, at Vladivostok on the Pacific Ocean. Vorontsov stayed in Siberia for thirteen years, returning to Moscow after being obliged to resign his institute directorship in Siberia because he refused to join the Communist Party. After 1977 he was a senior researcher at the Kol'tsov Institute of Developmental Biology in Moscow.

In 1989 he was elected to the legislature of the Soviet Union, and he served in four different legislatures, through the time when the Soviet Union collapsed and Russia emerged as an independent state. He was influential in the legislature in matters relating to science, serving as chairman on the sub-committee on science. In 1989 Mikhail Gorbachev appointed him Minister of the Environment, the first time a non-communist had ever been selected for such a high governmental post. In that position he did much to make the public more aware of environmental problems. His ministry began to publish detailed annual reports on the conditions of the environment. As minister of environment Vorontsov also expanded the protected areas (*zapovedniki*) of the Soviet Union. When the attempted pro-communist coup against Yeltsin was launched in August 1991 Vorontsov was the only member of the Council of Ministers to rally to the support of the reformist government against the men who wished to restore communism. He went to the barracks of soldiers and urged them to defend democracy, and he mounted a tank next to Yeltsin in front of the besieged White House to defend the reform movement. Photographs and TV cameras all over the world recorded his brave act. If the leaders of the putsch had succeeded, Vorontsov and others on the tank would surely have been imprisoned. However, the putsch failed, and Vorontsov continued his democratic efforts in the parliament (Russian Duma), of which he was a member from 1991 to 1996. He was an opponent of nuclear testing in the atmosphere, not only by the Soviet Union, but by all countries, and went to the Pacific in 1992 on the Greenpeace ship *Rainbow* to protest nuclear testing by France. He also became active in the history of science, writing a history of evolutionary theory. He died on March 3, 2000. His funeral is described in this book.

YAKOVLEV, ALEKSANDR NIKOLAEVICH (1923– 2005) Aleksandr Yakovlev is often called the "architect of *perestroika*," or the father of Soviet reform. As described in this book, he had in his life made the incredible transition from a Stalinist to one of the strongest defenders of democracy and human rights in Russia.

Yakovlev was born on December 2, 1923, in a peasant village near Yaroslavl. He served in the military during World War II and was severely wounded fighting the Germans. After the war he made a career in the Communist Party, serving as editor of several Party publications. In 1958–1959 he participated in the first year of the scholarly exchanges between the USSR and the USA and studied history at Columbia University, where Loren and Pat Graham first met him. On his return to Moscow he rose to head the Department of Ideology and Propaganda of the Communist Party (1969–1973). In 1972 he boldly criticized the Russian chauvinism and anti-Semitism that were becoming common in Soviet publications and was removed from his position as a result. As a demotion, he was sent to be ambassador to Canada, a position he held for ten years. During these years he was already seen as a reformer in Party politics, but for many years he continued to publish books and articles that were extremely critical of the United States. In the early 1980s he came to know Mikhail Gorbachev, at that time in charge of Soviet agriculture. Their friendship was cemented during a tour of farms and agricultural enterprises in Canada.

Upon his return to the Soviet Union, Gorbachev called Yakovlev back to Moscow, where he directed at first the Institute of International Relations and World Economy of the Soviet Academy of Sciences. When Gorbachev rose to the leadership of the Soviet Union in 1985 he appointed Yakovlev his senior advisor. At first Yakovlev was considerably more reform-minded than Gorbachev, but gradually the two men mutually decided to take the path of dramatic reform, based on *glasnost*, or openness. Yakovlev accompanied Gorbachev at five summit meetings with President Ronald Reagan of the United States. In 1987 Yakovlev became a member of the Politburo of the Communist Party, and thus was a member of the small group of men in charge of the entire country. However, his increasingly liberal views offended some of his colleagues on the Politburo, and he was expelled from both the Party and the Politburo shortly before the August 1991, attempted coup. Yakovlev opposed the leaders of the police and military who unsuccessfully tried to restore communism. In later years, after Gorbachev fell from power, the two men drifted apart. He later headed the Presidential Committee for the Rehabilitation of the Victims of Political Repression, and the Democracy Foundation. He continued to publish widely, revealing the horrors of Soviet repressions and calling for full democracy in Russia. As the policies of President Vladimir Putin became increasingly restrictive of democracy, Yakovlev moved once again into a position of opposition. Yakovlev died in 2005.

ACKNOWLEDGMENTS

———

SINCE THIS BOOK COVERS a good portion of my life, certainly that part of it connected with Russia, it is truly impossible to pay all the debts to that large group of people who have been generous to me with their time, their advice, and their assistance. My wife and daughter, Patricia and Marguerite, are at the top of that list. They are intellectuals and literary critics, and I have benefited enormously from them both personally and professionally. Among the friends who have read the manuscript and helped me shape it, I specifically wish to thank Elisabeth Hansot, David Tyack, Steve and Kit Marcus, Sheila Biddle, Michael Gordin, and Donald Blackmer. Kathie and Phil Carlson, and Char and Cliff Erickson are old friends from a place in Michigan important to us all who have both cheered and assisted me in my work. Everett Mendelsohn and Mary Anderson are close friends who have discussed many parts of the manuscript with me. Steve Cohen and Katrina van den Heuvel were also helpful friends. James Wade has assisted me stylistically. Howard Boyer was with the project at a very early point and made many suggestions. Tim Colton, Lis Tarlow, Marshall Goldman, Sonia Ketchian, Susan Gardos, Donna Griesenbeck, Donald Fanger, Ned Keenan, Mark Kramer, Priscilla McMillan, and Helen Repina are among the many people at the Davis Center for Russian and Eurasian Studies at Harvard University who have assisted me on specific points. Paul Doty of Harvard has often introduced me to his scientific colleagues from Russia. Rosalind Williams, Roe Smith, Ken Keniston, Leo Marx, Carl Kaysen, and Slava Gerovitch are among the many colleagues at the Program on Science, Technology and Society at MIT who have intellectually energized me. Peter Buck, Karl Hall, and Paul Josephson have been great friends at MIT and Harvard. Murad Akhundov and Ludmilla Oleinichenko have been at my side often in both Russia and the United States, as have Gerson Sher and Victor Rabinowitch. Susan and Nick Noyes have often encouraged me on, and once showed me new aspects of Russia through the eyes of their children.

I have been fortunate to have close scholarly contacts in a number of countries: the United States, Russia, France, the United Kingdom, Germany, Israel, and elsewhere. I cannot name them all, but I am grateful to everyone. Many Russian scholars have been friends and helpers; I would like to mention in particular Irina Dezhina, Nikolai Vorontsov, Elena Lyapunova, Masha Vorontsova, Daniel and Lira Aleksandrov, Aleksandr Yakovlev, Sergei Kapitsa, and Anton Struchkov. A French scholar with whom I am working closely at the present moment on a subsequent project, and greatly appreciating, is Jean-Michel Kantor of the Poincaré Institute in Paris.

I have been fortunate in my life to have the assistance of a number of institutions and philanthropic organizations. I would like to thank in particular the Danforth Foundation, the International Research and Exchanges Board, the John D. and Catherine T. MacArthur Foundation, the Civilian Research and Development Foundation, the International Science Foundation (and its creator, George Soros), the Sloan Foundation, the Carnegie Corporation, the National Science Foundation, the National Endowment for the Humanities, the Guggenheim Foundation, the Rockefeller Foundation, and the Institute of the History of Science and Technology, and the Institute of Philosophy, both in Moscow.

I would like also to thank Janet Rabinowitch, Director of the Indiana University Press, both for her help to me personally and also for the great work that she has done in promoting scholarship on Russia for many years.

I of course take all responsibility for errors of fact and judgment that may remain.

Loren Graham
Grand Island, Lake Superior
October 2005

CITATIONS

From the time of my first trip to the Soviet Union, in the fall of 1960, to the present day I have taken notes on notable things that happened on each trip which I placed in manila folders in chronological order. Today I have in my files fifty or sixty such folders. For this book I selected the twenty-three most interesting of the episodes. Most of the stories are based on these notes, which often contain detailed descriptions of conversations and events.

8 **he joined the Communist Party:** *The Harvard Crimson*, February 3, 1954.

12 **"Call the American Civil Liberties Union and Gerald Berlin!":** From a conversation with Gerald Berlin, September 20, 2005.

36 **this book became a standard work:** Leonard Schapiro, *The Communist Party of the Soviet Union* (New York: Random House, 1960).

103 **I have explored the history of science in Russia from the time of Peter the Great to the present:** See list of other books by Loren R. Graham, p. 306.

112 **"Do Mathematical Equations Express Social Attributes?"** *The Mathematical Intelligencer*, 22, no. 3 (2000), pp. 31–36; Loren R. Graham and Jean-Michel Kantor, "A Comparison of Two Cultural Approaches to Mathematics: France and Russia, 1890–1930," scheduled for publication in the March 2006 issue of the history of science journal *ISIS*.

116 **after writing a book about his experiences:** Victor Herman, *Coming Out of the Ice: An Unexpected Life* (New York: Harcourt Brace Jovanovich, 1979).

118 **His son, Paul Robeson Jr. . . . later said:** Martin B. Duberman, *Paul Robeson* (New York: Knopf, 1988), p. 499.

119 **Although a few publications about him have appeared in the West:** An example is Mark Kuchment, "Active Technology Transfer and the Development of Soviet Microelectronics," in Charles Perry and Robert Pfaltzgraff Jr., eds., *Selling the Rope to Hang Capitalism?: The Debate on West-East Trade and Technology Transfer* (Washington, D.C.: Pergamon-Brassey, 1987), pp. 60–69.

137 **his research assistant, Pavel Rubinin, . . . discovered in his mentor's personal archive:** Personal communication with the author.

150 Arthur Koestler, *Darkness at Noon* (New York: Macmillan, 1941).

150 **Stephen Cohen in his biography:** Stephen F. Cohen, *Bukharin and the Bolshevik Revolution: A Political Biography, 1888–1938* (New York, Knopf, 1973).

152 Anton Antonov-Ovseyenko, *The Time of Stalin: Portrait of a Tyranny* (New York: Harper & Row, 1981).

153 Alexander Rabinowitch, *The Bolsheviks Come to Power: The Revolution of 1917 in Petrograd* (New York: W. W. Norton, 1976).

153–154 **this remarkable letter:** Anna Larina, *This I Cannot Forget: The Memoirs of Nikolai Bukharin's Widow,* introduction by Stephen F. Cohen, translated by Gary Kern (New York: W. W. Norton, 1993), pp. 355–56.

158 **We arranged a film interview:** "How Good Is Soviet Science?" *NOVA* episode, prod. by Martin Smith, 58 min., WGBH, 1987.

171 Thomas Riha, ed., *Readings in Russian Civilization,* 3 vols. (Chicago: University of Chicago Press, 1964).

172 **The Boulder police also said:** David Wise, *The American Police State: The Government Against the People* (New York: Random House, 1976), pp. 261–62, 264–73.

173 **The CIA and the FBI began quarreling:** ibid.

173 **Donald Fanger . . . wrote an obituary:** *Slavic Review,* 30, no. 4 (December 1971) pp. 942–46.

192 **featured in the novel of that name:** Iurii Trifonov, *Another Life, and The House on the Embankment,* translated by Michael Glenny (New York: Simon and Schuster, 1983).

208 **According to Western press reports:** Stuart Millar and Duncan Campbell, "Fayed, the spies and the $20m plot to show Palace was behind Diana's death," *The Guardian Unlimited,* July 23, 1999; and Stuart Millar and Kate Connolly, "Fayed caught in 'murder plot' row," *The Guardian Unlimited,* August 28, 1999.

210 **Perhaps it was a letter of mine in the New York Times:** Loren R. Graham, "Another Lidice?" Letter to the Editor, *New York Times,* November 28, 1969, p. 38.

216 **a joint university committee:** The Inter-University Committee on Travel Grants (IUCTG).

218 **13 out of 580 candidates:** Files of the investigative committee of the IUCTG in 1968, chaired by Professor Ivo Lederer, Yale University. Files in author's possession.

219 **As the 1968 report stated:** Ibid.

226 **Yakovlev later described the event:** Aleksandr Yakovlev, *Muki, prochteniia, bytiia; perestroika: nadezhdy i real'nosti* (Moscow: Novosti, 1991), p. 29, from an interview of Yakovlev by Hedrick Smith of the *New York Times.* Translation by Loren R. Graham.

227–228 **In the last book he described the United States:** Aleksandr N. Yakovlev, *Pax Americana: Imperskaia ideologiia — istoki, doktriny* (Moscow: Molodaia gvardiia, 1969), p. 3.

228 **Writing in 1967, he maintained:** A. N. Yakovlev, *Ideologiia amerikanskoi "imperii": problemy voiny, mira i mezhdunarodnykh otnoshenii v poslevoennoi amerikanskoi burzhuaznoi politicheskoi literature* (Moscow: Mysl', 1967), p. 442.

228 **"The U.S. is a nation governed more by deception . . .":** A. N. Yakovlev, *On the Edge of an Abyss: From Truman to Reagan: The Doctrines and Realities of the Nuclear Age* (Moscow: Progress Publishers, 1986), p. 17.; published two years earlier in Russian as *Ot Trumana do Reigana: doktriny i real'nosti iadernogo veka* (Moscow: Molodaia gvardiia, 1984).

229 **Yakovlev wrote a long article:** A. Iakovlev, "Protiv antiistorizma," *Literaturnaia gazeta,* November 15, 1972, pp. 4–5.

233 **Entitled *The Sowing of Crosses:*** Aleksandr Yakovlev, *Krestosev* (Moscow: Vagrius, 2000), pp. 264–66. Translations by Loren R. Graham. This book was later republished in other languages, including Alexander Yakovlev, *A Century of Violence in Soviet Russia,* translated by Anthony Austin (New Haven: Yale University Press, 2002).

257 Douglas R. Weiner, *A Little Corner of Freedom: Russian Nature Protection from Stalin to Gorbachev* (Berkeley: University of California Press, 1999).

273 **a particularly paranoiac article:** *Moskovskii Komsomolets,* March 2001. Translation by Loren R. Graham.

274 Quotations by George Soros from George Soros, *Soros on Soros: Staying Ahead of the Curve* (New York: John Wiley & Sons, 1995), pp. 15, 143. Copyright © 1995 by George Soros. Reprinted with permission of John Wiley & Sons, Inc.

276 **Quotations by Dirk Struik:** Arthur B. Powell and Marilyn Frankenstein, "In His Prime: Dirk Jan Struik Reflects on 102 Years of Mathematical and Political Activities," *The Harvard Educational Review,* 69, no. 4 (Winter 1999), p. 417. Also, James Tattersall, "An Interview with Dirk Struik on the Eve of His Hundreth Birthday," *College Mathematics Journal* (May 2002), p. 5.

INDEX

Loren R. Graham is Professor of History of Science at the Massachusetts Institute of Technology and member of the Executive Committee of the Davis Center for Russian and Eurasian Studies at Harvard University. A specialist in the history of science in Russia, in addition to MIT he has taught at Indiana, Columbia, and Harvard universities. He is a member of the board of trustees of the European University in St. Petersburg and of the governing council of the program on Basic Research and Higher Education, which funds the efforts of Russian universities to bring teaching and research closer together. His numerous publications include two award-winning books (see below). Graham lives in Cambridge, Massachusetts, in the winter and in a remote lighthouse on an island in Lake Superior in the summer where he has written many of his books.

Publications by Loren R. Graham:

Moscow in May 1963: Education and Cybernetics (with Oliver Caldwell). Washington, D.C.: U.S. Department of Health, Education, and Welfare, 1964.

The Soviet Academy of Sciences and the Communist Party, 1927–1932. Princeton: Princeton University Press, 1967.

Science and Philosophy in the Soviet Union. New York: Alfred A. Knopf, 1972. National Book Award finalist.

Between Science and Values. New York: Columbia University Press, 1981.

Functions and Uses of Disciplinary Histories (coeditor with Wolf Lepenies and Peter Weingart). Dordrecht: D. Reidel, 1983.

Red Star: The First Bolshevik Utopia (coeditor with Richard Stites, translated by Charles Rougle). Bloomington: Indiana University Press, 1984.

Science, Philosophy and Human Behavior in the Soviet Union. New York: Columbia University Press, 1987.

Science and the Soviet Social Order (editor). Cambridge: Harvard University Press, 1990.

The Ghost of the Executed Engineer: Technology and the Fall of the Soviet Union. Cambridge: Harvard University Press, 1993.

Science in Russia and the Soviet Union: A Short History. New York: Cambridge University Press, 1993.

A Face in the Rock: The Tale of a Grand Island Chippewa. Berkeley: University of California Press, 1998. Winner of the Follo and Gross awards.

What Have We Learned about Science and Technology from the Russian Experience? Stanford: Stanford University Press, 1998.